Corruption and the Russian Economy

Corruption and the Russian Economy examines why the number of entrepreneurs is declining so rapidly in contemporary Russia, how many economic opportunities are being irrevocably lost each year because of administrative corruption, and why entrepreneurship has become one of the most dangerous occupations in the country over the last decade. Based on extensive research, including in-depth interviews with entrepreneurs and case studies, it reveals a corrupt system of government agencies at both the regional and local levels, and the increasing involvement of public officials in unlawful seizures of businesses. One major conclusion is that the vast majority of informal payments by entrepreneurs to regulatory agencies are made not to achieve illegal advantages, but rather to secure the property rights that they are entitled to under the law.

Yulia Krylova completed her doctorate at George Mason University, Arlington, VA. She currently works as a consultant for the World Bank Group. She is also a researcher at the Terrorism, Transnational Crime and Corruption Center at George Mason University, Fairfax, VA.

Routledge Transnational Crime and Corruption Series

Published in association with the Terrorism, Transnational Crime and Corruption Center, Schar School of Policy and Government, George Mason University, USA

1 **Russian Business Power**
   The role of Russian business in foreign and security relations
   Edited by Andreas Wenger, Jeronim Perovic and Robert W. Orttung

2 **Organized Crime and Corruption in Georgia**
   Edited by Louise Shelley, Erik Scott and Anthony Latta

3 **Russia's Battle with Crime, Corruption and Terrorism**
   Edited by Robert W. Orttung and Anthony Latta

4 **Human Trafficking and Human Security**
   Edited by Anna Jonsson

5 **Irregular Migration from the Former Soviet Union to the United States**
   Saltanat Liebert

6 **Human Security, Transnational Crime and Human Trafficking**
   Asian and Western perspectives
   Edited by Shiro Okubo and Louise Shelley

7 **Labour Migration, Human Trafficking and Multinational Corporations**
   The commodification of illicit flows
   Edited by Ato Quayson and Antonela Arhin

8 **Environmental Crime and Corruption in Russia**
   Federal and regional perspectives
   Edited by Sally Stoecker and Ramziyá Shakirova

9 **Disengaging from Terrorism – Lessons from the Turkish Penitents**
   Kamil Yilmaz

10 **The Political Economy of Corporate Raiding in Russia**
    Ararat Osipian

11 **Corruption and the Russian Economy**
    How Administrative Corruption Undermines Entrepreneurship and Economic Opportunities
    Yulia Krylova

Corruption and the Russian Economy

How Administrative Corruption Undermines Entrepreneurship and Economic Opportunities

Yulia Krylova

LONDON AND NEW YORK

First published 2018
by Routledge
2 Park Square, Milton Park, Abingdon, Oxon OX14 4RN

and by Routledge
711 Third Avenue, New York, NY 10017

Routledge is an imprint of the Taylor & Francis Group, an informa business

© 2018 Yulia Krylova

The right of Yulia Krylova to be identified as author of this work has been asserted by her in accordance with sections 77 and 78 of the Copyright, Designs and Patents Act 1988.

All rights reserved. No part of this book may be reprinted or reproduced or utilized in any form or by any electronic, mechanical, or other means, now known or hereafter invented, including photocopying and recording, or in any information storage or retrieval system, without permission in writing from the publishers.

Trademark notice: Product or corporate names may be trademarks or registered trademarks, and are used only for identification and explanation without intent to infringe.

British Library Cataloguing-in-Publication Data
A catalogue record for this book is available from the British Library

Library of Congress Cataloging-in-Publication Data
Names: Krylova, Yulia, author.
Title: Corruption and the Russian economy : how administrative corruption undermines entrepreneurship and economic opportunities / Yulia Krylova.
Description: Abingdon, Oxon ; New York, NY : Routledge, 2018. | Includes index.
Identifiers: LCCN 2017060481| ISBN 9780815394662 (hardback) | ISBN 9781351185318 (ebook) | ISBN 9781351185288 (mobipocket)
Subjects: LCSH: Political corruption–Russia (Federation) | Entrepreneurship–Russia (Federation) | Economic development–Moral and ethical aspects–Russia (Federation) | Russia (Federation)–Economic conditions–1991– | Russia (Federation)–Politics and government–1991–
Classification: LCC JN6695.A55 C65548 2018 | DDC 338/.040947–dc23
LC record available at https://lccn.loc.gov/2017060481

ISBN: 978-0-8153-9466-2 (hbk)
ISBN: 978-1-351-18531-8 (ebk)

Typeset in Times New Roman
by Wearset Ltd, Boldon, Tyne and Wear

To my father

Contents

List of Figures		viii
List of Tables		ix
About the Author		x
Acknowledgments		xi
1	Introduction: Endangered Entrepreneurs and Their Struggle for Survival in Contemporary Russia	1
2	From State Capture to "Market Capture": The Russian Entrepreneurial Environment	16
3	From Kleptocracy to "Regulocracy": Administrative Barriers to Doing Business in Russia	44
4	"No Grease, No Ride": Facilitation Payments in the Relations between Entrepreneurs and Regulatory Agencies	72
5	"Stand and Deliver, Your Money or Your Life": Illegal Raiding Against Businesses by Public Officials	91
6	"Entrepreneurial Spring": Collective Resistance to Administrative Corruption	112
7	Conclusion: Protecting Endangered Entrepreneurs	137
	Appendix 1 Interview Questions	157
	Appendix 2 Survey Questions	158
	Index	161

Figures

3.1	Spheres where entrepreneurs face the severest problems while dealing with regulatory agencies (the number of mentions in the interviews)	52
3.2	The number of entrepreneurs per 1,000 employed at the regional level, 2015	60
6.1	The number of charters adopted by business organizations in the Russian Empire in 1861–1916	121
6.2	The number of signatories of the Anti-Corruption Charter of Russian Businesses, 2015	126

Tables

2.1	Russia's scores on indicators of entrepreneurial activity in comparison with other post-communist countries, 2016	33
2.2	Scores on the perceived quality of the Russian entrepreneurial ecosystem in comparison with other post-communist countries, 2016	35
2.3	Russia's scores on the Global Entrepreneurship Index and three sub-indices of attitudes, abilities, and aspirations from 2006 to 2017	37
3.1	Average numbers of inspections of businesses and entrepreneurs by federal regulatory agencies in 2011 and 2012	50
3.2	Percentage of unannounced inspections in 2011 and 2012	51
3.3	Ratings of the effectiveness of regional governance in Moscow, Saint Petersburg, and Karelia	55
3.4	Comparative analysis of information published on official websites of the regional committees for small business development, 2016	58
3.5	Descriptive statistics	62
3.6	Results of the OLS and spatial error regression models	63
4.1	Descriptive statistics	79
4.2	Results of the ordered logistic regression	80
4.3	Predicted probabilities of the frequency of "grease" payments for female and male entrepreneurs	81
4.4	Predicted probabilities of the frequency of "grease" payments for members and non-members of business associations	82
5.1	Stages of illegal raiding and the related crimes under the Russian Criminal Code	95
5.2	Top ten regions by count: victim complainants in 2014 and 2015	97
6.1	Types of accountability	114
6.2	Types of contemporary self-regulatory organizations in Russia	124

About the Author

Yulia Krylova holds a PhD degree in Political Science from George Mason University and a PhD degree in Economics from Saint Petersburg State University. She currently works as a consultant for the World Bank Group. She is also affiliated with the Terrorism, Transnational Crime and Corruption Center (TraCCC) at George Mason University. She began her research into corruption and anti-corruption regulation as a Fulbright exchange scholar at Duke University, NC, and Georgetown University Law Center in 2009–2010. Her research interests lie at the intersection of the fields of entrepreneurship, anti-corruption policies, gender inequality, and international development. Her works have been published in such journals as *Global Policy*, *The Journal of Small Business and Entrepreneurship*, *The Economic Analysis of Law Review*, *East European Politics*, *The Journal of Eurasian Studies*, *Region: Regional Studies of Russia, Eastern Europe, and Central Asia*, and *The Journal of Contemporary Central and Eastern Europe*.

Acknowledgments

This book is based on my doctoral research completed at George Mason University in Virginia, from 2012 to 2017. I owe the most to my scientific advisor Dr. Louise Shelley, whose expertise, guidance, and innovative insights into corruption and organized crime deepened and enriched my understanding of these problems from both a theoretical and practical perspective. The book would never have been written without her encouragement and without the support of the Center for Terrorism, Transnational Crime, and Corruption Studies (TraCCC), which she founded at George Mason University. TraCCC served as a thought-provoking and intellectually stimulating home throughout the research process. One of the most valuable advantages was the intensive process of dialog with international scholars and anti-corruption practitioners whom I was lucky to meet at numerous events, conferences, and lectures organized by TraCCC. This fascinating and energizing experience strengthened my belief that international cooperation in the field of anti-corruption programs has enormous potential to create mechanisms for social control and promote action for responsible public administration.

During my research, many people and organizations were instrumental in shaping my ideas about corruption and entrepreneurship. In particular, the Mercatus Center at George Mason University was a supportive community for my research. My gratitude is extended to Dr. Peter Boettke, Dr. Jayme Lemke, and many other scholars from the Mercatus Center. I owe a special debt to all of them for helpful and extremely useful discussions and new insights into private enterprise and entrepreneurship. I am also deeply grateful to the anti-corruption experts at the Center for International Private Enterprise (CIPE) for opportunities to discuss my research on business associations and collective action against corruption. I am especially indebted to Frank Brown and Dr. Kim Bettcher who provided anti-corruption expertise that greatly assisted the research.

I would also like to include a special note of thanks to my colleagues at the World Bank. Working on the World Bank's Entrepreneurship Project was a magnificent and challenging experience for me. I convey my deep regards to Valentina Saltane who generously shared her research.

I owe more than I could say to numerous entrepreneurs whom I met during my fieldwork in Russia in 2015. They generously gave me their precious time, filling out surveys, answering questions during long interviews, sharing their fascinating ideas about anti-corruption policies, explaining their problems and challenges, and trusting me to tell their stories. It is now a great honor for me to let their voices be heard through this book. The experiences of those Russian entrepreneurs show a growing need to document a range of best practices and anti-corruption policies capable of countering bureaucratization and government imperfections which impede social and economic development. Having grown up in Russia, it has always been hard for me to observe the devastating and distorting impact of corruption on ordinary citizens and entrepreneurs. Yet, this experience has given me a powerful impetus, strengthening my determination to devote my research efforts to the development of anti-corruption programs which could be implemented in Russia and other countries. In this respect, it was my greatest privilege to work with every Russian entrepreneur who participated in this study and whose contributions to this book have proven invaluable.

My final thanks go to my family and friends for their support and encouragement during my research. The book would never have gotten off the ground had not my father given me the courage to take the first steps in my doctoral studies. I am also grateful to my friend Sajith Kumar, who restored a significant part of my research when both the original file and a backup copy of my archival work containing 150 pages mysteriously disappeared from my laptop. Without his help, some of the valuable data collected during my fieldwork in Russia would have been irrevocably lost and it would have been extremely hard to finish this book in a timely manner.

1 Introduction

Endangered Entrepreneurs and Their Struggle for Survival in Contemporary Russia

Many economic opportunities are being irrevocably lost each year in Russia because of administrative corruption, excessive regulation, and discretionary abuses by regulatory agencies and law enforcement authorities. The combination of these problems together with recent economic crises has created a considerable drag on entrepreneurial activity, amounting to a tremendous reduction in the number of entrepreneurs in Russia in the last decade. The decline of an entrepreneurial spirit is also compounded by threats of unlawful property seizures and the danger of unjust imprisonment by public authorities. These negative trends keep Russia's economy on an unproductive trajectory of a resource-dependent country that lacks modern technology and diversified production.

In contemporary Russia, entrepreneurs might be considered an endangered species. The number of registered entrepreneurs decreased from 8.3 million in 2008 to 2.8 million in 2015.[1] This constitutes a 66 percent decline in their population over the course of eight years. The largest decline was observed at the end of 2015 when Russia's economy lost more than 50 percent of the 5.6 million entrepreneurs registered at the beginning of that year. A confluence of different factors is responsible for this trend. Among them, one can list volatile politics, geopolitical tensions, the weakened currency, and a sharp decline in oil prices. The 2014 financial crisis and economic sanctions imposed by Western countries against Russia also played a critical role in this process. Yet, as the 2015 Moscow Economic Forum showed, many Russian entrepreneurs blame public authorities for putting their survival at risk. An alarming trend is the increasing rent-seeking activities by public agencies in the form of bribe extortion and illegal seizures of businesses. In turn, a long-term recession creates additional incentives for public officials to quickly regain their economic losses through informal venues.

In December 2015, the annual Moscow Economic Forum organized a special roundtable entitled "Changing Economic Policy as a Response to External Threats." Contrary to the roundtable's title, representatives of the entrepreneurial community in attendance indicated that Russian businesses suffer much more from internal threats than from economic sanctions. According to Dmitry Potapenko, the founder of several retail chains, the main enemies of the Russian business community are public officials:

For the past 20 years, the dialogue between business and authorities has been that of a butcher looking tenderly into the eyes of a cow, holding a knife at its throat and asking, "What do we have today, beef or milk?"[2]

Another participant of the roundtable, Pavel Grudinin, the Director of the Lenin Farm, indicated that corruption, pocket lining, and red tape are strangling Russian businesses.[3] Both businessmen accused the government and public officials of predations on businesses.

Potapenko's and Grudinin's experiences with corruption are no exception. In recent decades, Russia's corruption ranking has remained one of the worst in the world. In 2016, Transparency International ranked Russia 131st out of 176 countries on the Corruption Perception Index, with a score of 29 on a scale of 0 (highly corrupt) to 100 (very clean).[4] Surveys of Russian small businesses and entrepreneurs demonstrate that most of them suffer under administrative corruption. For example, in the 2011 survey conducted by the Association of Entrepreneurs OPORA Russia, the majority of respondents indicated that corruption represents a significant obstacle to their development and survival. According to the survey, 39 percent of entrepreneurs characterized the level of corruption as extremely high and burdensome for their businesses, 26 percent indicated that they suffer from corruption, and only 5 percent answered that they did not face corruption in their relations with regulatory agencies.[5]

The aim of this book is to assess the impact of administrative corruption on entrepreneurs and identify methods they can use to decrease the scope of this problem in the Russian economy. Specifically, the book addresses the questions of how much incentive there is within Russia's business community to organize collective action against corruption and how entrepreneurial organizations can increase their role in anti-corruption efforts. The question about entrepreneurial incentives to fight against corruption is particularly important. One of the serious fallacies of Russia's anti-corruption initiatives is that they do not directly involve the private sector and civil society despite the economic opportunities of the former and moral authority of the latter. As Louise Shelley argues, "Those efforts will likely be short-lived and perhaps even counterproductive as scarce opportunities and citizen support are wasted."[6] Financial and administrative difficulties of businesses in Russia are exacerbated by weak enforcement of anti-corruption laws. Entrepreneurs in Russia comprise a potentially large community to be actively involved in anti-corruption efforts. At the same time, they demonstrate a low level of cohesion and are not actively involved in collective entrepreneurial organizations.

The importance of this research is related to the fact that corruption is a key factor explaining the failures of small businesses and entrepreneurs, especially in developing and emerging markets.[7] Numerous empirical studies show that corruption has adverse consequences for economic development, including reduced investment, low economic growth, increased income inequality, and inefficient public spending. Yet, the negative effects of corruption go far beyond economic damages. Corruption of the public administration system has various distorting effects on society-state relations: undermining the integrity of the political system, destroying the rule of law, diminishing citizens' trust in the state, demoralizing society as a whole, and facilitating organized crime, insurgent and terrorist organizations.[8] In contemporary Russia, corruption prevents the development and growth of the entrepreneurial sector, keeping the economy on an unproductive path, and unless the business community recognizes its critical role in the fight against corruption, this situation is unlikely to change.

Research Focus and Terminology

This book focuses on administrative corruption in Russia and its impact on individual entrepreneurs. Russia's Civil Code defines individual entrepreneurs as persons who are registered in accordance with the procedure established by law and who are carrying out entrepreneurial activities without forming a legal entity. An important feature of individual entrepreneurs is that they are responsible for their obligations with personal property. This distinguishes individual entrepreneurs from limited liability companies whose owners are responsible for the obligations only within their shares in the company's capital. The state registration and activities of entrepreneurs are regulated by the Federal Law of the Russian Federation entitled "On State Registration of Legal Entities and Individual Entrepreneurs," the Civil Code, and other federal laws and resolutions of the Government. Individual entrepreneurs can be self-employed or they can have employees. On average, individual entrepreneurs had three employees under their supervision in 2015.[9]

The research focuses on entrepreneurs because they are disproportionately affected by corruption in the public administration system. In comparison with large and medium-sized enterprises, they have fewer opportunities and less financial possibilities to counteract corrupt public officials. According to Government Decree #702 of 2015, individual entrepreneurs are classified into three groups based on their revenues: (1) microenterprises, with annual revenues of less than 120 million rubles (about $1.7 million); (2) small businesses, with annual revenues ranging from 120 million to 800 million rubles (from $1.7 million to $11.4 million); and (3) medium-sized businesses, with annual revenues ranging from 800 million to 2 billion rubles (from $11.4 million to $28.6 million). In 2016, 98.9 percent of Russian entrepreneurs represented microenterprises, with annual revenues of less than $1.7 million.[10]

The majority of individual entrepreneurs in Russia are engaged in retail and wholesale trade. They comprise 48.4 percent of the total number of individual entrepreneurs, followed by real estate (14.8 percent) and transport and communications (12.3 percent).[11] The remaining entrepreneurs operate in different industries: communal services (6.6 percent), agriculture (4.9 percent), construction (3.2 percent), education (0.7 percent), health (0.7 percent), fishing (0.1 percent), and manufacturing (0.1 percent).[12] Individual entrepreneurs in all industries encounter the rent-seeking practices of regulatory agencies and public officials who extort facilitating payments to issue the permits and licenses required for business activities, process governmental documents, provide inspections, and protect property rights. Although administrative corruption is not limited to these practices, they constitute a significant part of the informal sector in Russia.

There are many definitions of corruption which focus on the violation of trust and misuse of power by individuals or organizations. For example, Samuel Huntington defines corruption as the "behavior of public officials which deviates from accepted norms in order to serve private ends."[13] In countries that lack an effective system of checks and balances, bureaucrats performing public duties tend to abuse their position and office for illicit enrichment. In such countries, it is not rare for bureaucrats and regulatory agencies to impose additional administrative procedures for doing business to extort informal payments from entrepreneurs. Another definition offered by Nathaniel Leff describes corruption as "an extra-legal institution used by individuals or groups to gain influence over the actions of the bureaucracy."[14] This definition highlights the fact that private actors can initiate corrupt transactions in order to receive illegal advantages for themselves or their businesses. While the first definition concentrates on the demand side of corruption, the second focuses on the supply side. These definitions illustrate the selfish motives of different private and public actors who initiate corrupt deals.

Following these definitions, I define administrative corruption in this book as the abuse of office for personal gain by regulatory agencies that perform oversight and maintain control over business entities and entrepreneurs. This narrow definition of administrative corruption helps distinguish it from other types of corrupt activities that do not directly influence entrepreneurship. For example, the research does not include petty "household" corruption that involves citizens who deal with public officials representing social security authorities, traffic police, administrative staff in hospitals and educational bodies. Another type of informal activities excluded from the analysis is private-sector corruption that involves bribery, undue influence, fraud, money laundering, and collusion committed without involvement of public officials. Taking the book's objective into account, my analysis of corrupt practices centers exclusively on the abuse of power by public officials that has a direct impact on entrepreneurs.

Administrative corruption can take many forms. In most developing countries, entrepreneurs are forced to provide informal payments to public officials in order to speed up bureaucratic procedures and gain access to property rights that they are eligible to receive under the law. However, there are also country-specific forms of administrative corruption. For example, Russian entrepreneurs increasingly fall victim to the illegal business raiding committed by regulatory agencies and public officials who want to seize valuable assets. In the Russian language, the practice of illegal raiding is often referred to as *reiderstvo*. It has become an increasingly profitable new type of organized crime in Russia.[15] Thousands of illegal raids on businesses are committed by public officials every year through the use of illegal methods, such as forgery of registration documents, abuse of inspections and regulations, police violence, and criminal prosecution of legal owners on nonexistent grounds. Alarming statistics come from Boris Titov, Russia's ombudsman for business rights, who estimates that nearly three million entrepreneurs were unjustly imprisoned and lost their businesses over the last decade.[16]

The low participation of small businesses in collective action makes them easy prey for corrupt public officials and regulatory agencies. Taking this into account, this book emphasizes the importance of collective action theory for the development of anti-corruption programs and initiatives. Despite many entrepreneurs' frustration with administrative corruption, their potential force is limited by insufficient coordination and cooperation in anti-corruption efforts. This makes them particularly vulnerable to extortion of bribes and illegal business raiding. In this respect, collective organizations of entrepreneurs can better protect their rights against violations by public authorities. This book refers to them as self-regulatory organizations. In a broad sense, self-regulatory organizations represent collective organizations in the private sector that exercise some degree of regulatory authority over a particular profession, industry, or business entity. In Russia, they are represented by inter-industry cross-sector associations of entrepreneurs, chambers of commerce, and professional business associations.

Recognizing the importance of private-sector involvement in providing accountability for public administration, this book moves beyond "mainstream" studies of corruption in Russia that focus on the demand side represented by the political elite and public officials who manipulate legal and regulatory institutions to their advantage. In contrast, this research focuses on the supply side represented by Russian entrepreneurs. This allows for the identification of specific factors facilitating corruption, which are often ignored by policy-makers in charge of anti-corruption reforms. Contrary to the widely accepted views about the cultural predisposition of Russian businesses to pay bribes, the book argues that the vast majority of informal payments are made by entrepreneurs not to achieve illegal advantages, but to obtain property rights that are denied to them by regulatory agencies. The book also provides new insights into linkages between political and administrative corruption that represent interdependent parts integrated into the hierarchical structure of informal payments within the Russian state. In order to mitigate the problem of corruption, it is imperative to take a comprehensive look at the role of entrepreneurs and their collective organizations in anti-corruption efforts.

Methodology and Fieldwork in Russia

The research presented in this book is based on a combination of qualitative and quantitative data that were collected during my four-month fieldwork in Russia from August to November 2015. Depending on its objective and specific topic, each chapter of the book applies various methods to study a particular problem faced by entrepreneurs. These methods include a survey on the use of informal payments in the relations with regulatory agencies, in-depth interviews with representatives of business associations and chambers of commerce, regional case studies, archival research, and statistical analysis.

The book pays particular attention to gender-specific attitudes toward corruption. The importance of gender-specific aspects of informal practices is underlined in numerous studies providing evidence that women are less tolerant of corruption and less likely to be involved in illegal activities.[17] In this respect, both the survey and the interviews presented in this book included female entrepreneurs as respondents. Specifically, six of the 12 in-depth interviews with entrepreneurs and representatives of self-regulatory organizations were conducted with female respondents. On average, each interview took one and a half hours. The full list of questions can be found in Appendix 1. In addition, 24 female entrepreneurs participated in the survey about the use of informal payments, which constituted 26 percent of the total received responses. Chapter 4 provides more detailed explanations of the survey methodology. The survey questions can be found in Appendix 2. An analysis of women's experiences with corruption helps identify specific problems and challenges that Russian female entrepreneurs experience while dealing with public authorities and competing in male-dominated industries. This analysis also shows the importance of women's organizations for the development and implementation of anti-corruption programs and initiatives in Russia and other developing countries. Specifically, the analysis of gender-specific dimensions of corruption proves to be a useful tool to facilitate the creation of social and political institutions that both impede informal practices and empower women entrepreneurs at the local and regional levels.

The book incorporates regional aspects into the study of corruption. Specifically, it explores the impact of administrative corruption on entrepreneurial employment in 83 Russian regions based on spatial regression analysis. The key data sources for this analysis include the Federal Statistics Service of the Russian Federation, the Association of Russian Lawyers for Human Rights, and the Agency of Strategic Initiatives. This analysis is combined with my original survey and interviews with entrepreneurs conducted in three Russian regions: Moscow, Saint Petersburg, and the Republic of Karelia. The choice of these regions is explained by their different levels of entrepreneurial activities. Moscow has a high level of entrepreneurial activities, Saint Petersburg a medium level, and Karelia the lowest level among these regions.[18] Moscow, Saint Petersburg, and Karelia also differ significantly in regional policies related to the development of the entrepreneurial sector. Their comparisons help trace specific factors either facilitating or impeding entrepreneurship in different institutional environments.

The importance of incorporating regional aspects into the research on collective action is underlined in a study of Russia's civil society conducted by the Levada Center, an independent non-governmental polling and sociological research organization based in Moscow. It demonstrates that the most active representatives of Russia's civil society are concentrated in large cities, such as Moscow, Kaliningrad, Saratov, Perm, Krasnoyarsk, and Vladivostok.[19] Interviews with civil society activists from these cities conducted by the Levada Center showed that most non-governmental organizations (NGOs) in the field of human rights and democratic development suffered from repression at the hands of state agencies. These organizations pointed to corruption among public officials as a serious threat to civil society. They also expressed concerns about the lack of public mechanisms to resolve conflicts with state agencies due to corruption in the courts.[20] The Levada Center's study of Russian civil society involved NGOs operating in various spheres, including political, cultural, ecological, and human rights activities. It did not, however, pay sufficient attention to the role of business associations in the development of civil society. To fill this gap, this book focuses on business communities and their collective organizations as protectors of both entrepreneurial and human rights.

Throughout the book, the research employs a comparative historical analysis to identify patterns and problems of entrepreneurial development in Russia. To explore the role of self-regulatory organizations in the reduction of corruption, the research pays particular attention to pre-revolutionary business practices. The comparative historical analysis traces the development of collective entrepreneurial organizations in the Russian Empire that was interrupted by the Revolution of 1917 and re-emerged after the collapse of the Soviet Union. This method identifies path-dependent factors in policy-making and certain corruption patterns in the entrepreneurial sector. Similar to contemporary businesses, entrepreneurs in the Russian Empire faced serious administrative problems, which they often could not solve on their own. These problems were especially burdensome for entrepreneurs located in large cities. This gave them a strong impetus to form collective organizations to represent their interests in their relations with state agencies. Interestingly, in the Russian Empire, the level of corruption was especially high in Saint Petersburg, then Russia's capital.[21] This study shows the same pattern. Specifically, entrepreneurs in Moscow, Russia's current capital, tend to be subject to corrupt practices more often than in other regions.

Studies of corruption have proven to be extremely challenging for researchers. Most surveys and interviews about the use of informal payments and other corrupt practices are based on self-reporting by respondents. A certain disadvantage of the self-reporting technique is related to the reluctance of respondents to give honest answers about informal activities. Based on the World Bank's enterprise survey data on 44,000 firms in 72 countries between 2000 and 2015, Nathan Jensen, Quan Li, and Aminur Rahman find that "in politically repressive environments, firms use nonresponse and potential false response as self-protection mechanisms."[22] This leads to underestimation of the scope of corruption at the national and regional levels. Specifically, self-reported answers about the scope of corruption might understate the frequency of informal payments. Entrepreneurs are often reluctant to reveal their own participation in informal activities due to possible legal consequences. This is why disclosure of their honest responses regarding personal involvement in corrupt transactions can cause harm. In order to mitigate this issue and protect respondents, data for this book were collected anonymously through an emailed survey constructed with a

Google Docs tool without a follow-up procedure. This made it impossible to link the received responses with respondents' identities. During the interview stage, entrepreneurs were identified only by general characteristics, such as their status (entrepreneur or representative of self-regulatory organizations), region, and gender.

Anonymity of the survey and protection of respondents' identities were meant to mitigate a self-reporting bias. Yet, this bias might persist due to subjective fears of respondents. These fears are associated with Russia's current political regime. Since 2004, Freedom House, an independent non-governmental human rights organization, has classified Russia's regime as "not free." As Phyllis Dininio and Robert Orttung indicate, authoritarian regimes are associated with distortions in perceptions of corruption caused by state-controlled media or by fear of retaliation by corrupt officials.[23] Similarly, Nathan Jensen, Quan Li, and Aminur Rahman find that respondents in countries with less press freedom are more likely to provide false responses or nonresponse on corruption-related questions.[24] According to Freedom House, Russia's press status is not free. As Freedom House indicates, Russia maintains "a tight grip on locally based print and broadcast media, while also seeking to control the more independent views provided either online or by foreign news sources."[25] For example, in 2016, RBC, one of Russia's few independent media groups, came under enormous pressure from public authorities after covering a corruption case related to the family and associates of President Putin.[26] Three of the RBC editors lost their jobs as a result. The actions of public authorities against RBC signaled a warning to other media participants about the negative consequences related to publishing about corruption.

Investigative journalism requires a lot of courage in contemporary Russia. Today, writing about Russian politics is more dangerous than covering stories first-hand in the most conflict-ridden parts of the world. In his speech at the International Press Freedom Award ceremony organized by the Committee to Protect Journalists, Mikhail Zygar, a renowned Russian journalist, compared his work at the TV station Dozhd with a war zone. In his own words,

> About five years ago, I quit war reporting and turned to politics and society. I thought it would make my life easier. I was wrong. Running the only independent TV channel in Russia is just like walking through a mine field.[27]

The Civil Initiatives Committee, an NGO which promotes human rights in Russia, indicates that the level of press freedom differs significantly at the regional level.[28] In some regions, local administrations put additional pressure on the media. In such regions, perceptions of citizens and entrepreneurs on corruption levels are distorted since media outlets are not willing or not ready to cover abuse of power by public authorities. For example, interviews with entrepreneurs provide certain evidence that this is the case in Karelia. To mitigate regional distortions in entrepreneurial assessments of corruption, the book combines the original survey with various secondary sources and reports published by such organizations as the Association of Russian Lawyers for Human Rights, Transparency International, the World Economic Forum, and the World Bank. The triangulation of sources facilitates validation of corruption-related data through cross-verification.

The use of different types of respondents in corruption studies also proves effective. In his research on corruption in Vietnam, Anh Tran demonstrates that it is possible to persuade sources to talk openly about this topic. To collect data about the scope of corruption, Tran developed a network with dozens of businesses and public officials in Vietnam, who were willing to provide information about informal activities.[29] Tran explains their honest responses about their involvement in such activities by referencing the low probability of being caught and prosecuted for bribery in a highly corrupt environment, where almost everyone is engaged in informal practices. As Tran indicates, "Firm owners and workers share information with me as a favor and don't fear reprisal ... It is not really a closely guarded secret if you know how and who to ask."[30] Similar to Tran's experience, the interviews conducted for this book demonstrated that many Russian entrepreneurs are willing to talk about corruption. Importantly, members of grassroots organizations that were created by entrepreneurs at the local level are more likely to speak freely about corruption than representatives of large elite business associations. Most refusals to participate in the study were received from representatives of large self-regulatory organizations at the national level. In general, the willingness of many entrepreneurs to participate in this study demonstrates that there are internal incentives within the business community to counteract corruption.

Structure of the Book

Each chapter of the book addresses a particular problem experienced by Russian entrepreneurs in the process of operating their businesses. These problems include administrative overregulation, extortion of informal payments by public authorities, illegal raiding of businesses, the inefficiency of self-regulatory organizations, and challenges in organizing collective action against corruption. The assemblage of various facets of administrative corruption allows the reader to see the big picture of this complicated phenomenon and to trace its impact on entrepreneurship and economic development.

Chapter 2, "From State Capture to 'Market Capture'," explores the development of business institutions and the evolution of entrepreneurship after the collapse of the Soviet Union. It pays particular attention to government failures and administrative problems which have affected entrepreneurial development over the course of the last 25 years. The chapter argues that entrepreneurs became particularly vulnerable to administrative corruption under Putin's regime. In the post-perestroika period, capture of key state institutions by informal clientelistic groups led to the corrosion of the public administration system and destruction of its ability to provide the security of property rights. Since 2000, another trend became especially apparent in Russia, with the ruling elite monopolizing wealth redistribution in the national economy. In this context, "market capture" refers to the predatory nature of the Russian political elite actively engaged in seizing economic resources and businesses through the use of quasi-legal and illegal instruments. The resulting hostile business environment creates a considerable drag on entrepreneurial activity, amounting to a tremendous reduction in the number of entrepreneurs. Based on several international rankings, such as the Global Entrepreneurship Monitor, the Global Entrepreneurship Index, and the Female Entrepreneurship Index, this chapter provides evidence that Russia is lagging in terms of entrepreneurial development not only behind developed economies, but also behind other post-communist countries of the former Eastern Bloc.

Chapter 3, "From Kleptocracy to 'Regulocracy'," analyzes the administrative barriers to doing business in Russia. This chapter examines the impact of corruption in the higher echelons of power on street-level bureaucrats. The famous Russian expression "the fish rots from the head" vividly illustrates the demoralizing effect of kleptocratic rulers on low-ranking officials responsible for exercising authority over entrepreneurial activity. Russia's kleptocratic regime led to the creation of a "regulocracy," a corrupt system of government agencies at the regional and local levels that systematically exploit their office for personal gain. "Regulocrats" are responsible for creating numerous administrative barriers to doing business in Russia, such as excessive and costly procedures required to start a new business, obtain construction permits, register property, get credit, or engage in trade across borders. To show how the existence of powerful "regulocracy" blocks deregulation reforms in Russia, the chapter analyzes recent attempts to improve the inspection regime for entrepreneurs and small businesses. Another negative consequence of overregulation and corruption is the decrease in entrepreneurial employment at the regional level. Spatial regression analysis identifies a negative relationship between administrative corruption and the number of entrepreneurs registered in Russian regions.

Chapter 4, "'No Grease, No Ride'," analyzes the use of informal payments in the relations between entrepreneurs and regulatory agencies. The Russian saying, "no grease, no ride" illustrates the embeddedness of informal payments in the economy. The problem of overregulation in the entrepreneurial sector is directly related to rent-seeking activities by regulatory agencies. In fact, government agencies often adopt new burdensome regulations to extort payments from entrepreneurs for speeding up or facilitating bureaucratic procedures. Such payments are called facilitation or "grease" payments. Recent surveys of entrepreneurs show that the frequency of facilitation payments remains very high in Russia. The chapter explores the attitudes of Russian entrepreneurs toward facilitation payments. The empirical evidence comes from the original survey and interviews conducted in 2015 in three Russian regions: Moscow, Saint Petersburg, and Karelia. The interviews not only give an opportunity to hear the victims' voices, but also help identify key factors behind the prevalence of facilitation payments in the entrepreneurial sector.

Chapter 5, "'Stand and Deliver, Your Money or Your Life'," addresses the question of why entrepreneurship is considered one of the most dangerous occupations in contemporary Russia. State predations on Russian businesses are not limited to extortion of facilitation payments. The increasing appetites of corrupt public officials involve unlawful seizures of entrepreneurial assets and businesses. The active involvement of regional and local government agencies in cases of unlawful business raiding is directly linked to Putin's "vertical of power." The existing kleptocratic regime is based on the notion of loyalty of public officials measured by the amount of illegal proceeds distributed by low-level bureaucrats to their superiors. Although illegal business raiding can be traced back to the collapse of the Soviet Union, its nature has transformed significantly since Putin's rise to power in 2000. Public officials often hire criminals to conduct illegal raids on Russian entrepreneurs. Another commonly used raiding method is the fabrication of criminal cases against legal owners of targeted businesses. Entrepreneurs who dare resist powerful state raiders often risk their freedom or even their lives. Based on an analysis of recent raiding cases against entrepreneurs, the chapter explores the roles of law enforcement, of the judiciary, and of regulatory agencies in the process of illegal asset seizures.

Chapter 6, "'Entrepreneurial Spring'," is devoted to an analysis of collective resistance to administrative corruption. This chapter examines defense mechanisms that the entrepreneurial community can use to protect itself against both administrative corruption and state predations on businesses. A historical analysis shows that pre-revolutionary business associations in Russia were powerful representative institutions that directed economic policy in the interests of business groups. They served as effective mediators between the state and businesses, setting a good example for contemporary entrepreneurial organizations in Russia. In addition, this chapter analyzes best anti-corruption practices in other developing countries, which provide evidence that collective resistance is an effective strategy for entrepreneurs to decrease barriers to doing business. Social movements and civil society protests against corruption in the Arab Spring countries demonstrate the great potential of collective action in bringing kleptocrats and "regulocrats" to justice. In Russia, entrepreneurs fail to mobilize against corruption. Recent protests of Russian entrepreneurs against administrative harassment failed to attract massive numbers of participants. Not only does the failure of the "entrepreneurial spring" in Russia demonstrate a low level of cohesion within the Russian business community, but it also indicates the lack of effective leadership on the part of their collective organizations and professional networks.

The Conclusion, "Protecting Endangered Entrepreneurs," provides a review of important anti-corruption laws in Russia and makes several proposals to improve public policies in this sphere. The chapter also looks at how public–private partnerships can be used to combat corruption in the economy. In addition, the chapter provides suggestions on how Russian business associations and professional networks can increase their effectiveness in mobilizing entrepreneurs and organizing collective action against corruption. Particular attention is paid to successful international initiatives against corruption that can be used as role models by Russian business associations. Collective entrepreneurial organizations have a wide range of opportunities to organize public–private dialogue and put pressure on public officials to alter inefficient regulations. The chapter concludes that collective action against corruption can be a potential force leading to synergies that individual entrepreneurs would not be able to achieve independently.

Notes

1 Federal Statistics Service of the Russian Federation. Individual'nye predrinimateli [in Russian]. (2017). Available at: www.gks.ru/wps/wcm/connect/rosstat_main/rosstat/ru/statistics/enterprise/reform/
2 Cited in Schreck, C., & Shakirov, M. Russian Businessman Lashes out at Kremlin, Becomes Cause Célèbre. *Radio Free Europe/Radio Liberty*, December 11, 2015. Available at: www.rferl.org/a/russia-businessman-rails-against-official-extortion/27420874.html
3 Hartog, E. Angry Russian Businessmen Turn on Kremlin. *The Moscow Times*, December 18, 2015.
4 Transparency International. Corruption Perceptions Index 2016 – Results. (2016). Available at: www.transparency.org/news/feature/corruption_perceptions_index_2016
5 OPORA. *Opora Indeks 2010–2011* [in Russian] (Moscow: OPORA, 2012), p. 27.
6 Shelley, L. Civil Society Mobilized against Corruption: Russia and Ukraine. In M. Johnston (Ed.), *Civil Society and Corruption: Mobilizing for Reform* (pp. 3–21) (Lanham, MD: UPA, 2005), p. 3.
7 World Bank. *Fighting Corruption Through Collective Action: A Guide for Business* (Washington, DC: The World Bank, 2008).
8 See, for example, Rose-Ackerman, S. *Corruption and Government: Causes, Consequences, and Reform* (Cambridge: Cambridge University Press, 1999); Shelley, L. Post-Soviet Organized Crime, *Demokratizatsiya*, 2(31) (1994), 341–358; Shelley, L. Corruption in the Post-Yeltsin Era, *East European Constitutional Review*, 9 (2000), 70–74; Shelley, L. *Dirty Entanglements: Corruption, Crime, and Terrorism* (Cambridge: Cambridge University Press, 2014); Holmes, L. *Rotten States: Corruption, Post-Communism, and Neoliberalism* (Durham, NC: Duke University Press, 2006); Lambsdorff, J. *The Institutional Economics of Corruption and Reform: Theory, Evidence, and Policy* (Cambridge: Cambridge University Press, 2007); Rollins, J., & Wyler, L. S. *International Terrorism and Transnational Crime: Security Threats, US Policy, and Considerations for Congress* (Washington, DC: Congressional Research Service, 2010); Williams, P. Lawlessness and Disorder: An Emerging Paradigm for the 21st Century, in M. Miklaucic & J. Brewer (Eds.), *Convergence: Illicit Networks and National Security in the Age of Globalization* (pp. 15–36) (Washington, DC: NDU Press, 2013).
9 Resource Center for Small Entrepreneurship. Statistika MSP [in Russian]. (2017). Available at: http://rcsme.ru/ru/statistics
10 Single Registry of Small and Medium Enterprises. Kolichestvo individual'nykh predrinimatelei [in Russian]. (2017). Available at: www.nalog.ru/rn77/related_activities/regbusiness/
11 Federal Statistics Service of the Russian Federation. Gruppirovka individual'nykh predrinimatelei po vidam ekonomicheskoi deiatel'nosti [in Russian]. (2017). Available at: www.gks.ru/free_doc/new_site/business/prom/small_business/itog2015/8-ip.htm
12 Ibid.
13 Huntington, S. P. *Political Order in Changing Societies* (New Haven, CT: Yale University Press, 2006), p. 2.
14 Leff, N. H. Economic Development Through Bureaucratic Corruption. *American Behavioral Scientist*, 8(3) (1964), 8.

15 Kleiner, V. Antikorruptsionnaya strategiya biznesa v Rossii [in Russian]. *Voprosy Ekonomiki*, *4* (2011), 32–46.
16 Kesby, R. (2012, July 5). Why Russia Locks up So Many Entrepreneurs. *BBC News*. Available at: www.bbc.com/news/magazine-18706597
17 See, for example, Deshpande, S. P., Joseph, J., & Maximov, V. V. Perceptions of Proper Ethical Conduct of Male and Female Russian Managers, *Journal of Business Ethics*, *24*(2) (2000), 179–183; Dollar, D., Fisman, R., & Gatti, R. Are Women Really the "Fairer" Sex? Corruption and Women in Government, *Journal of Economic Behavior & Organization*, *46*(4) (2001), 423–429; Alatas, V., Cameron, L., Chaudhuri, A., et al. Gender, Culture, and Corruption: Insights from an Experimental Analysis, *Southern Economic Journal*, *75*(3) (2009), 663–680; Krylova, Y. Corruption and Gender Inequality: The Case of Nicaragua, *International Journal of Ethics*, *12*(3) (2016), 273–289; Esarey, J., & Chirillo, G. "Fairer Sex" or Purity Myth? Corruption, Gender, and Institutional Context, *Politics & Gender*, *9*(4) (2013), 361–389.
18 Federal Statistics Service of the Russian Federation. Individual'nye predrinimateli, op. cit.
19 Volkov, D. *Perspektivy grazhdanskogo obshchestva v Rossii* [in Russian] (Moscow: Levada Center, 2011), p. 3.
20 Ibid., p. 50.
21 Tikhomirov, Y. Predprinimatel'skie organizatsii Sankt-Peterburgskoi burzhuazii kontsa XIX – nachala XX vv (doctoral dissertation autoreferat) [in Russian] (Leningrad: Institute of the USSR History of the Academy of Sciences, 1990), p. 8.
22 Jensen, N. M., Li, Q., & Rahman, A. Understanding Corruption and Firm Responses in Cross-National Firm-Level Surveys. *Journal of International Business Studies*, *41*(9) (2010), 1481.
23 Dininio, P., & Orttung, R. Explaining Patterns of Corruption in the Russian Regions. *World Politics*, *57*(4) (2005), 500–529.
24 Jensen et al., op. cit., p. 1481.
25 Freedom House. *Freedom of the Press 2015* (Washington, DC: Freedom House, 2015), p. 2.
26 Freedom House. *Freedom of the Press 2017* (Washington, DC: Freedom House, 2017), p. 19.
27 Zygar, M. (2014). The International Press Freedom Award Acceptance Speech. Available at: https://cpj.org/awards/2014/mikhail-zygar-russia.php
28 Civil Initiatives Committee. Indeks razvitiya mediasfery v regionakh Rossii [in Russian]. (2017). Available at: https://komitetgi.ru/upload/indexsmi/dopmaterial.pdf
29 Cited in Shere, J. Vietnam: Complex Combinations, Dynamic Partnerships. *SPEA Magazine*, Spring. (2011). Available at: https://spea.indiana.edu/magazine/Spring-2011/articles/vietnam.shtml
30 Ibid.

References

Alatas, V., Cameron, L., Chaudhuri, A., Erkal, N., & Gangadharan, L. (2009). Gender, Culture, and Corruption: Insights from an Experimental Analysis. *Southern Economic Journal*, *75*(3), 663–680.

Civil Initiatives Committee. (2017). Indeks razvitiya mediasfery v regionakh Rossii [in Russian]. Available at: https://komitetgi.ru/upload/indexsmi/dopmaterial.pdf

Deshpande, S. P., Joseph, J., & Maximov, V. V. (2000). Perceptions of Proper Ethical Conduct of Male and Female Russian Managers. *Journal of Business Ethics*, *24*(2), 179–183.

Dininio, P., & Orttung, R. (2005). Explaining Patterns of Corruption in the Russian Regions. *World Politics*, *57*(4), 500–529.

Dollar, D., Fisman, R., & Gatti, R. (2001). Are Women Really the "Fairer" Sex? Corruption and Women in Government. *Journal of Economic Behavior & Organization, 46*(4), 423–429.

Esarey, J., & Chirillo, G. (2013). "Fairer Sex" or Purity Myth? Corruption, Gender, and Institutional Context. *Politics & Gender, 9*(4), 361–389.

Federal Statistics Service of the Russian Federation. (2017a). Gruppirovka individual'nykh predrinimatelei po vidam ekonomicheskoi deiatel'nosti [in Russian]. Available at: www.gks.ru/free_doc/new_site/business/prom/small_business/itog2015/8-ip.htm.

Federal Statistics Service of the Russian Federation. (2017b). Individual'nye predrinimateli [in Russian]. Available at: www.gks.ru/wps/wcm/connect/rosstat_main/rosstat/ru/statistics/enterprise/reform/.

Freedom House. (2015). *Freedom of the Press 2015*. Washington, DC: Freedom House.

Freedom House. (2017). *Freedom of the Press 2017*. Washington, DC: Freedom House.

Hartog, E. (2015, December 18). Angry Russian Businessmen Turn on Kremlin. *The Moscow Times*.

Holmes, L. (2006). *Rotten States: Corruption, Post-Communism, and Neoliberalism*. Durham, NC: Duke University Press.

Huntington, S. P. (2006). *Political Order in Changing Societies*. New Haven, CT: Yale University Press.

Jensen, N. M., Li, Q., & Rahman, A. (2010). Understanding Corruption and Firm Responses in Cross-National Firm-Level Surveys. *Journal of International Business Studies, 41*(9), 1481–1504.

Kesby, R. (2012, July 5). Why Russia Locks up So Many Entrepreneurs. *BBC News*. Available at: www.bbc.com/news/magazine-18706597.

Kleiner, V. (2011). Antikorruptsionnaya strategiya biznesa v Rossii [in Russian]. *Voprosy Ekonomiki, 4*, 32–46.

Krylova, Y. (2016). Corruption and Gender Inequality: The Case of Nicaragua. *International Journal of Ethics, 12*(3), 273–289.

Lambsdorff, J. (2007). *The Institutional Economics of Corruption and Reform: Theory, Evidence, and Policy*. Cambridge: Cambridge University Press.

Leff, N. H. (1964). Economic Development Through Bureaucratic Corruption. *American Behavioral Scientist, 8*(3).

OPORA (2012). *Opora Indeks 2010–2011* [in Russian]. Moscow: OPORA.

Resource Center for Small Entrepreneurship. (2017). Statistika MSP [in Russian]. Available at: http://rcsme.ru/ru/statistics.

Rollins, J., & Wyler, L. S. (2010). *International Terrorism and Transnational Crime: Security Threats, US Policy, and Considerations for Congress*. Washington, DC: Congressional Research Service.

Rose-Ackerman, S. (1999). *Corruption and Government: Causes, Consequences, and Reform*. Cambridge: Cambridge University Press.

Schreck, C., & Shakirov, M. (2015, December 11). Russian Businessman Lashes out at Kremlin, Becomes Cause Célèbre. *Radio Free Europe/Radio Liberty*. Available at: www.rferl.org/a/russia-businessman-rails-against-official-extortion/27420874.html.

Shelley, L. (1994). Post-Soviet Organized Crime. *Demokratizatsiya, 2*(31), 341–358.

Shelley, L. (2000). Corruption in the Post-Yeltsin Era. *East European Constitutional Review, 9*, 70–74.

Shelley, L. (2005). Civil Society Mobilized against Corruption: Russia and Ukraine. In M. Johnston (Ed.), *Civil Society and Corruption: Mobilizing for Reform* (pp. 3–21). Lanham, MD: UPA.

Shelley, L. (2014). *Dirty Entanglements: Corruption, Crime, and Terrorism*. Cambridge: Cambridge University Press.
Shere, J. (2011). Vietnam: Complex Combinations, Dynamic Partnerships. *SPEA Magazine*, Spring. Available at: https://spea.indiana.edu/magazine/Spring-2011/articles/vietnam.shtml
Single Registry of Small and Medium Enterprises. (2017). Kolichestvo individual'nykh predrinimatelei [in Russian]. Available at: www.nalog.ru/rn77/related_activities/reg-business/.
Tikhomirov, Y. (1990). Predprinimatel'skie organizatsii Sankt-Peterburgskoi burzhuazii kontsa XIX – nachala XX vv (doctoral dissertation autoreferat) [in Russian]. Leningrad: Institute of the USSR History of the Academy of Sciences.
Transparency International. (2016). Corruption Perceptions Index 2016 – Results. Available at: www.transparency.org/news/feature/corruption_perceptions_index_2016.
Volkov, D. (2011). *Perspektivy grazhdanskogo obshchestva v Rossii* [in Russian]. Moscow: Levada Center.
Williams, P. (2013). Lawlessness and Disorder: An Emerging Paradigm for the 21st Century. In M. Miklaucic & J. Brewer (Eds.), *Convergence: Illicit Networks and National Security in the Age of Globalization* (pp. 15–36). Washington, DC: NDU Press.
World Bank. (2008). *Fighting Corruption Through Collective Action: A Guide for Business*. Washington, DC: The World Bank.
Zygar, M. (2014). The International Press Freedom Award Acceptance Speech. Available at: https://cpj.org/awards/2014/mikhail-zygar-russia.php

2 From State Capture to "Market Capture"
The Russian Entrepreneurial Environment

While the research on entrepreneurship in Western countries is more than a century old, the study of entrepreneurial activity in Russia is a relatively new phenomenon. Entrepreneurship as a free-enterprise activity was not allowed in the Soviet Union. Economic and political reforms initiated by the General Secretary of the Communist Party Mikhail Gorbachev in the late 1980s were crucial for the formation of the entrepreneurial sector in Russia. Although Gorbachev saw these reforms as an opportunity to improve the USSR's stagnating economy, quite unexpectedly, they failed to save the Soviet system from further deterioration and instead brought it to its end. The perestroika era gave hope to many emerging private businesses and entrepreneurs. In 1991, the Supreme Council, the key legislative body in the Soviet Union, adopted a set of laws that revived entrepreneurship and led to the mass privatization of state enterprises and property. The Yeltsin era ensured further expansion of the private sector and entrepreneurial activity.

Privatization policies offered opportunities to transfer property from the public sector toward private capital. However, large-scale corruption and the involvement of organized crime during the privatization process became the main obstacles to the efficient allocation of resources. In the post-Soviet period, state institutions were captured by organized crime and private interest groups who took advantage of their collusion with public officials to gain access to valuable assets in the economy. The resulting insecurity of property rights and administrative abuses of power by public officials became key impediments to the development of the entrepreneurial sector in Russia. In addition, the process of industrial concentration and the formation of large corporations affiliated with the government limited the access of small businesses and entrepreneurs to financial resources and public procurement. These negative trends became especially noticeable in the 2000s during the formation of the contemporary system of crony state capitalism. In this context, this chapter explores the historical, socio-economic, and political factors that impede the growth of entrepreneurship in Russia.

Literature Review

The analytical framework of this research lies at the intersection of two large bodies of literature. The first stream focuses on the study of corruption in the post-Soviet countries, while the second is related to entrepreneurial development in post-communist transition economies. The integration of these fields offers a valuable opportunity to understand the interdependences and connections between the two phenomena in cross-national contexts. Despite the great explanatory potential of such integrated research into the impact of corruption on the entrepreneurial sector, it remains scattered and unfocused largely because the study of entrepreneurship in Russia is a relatively new phenomenon. During the Soviet era, this phenomenon received little attention because the state both limited economic freedoms in the formal sector of the economy and denied the existence of the shadow sector, which emerged as a reaction to restrictions imposed by the government on entrepreneurial activity.

The last two decades have witnessed the emergence of a substantial body of literature on corruption in the post-Soviet space. The pioneering studies of organized crime and corruption in Russia and other ex-Soviet republics were published in *Demokratizatsiya, the Journal of Post-Soviet Democratization*. As Louise Shelley indicates, "exposing the crime issue in the mid-1990s required courage on the part of the journal [*Demokratizatsiya*] and the Helen Dwight Reid Educational Foundation, which published the journal."[1] At the present time, the seriousness of the problem of corruption and organized crime in the post-Soviet space is widely recognized.[2] Post-communist Russia inherited many corrupt practices from the Soviet era. These practices go beyond traditional forms of corruption, such as bribery, extortion, embezzlement, nepotism, and favoritism. The Soviet system gave rise to a wide range of specific informal practices. Improper use of socialized property, for example, spread across the Soviet Union. Another form of informal practices common for the Soviet people was *krugovaya poruka* (collective [ir]responsibility), which generally means collective support for circumventing formal institutions and regulations.[3] Informal practices were also widely spread in the judicial branch. For example, decisions in courts were often based on so-called "telephone justice," meaning informal influence executed by public officials in the judiciary.[4]

Centralized restrictions imposed on the industrial and private sectors led to the emergence of a black market and a class of middlemen engaged in arranging unofficial barter and trade between enterprises and individuals. In the Russian language, these middlemen were often referred to as *tolkachi*.[5] They played an important entrepreneurial role in the shadow economy. Yet, their illegal status was responsible for the negative connotation of the term *tolkachi* and negative attitudes toward them among the general public. Interestingly, there is a historical continuity in suspicion against entrepreneurs. In post-Soviet Russia, entrepreneurs are often called "new robber barons" or "new Russians." According to Sophie Boutillier, negative perceptions about entrepreneurs emerged because their success "was chalked up either to the dubious support of the Russian mafia or to less violent but equally pervasive government corruption."⁶ The term "new Russians" is derogatory, meaning businessmen who gain their wealth though the exploitation and impoverishment of the Russian people.⁷ Such negative public opinion about entrepreneurs stems from the mass privatization of state enterprises in the 1990s that was based on nontransparent and informal procedures, which allowed insiders close to high-ranking public officials to accrue valuable assets for almost nothing.

The centralized planned economy was responsible for widespread report padding in the Soviet Union. This term means false reporting or overstatements generally found in centralized economies, where enterprises are encouraged to demonstrate the fulfillment of production plans. For example, according to the 1984 Uzbek Central Committee report, "the ability to fulfill the plan at any cost was valued over all else. As a result, such alien and immoral phenomena as report-padding, hoodwinking and bribery have penetrated our lives."⁸ The domination of production plans in the economy and their importance for communist authorities explain why report padding was ubiquitous among Soviet enterprises.

Alena Ledeneva examines another type of informal practice pervasive in the Soviet Union, which is known as *blat*.⁹ In a broad sense, *blat* means the use of personal networks and informal relations to obtain goods and services under the rationing system. The collapse of the state-centralized economy and the emergence of new market conditions resulted in "the monetization of *blat*" in post-Soviet Russia, where bribes and "grease" money paid by citizens and businessmen replaced the personal favors commonly used in the Communist era.¹⁰ According to Ledeneva's estimates, "about 90 percent of bribes in Russia are paid by businessmen for export licensing and quotas, state budget transactions, tax transfers, custom duties, privatization deals, and servicing debts to the federal budget."¹¹ Importantly, in the post-perestroika period, the problem of corruption significantly increased due to the insecurity of property rights, the highly unstable institutional environment, policy uncertainty, constant changes in legislation and its manipulations by powerful interest groups and individuals interested in gaining access to transitional rents through the privatization process. During the transitional period, the disruption of the public administration system was also facilitated by the low salaries of public servants and a low level of administrative control over numerous regulatory agencies.

As indicated by Andrei Shleifer and Robert Vishny, in Soviet Russia, the industrial organization of corruption was monopolized by the Communist Party, and bribes from state enterprises were channeled through local Communist Party committees.¹² Corruption schemes outside this system were penalized by the Soviet bureaucracy, which significantly limited their occurrence. This situation radically changed in post-Soviet Russia, where numerous regulatory agencies began to compete with each other for informal rents in the form of bribes and "grease" payments. Currently, Russian businesses are subject to numerous inspections by regulatory agencies, including tax, fire safety, sanitation, labor protection, technical supervision, and social security, among others. Competing public agencies introduce their own regulations and set their own bribe rates, which increases the level of uncertainty for doing business.

Studies of Russian entrepreneurship show that inefficient government policies were a significant obstacle for its development and growth throughout history. There is a widely shared opinion among scholars regarding a historical continuity in the state-centered nature of the Russian economy and entrepreneurship in particular. According to Cyril Black, "If the Russian and Soviet experience has a particular distinguishing feature, it is certainly the role of the state in entrepreneurial activity." Similarly, William Blackwell suggests that the state "is the 'red thread' of Russian entrepreneurial history, as deeply interwoven with this activity, as with other sectors of Russian life through centuries."[13] Unlike Western countries, the development of Russian entrepreneurship was dominated by state interests in various historical periods. This raises the question of how the domination of the state hindered entrepreneurial development in the national economy. Despite certain progress in this area, most microenterprises and small businesses show no tendency toward growth, balancing at some basic level of survival. Not surprisingly, some experts categorize the entrepreneurial sector in Russia as a *kiosk* [small shop] entrepreneurship.[14] This chapter addresses this question by focusing on various linkages between historical, socio-economic, and political factors that reinforce their impact on entrepreneurship.

History of Entrepreneurship in Russia

The history of entrepreneurship in Russia goes back to the establishment of the first ancient Slavic state called Kievan Rus'. The state was created in the ninth century by East Slavic tribes and existed until the mid-thirteenth century under the rule of the Rurik dynasty. The modern peoples of Belarus, Ukraine, and Russia can trace their heritage to Kievan Rus'. The first entrepreneurs in Kievan Rus' were mostly engaged in commerce, trade, and artisanry. These occupations were considered important and respected activities, and entrepreneurs enjoyed a high status in the social hierarchy. As William Blackwell notes, "not only did merchants and artisans have political power and substantial wealth, but almost everyone above the lowest level of peasants engaged in economic enterprise of one type or another."[15] In the tenth century, Kievan Rus' experienced a period of rapid economic expansion due to the establishment of trading routes with the Byzantine Greeks in the south-west and the Vikings in the north-west. Merchants also traveled extensively in the south-eastern direction, making trading partners in Persia and the countries of Central Asia.

In the late eleventh century, Kievan Rus' began slowly to decline. A confluence of various factors contributed to its final disintegration in the thirteenth century, including the Mongol invasion, dynastic power struggles, and rivalries between various regional principalities. Another prominent factor responsible for the decline of Kievan Rus' was the collapse of Constantinople, which at that time was one of the key commercial partners and trading routes of Kievan Rus'. In the late fifteenth century, the Grand Dukes of Moscow took over the eastern territories of the former state of Kievan Rus' and formed the Muscovy state that later became known as the Tsardom of Russia and then the Russian Empire. Most of early Muscovite industrial entrepreneurs were either of merchant background, like those in the Stroganov, Tretyakov, or Ryabushinski dynasties, or they were craftsmen, like the Demidov, Morozov, or Mamontov dynasties.[16]

In the late seventeenth and early eighteenth centuries, the development of Russian entrepreneurship experienced a boom under the rule of Peter the Great, who made significant attempts to create and support manufacturing in the mining, textile, and shipbuilding industries. To foster industrial development, Peter the Great brought many foreigners to Russia for their technical skills and competence. Russia's large unexplored market attracted many entrepreneurs from foreign countries and they quickly gained important positions in the country's economic life.[17] The guilds founded in the time of Peter the Great (the first prototypes of collective business organizations in contemporary Russia) facilitated the growth of entrepreneurship. However, further entrepreneurial development was significantly restricted by the existence of serfdom in Russia. The reforms introduced by Alexander the Second in the 1880s were aimed at solving this problem and stimulating economic development. The Emancipation Reform of 1861 that effectively abolished serfdom provided a strong impetus for industrial development in the Russian Empire, which led to the creation of the railroad industry, a reorganization of the machinery industry, and to the foundation of stock exchanges.

In the late nineteenth century, Russia witnessed the creation of the industrial base of entrepreneurship. In the early twentieth century, entrepreneurship became a widespread phenomenon in the Russian Empire. At the same time, the formation of entrepreneurs as a new class of private owners was heavily influenced by the state and foreign capital. During this period, various private joint-stock banks were opened in Russian cities. By the beginning of the twentieth century, two-thirds of all industrial output in the Russian economy was produced by enterprises.[18] Especially profitable were cotton production, trade, and credit. However, high profits were also a sign of the monopolization processes that were typical of Russia's industrial development. The syndicates Prodamet (metal production), Produgol (coal production), and Med (copper production) controlled 60–70 percent of the trade in their commodities.[19] Another example is the railroad industry that was controlled by the Prodvagon syndicate that included 14 factories manufacturing railroad cars for state-owned and private railroads.

After the February and October Revolutions of 1917, Russia took a course aimed at the elimination of market structures and the formation of a centralized economy. All large enterprises were nationalized. A new economic policy (NEP) that was implemented between 1921 and 1926 brought some revival in entrepreneurial activity. The NEP reforms intended to reintroduce market mechanisms. However, as Peter Boettke and Bridget Butkevich note:

> The Nepmen [capitalist entrepreneurs during the NEP] lived in fear of reprisals against their wealth ... like today's typical Russian businessmen,

the Nepmen's time horizon of investment was short, and many sought to hide their wealth or consume their assets in the short-term rather than expose those assets to confiscation in the near future.[20]

Russian history has confirmed that these fears were well-founded and justified. In the late 1920s, entrepreneurship was again curtailed by the Communist government, and the Soviet economy became subject to further centralization efforts. Only in the 1990s, after the collapse of the Soviet Union, did entrepreneurship re-emerge from scratch.

The formation of the first collective organizations of entrepreneurs in contemporary Russia began during the perestroika era in the late 1980s. In 1987, Mikhail Gorbatchev, then General Secretary of the Communist Party, introduced the most ambitious plan for reforming the private sector of the Soviet economy, which eventually undermined the socialist centralized system. New legal institutions initiated by Gorbachev and authorized by the USSR Supreme Council laid the foundation for the re-emergence of entrepreneurship in then Soviet Russia. They included the laws "On Individual Labor Activity," "On Cooperation," and "On Enterprises and Entrepreneurship." The Law "On Individual Labor Activity" was adopted in 1986 and came into force in 1987. It defined legal norms for the operation of private enterprise, yet, it did not intend to encourage entrepreneurship.

In 1987, the decree "On the Creation of Cooperatives in the Service Sphere for the Population" authorized the foundation of cooperatives. This decree, however, contained a special provision that significantly restricted economic freedoms of cooperative owners. Specifically, the provision allowed individuals to create cooperatives only under the authority of state enterprises, local government commissions, or similar organizations. One year later, the law "On Cooperation" removed this provision, thus opening a window of opportunity for entrepreneurial activity in Russia that had been constrained by the previous decree. According to this law, individuals were allowed to open cooperatives as private enterprises owned by at least three people. However, certain restrictions on cooperative activity remained in the legislature. For example, the foundation of cooperatives was limited in certain sectors of the economy. Furthermore, public officials were allowed to fix and set prices for the products of cooperatives. Finally, cooperative purchases were subject to special fees and charges. Regardless, the cooperative movement "has mushroomed, despite restrictive government policies and a hostile social climate."[21]

The big breakthrough in the legislature related to the private sector came in January 1991 when the law "On Enterprises and Entrepreneurship" was adopted by the USSR Supreme Council. For the first time since 1917, "private enterprise" was introduced as a legal term. The law "On Enterprises and Entrepreneurship" allowed any individual to open a private enterprise and own private property. Later, in April 1991, the USSR Supreme Council adopted another law, "On Principles of Entrepreneurship," which further clarified the legal terminology related to private enterprise. According to this law, private enterprise was defined as:

initiative-taking, self-development by citizens that is intended to obtain income or profit ... and is performed for oneself and at one's own risk and property responsibility, or is performed on behalf of and at the property responsibility of a legal person – an enterprise.[22]

According to the Goskomstat, the centralized statistics agency in the Soviet Union (now the Federal Statistics Service), over 700,000 small enterprises were registered in 1993, which accounted for 11.5 percent of total employment in Russia.[23]

In July 1991, the USSR Supreme Council adopted another groundbreaking law "On the Basic Principles of the Decentralization and Privatization of Enterprises," which specified procedures for transfers of state property to private owners. This law was followed by a set of other legislative acts that laid the foundation for the mass privatization of state enterprises and property in the early 1990s. These laws led to a dramatic transformation in Russia during the following two decades. Not only did they facilitate a rapid growth of private enterprises in the national economy, but they were also responsible for the creation of new industries, including investment, banking, and telecommunications. By 1998, seven years after the law "On the Basic Principles of the Decentralization and Privatization of Enterprises" came into power, the private sector represented 88.1 percent of industrial enterprise ownership, while government ownership constituted only 5.1 percent.[24]

The late 1980s also witnessed the formation of collective entrepreneurial organizations. Specifically, in 1988, the Association of Joint Ventures, International Partnerships, and Organizations began its work in Moscow. Its key objective was to facilitate the expansion of economic ties between business circles in Russia and foreign countries and protect the rights and interests of joint ventures and international organizations. In 1990, the Union of Public Associations of Entrepreneurs and Tenants was founded to protect economic and social interests of its members and provide legal, organizational, and informational support for their activities. Following an initiative proposed by several deputies in 1990, the Supreme Council created the USSR Scientific and Industrial Union by analogy with the Union of Industrial and Trade Enterprises of the Russian Empire that had existed at the beginning of the twentieth century. After the collapse of the USSR in 1991, the Scientific and Industrial Union was transformed into the International Confederation of Industrialists and Entrepreneurs and later into the Russian Union of Industrialists and Entrepreneurs. Similarly, the Union of Cooperatives of the USSR was transformed into the League of Cooperators and Entrepreneurs of Russia.

In 1993, the Russian government passed the law, "On Chambers of Commerce and Industry of the Russian Federation," which defined them as non-governmental, non-profit organizations. This law laid the legal foundation for representative and other functions performed by the Chamber of Commerce and Industry of the Russian Federation. At the same time, new entrepreneurial organizations were formed at the national, regional, and grassroots levels. Entrepreneurs in various industries formed professional associations that could represent their interests. One of the first among them was the Association of Russian Banks. The crisis of 1998, which was especially troublesome for individual entrepreneurs, revealed the need to establish collective organizations that focus specifically on protecting the interests of microenterprises and small businesses. At that time, there was no single organization that could unite individual entrepreneurs from various regions and sectors of the economy. To fill this vacuum, the Association of Entrepreneurs OPORA Russia was formed in 2001. In 2017, it included about 450,000 entrepreneurs and united more than 100 trade unions, associations, and guilds. Now, branches of this association operate in all regions of the Russian Federation.

The challenges of the development of a market economy in Russia, various inconsistencies of economic policies, and the increasing administrative burden on entrepreneurial activity predetermined the creation of business associations to protect their members from violations of their rights. Taking this into account, this book provides a new conceptual framework to analyze corruption in the administrative system as a violation of both entrepreneurial and human rights. This framework centers around business communities and collective entrepreneurial organizations as protectors of entrepreneurial and human rights. Entrepreneurs and their collective organizations represent an important part of civil society. Under the conditions of Russia's deteriorating political environment and shrinking civic space, collective business organizations can take the lead in the promotion of anti-corruption initiatives and broader human rights campaigns.

The Vertical of Power in Putin's Russia

Throughout its history, the Russian entrepreneurial sector has been constantly in turmoil. At the same time, some historical periods were more detrimental to the development of entrepreneurship than others. The state has always played a dominant role in Russia's economy; yet state-centered trends have been characterized by certain fluctuations. The post-perestroika era brought certain improvements in the institutional environment in the entrepreneurial sector. As a result, the number of small businesses rose in the 1990s. The situation changed in the 2000s, when the development of the entrepreneurial sector experienced a significant slowdown. This became particularly noticeable after 2008, with an exponential decay of the population of entrepreneurs. Although not the sole culprit, the change in Russia's political regime played a critical role in this process, bringing new challenges for entrepreneurs and small businesses.

In his attempt to centralize control over the state and economy, President Putin dedicated significant efforts to demolish the separation of powers, eliminate the independence of the judiciary, and put pressure on the media and civil society. The media became a primary target of the centralization campaign during Putin's first presidential term. As a result, Freedom House downgraded Russia's press status from "partly free" to "not free" in 2003. The centralization trend became obvious in almost all spheres of political and social activities in Russia during Putin's second and third presidential terms. In 2005, Freedom

House changed Russia's freedom status from "partly free" to "not free."[25] A serious setback for democratic institutions was the abolition of direct elections for regional governors. In 2013, Putin signed a law that allowed him to appoint candidates who would lead all Russia's regions.[26] During his third presidential term, Putin took advantage of United Russia's parliamentary majority to rewrite the Russian Constitution increasing the presidential term from four to six years.

Another step toward political centralization occurred with the introduction of repressive measures against civil society and human rights NGOs. These measures included restrictions on their funding, negative media campaigns, and state coercion. In 2012, Putin signed the Federal Law "On Amendments to Legislative Acts of the Russian Federation regarding the Regulation of the Activities of Non-Profit Organizations Performing the Functions of a Foreign Agent" (also known as the "foreign agent" law). According to this law, NGOs that receive foreign donations and engage in "political activity" must register and declare themselves as foreign agents. Historically and linguistically, the term "foreign agent" has negative connotations. It is comparable with such words as "spy" or "traitor," especially in the context of the rhetoric used during the Cold War period. The lack of clear specifications of what constitutes "political activity" led to a situation in which public officials had wide discretion in applying this law to any NGO that did not demonstrate its loyalty to the regime. Not only did this law have a negative impact on Russian civil society, it also had broader consequences for the country's deteriorating political environment. First of all, it increased registration barriers for NGOs classified as "foreign agents." Second, many NGOs engaged in providing accountability and transparency of public administration, such as Transparency International Russia, became subject to extensive audits and inspections. Third, government agencies were granted the authority to intervene in the internal operations of human rights organizations and suspend them for up to six months. Finally, the "foreign agent" law increased the overall administrative burden on NGOs representing civil society in Russia.

The Movement for the Defense of Voters' Rights *Golos* was one of the first NGOs fined under the "foreign agent" law. The Russian Justice Ministry required "Golos" to register itself as a "foreign agent" for accepting an award from the Norwegian Helsinki Committee. Even though the organization did not accept the prize, its offices were raided by the police and its operations were suspended for six months. The Levada Center, Russia's only independent polling agency, became another victim of the "foreign agent" law, despite the fact that it had suspended foreign funding in 2013.[27] In 2016, the Levada Center was classified as a foreign agent, which prevented it from working on the election. Other prominent human rights and civil society organizations that have been harassed by public authorities under the "foreign agent" law include the historical organization Memorial, the research and education Dynasty Foundation, the Russian Committee Against Torture, Transparency International Russia, the Institute for Information Freedom Development, and the Glasnost Defense Foundation. As of 2017, Russia's Justice Ministry had classified 158 groups as "foreign agents," and the courts had imposed fines on many of them for failing to comply with the law, and about 30 of them had to close their offices to avoid the forced registration.[28] Several international organizations, including the American MacArthur Foundation and the Center for International Private Enterprise, closed their Russian divisions, citing a hostile environment that followed the adoption of the "foreign agent" law.

The "foreign agent" law was criticized by national human rights activists and international organizations. In 2014, Russia's Human Rights Commissioner Vladimir Lukin, together with a number of non-governmental groups, filed an appeal with the Constitutional Court, complaining that this law violated constitutional provisions on freedom of association (Article 30). Russia's Constitutional Court ruled that the "foreign agent" law did not infringe on the right to association. Attempts by Russia's Presidential Council for Civil Society and Human Rights to call upon the Plenum of the Supreme Court to examine the application of the law were equally unsuccessful. A report from the Council of Europe Commissioner for Human Rights, Nils Muižnieks, found that the "foreign agent" law is not compatible with international and European human rights standards.[29] According to this report:

> The application of this law has had a chilling effect on the work of civil society organizations in the Russian Federation and has considerably interfered with the rights to freedom of association and freedom of expression of many non-commercial organizations and human rights defenders, sometimes with severe consequences.[30]

In 2016, one of the co-authors of the "foreign agent" law, Irina Yarovaya, initiated another widely criticized law that significantly restricted freedom of assembly in Russia. The Anti-Terror Package (also known as "the Yarovaya law") introduced severe sentences for organizers of unsanctioned protests and imposed the requirement on Internet providers and phone companies to keep their customers' communication data and report it to public authorities. The Yarovaya law was yet another attempt to harass and prosecute political opponents.

The Russian political system is often described as "the vertical of power." This term refers to a centralized vertical chain of hierarchical authority created by President Putin and his associates to monopolize power and maintain control over the electoral, legislative, judiciary, and economic spheres.[31] Putin placed his close friends and loyal supporters in high-ranking positions not only within public agencies but also within private and state corporations. In the last decade, the ruling elite was also actively engaged in taking over successful businesses and removing economic rivals. These activities involved the law enforcement system, including the prosecutor's office, police, and tax authorities that were responsible for making "offers that could not be refused."

An illustrative example is Russia's major titanium producer VSMPO-Avisma, whose co-owners were forced to transfer their company to the Russian state corporation Rostec, headed by Sergey Chemezov, who is Putin's close friend. Rostec's CEO Chemezov is a former security officer who served with Vladimir Putin in the KGB in East Germany in the 1980s. One of the former co-owners of VSMPO-Avisma described the deal in the following way:

> It was clear that the state was absolutely determined to take control over the company. My position was as follows: human life is finite, the state is forever. In a dialogue with the state, we can argue only to a certain point. Then, one has to reconcile his position.[32]

VSMPO-Avisma is only one company among many others whose owners have received threats from enforcement officers and public officials requiring "peaceful" transfers of business assets to the political elite.

An analysis of Russia's legislature demonstrates that many laws adopted in the last decade were tailored to specific individuals and groups closely related to the President. A good example is the so-called "Rotenberg tax," imposed in 2015 on drivers of trucks over 12 tons. The Rotenberg tax illustrates the detrimental effect of the vertical of power on small businesses and entrepreneurs. To collect all proceeds, the Russian Government established an electronic system called "Platon." Its operator became the company RT-Invest Transport Systems, whose owners were directly affiliated with President Putin. Specifically, 50 percent of the RT-Invest Transport Systems belonged to Igor Rotenberg, the son of Putin's childhood friend and judo partner, Arkady Rotenberg. The rest of the company was owned by the state corporation Rostec, headed by Chemezov. The introduction of this burdensome toll made many small truck driving businesses unprofitable and sparked their protests all across Russia. However, the protests failed to transform into a coherent social movement.

In terms of historical analogies, some business owners who lost their companies compare "Vladimir Putin's destruction of entrepreneurs and genuine entrepreneurial culture" with "Stalin's destruction of peasants in the 1930s."[33] The practice of illegal business raiding (known as *reiderstvo*) committed by corrupt public officials and criminal organizations has become a major threat to hundreds of thousands of Russian entrepreneurs. In this respect, the personal story of Igor Bitkov is illustrative of these destructive processes. Once the owner of a flourishing paper business in Kaliningrad, Bitkov had to flee Russia with his family when his company was seized by public officials. According to Bitkov, the seizure was politically motivated and his only mistake was to decline the offer of Kaliningrad's governor to collaborate with United Russia, the ruling political party in Russia.[34] After his refusal, his company was forced into bankruptcy and a criminal case was opened against the businessman. As Bitkov's wife describes the current situation in Russia, "They want businesspeople who have money, influence and success to support them. They won't let you be independent."[35] Entrepreneurs who try to stay independent face negative consequences.

Bitkov's story is typical of authoritarian regimes where neither business communities, nor civil society organizations can influence the state in any decisive way. Authoritarian regimes undermine the independence of private and public actors in every possible way and expand their control over businessmen. In Bitkov's words, this is what happens in contemporary Russia

> because Putin understands that it is precisely such people who are the real threat to his dictatorship. Having resources, influence and the support of the population, they could effectively struggle against the archaic, semi-feudal Putin regime which has blocked the development of the country and is pushing it on the path to degradation.[36]

The destruction of the middle class of entrepreneurs is also facilitated by a high level of monopolization of the Russian economy.

State Capture Versus "Market Capture"

The 1990s saw the formation of a class of Russian oligarchs who gained access to the country's economic resources through informal relations with public officials at the federal and regional levels. Informal relationships between private insider groups and politicians were mutually beneficial. On the one hand, oligarchs penetrated the political sphere in order to twist the legal and regulatory framework to their advantage. On the other hand, corrupt politicians received informal payments and other favors from oligarchs in return for providing opportunities for illicit enrichment and ensuring immunity from prosecution. The process of illicit enrichment of the economic and political elites is a symptom of weak and failed states where public institutions are captured by private interests and organized crime. Originally, the concept of state capture was developed in the early 2000s by researchers from the World Bank who analyzed political corruption in post-communist countries in Central Asia and Russia.[37] According to their definition, state capture represents "shaping the formation of the basic rules of the game (i.e. laws, rules, decrees, and regulations), through illicit and non-transparent private payments to public officials."[38] One of the negative consequences of state capture in the post-perestroika period was the corrosion of the public administrative system and destruction of its ability to provide secure property rights.

Since Putin's rise to power, the role of "captors" has been gradually taken over by high-ranking public officials. The way President Putin and his circle maintained their contacts with Russian organized crime and used their public positions to take control over the most valuable economic resources is well documented in the literature.[39] By appointing his close friends and associates to the leading positions in the private sector, Putin created a system of crony state capitalism characterized by the domination of private interests pursued by political actors and civil servants in the economic sphere. In parallel with state capture by informal clientelistic groups, "market capture" by the political elite shaped the formation of industries and the financial sector in Russia. In this context, the term "market capture" refers to the predatory nature of the Russian political elite engaged in seizing economic resources and businesses through the use of quasi-legal and illegal instruments. "Market capture" manifests itself in the monopolization of the wealth redistribution system by the ruling elite. In this respect, "market capture" has a double meaning. First, it is an allusion to market failure, a term widely used in economics to describe situations where the allocation of goods and services is not efficient. Second, similar to state capture by private interest groups, "market capture" by the political elite represents another side of the corrupt system of public administration.

In 2012, *Forbes* conducted an investigation to assess the degree of influence of "Putin's team" over the Russian economy. It should be noted that the term "Putin's team" refers not to a group of people who come together in a traditional way to achieve some common goal, but rather to people whose only common characteristic is their loyalty or long-term friendship with Russia's President. In most cases, they had previously worked together with Vladimir Putin during his professional career in the KGB in the 1980s or in the Administration of Saint Petersburg in the 1990s. According to *Forbes*, Putin's team plays a very important role in the Russian economy, controlling various industries, large state corporations, strategically important public projects, and lucrative procurement contacts. The *Forbes* investigation shows that in 2012, "the total revenue of companies controlled by Putin's managers amounted to 12.3 trillion rubles," which is "equivalent to about 22.6 percent of the total Russian GDP."[40] Interestingly, six out of Russia's ten largest companies (by revenue) were directly managed by Putin's friends, who during his rule significantly increased their personal wealth and power.[41] Nine managers of Putin's team controlled strategically important positions in various spheres, including the media, the financial sector, transportation, construction, defense, the gas, and oil industries. It is worth noting that few members of Putin's team had any previous experience in the industry they were appointed to lead.[42]

Some of Putin's friends head Russia's largest private corporations. For example, Alexey Miller is Deputy Chairman of the Board of Directors and CEO of the largest gas corporation, Gazprom. Another example is Arkady Rotenberg, who owns the Stroygazmontazh group, the largest construction company for gas pipelines and electrical power supply. Putin's friends were also appointed to the leading positions of Russia's largest state corporations. As a legal entity, state corporations have a privileged position and enjoy preferential treatment in Russia's economy. In fact, some researchers attribute their creation in the mid-2000s to an attempt by Putin's team to take control over the country's valuable assets.[43] In 2007, the Federal Law "On Nonprofit Organizations" was amended to include a new legal entity in the form of state corporations. The law defined state corporations as nonprofit organizations, without membership, constituted by the Russian Federation on the basis of a property contribution and created to perform social, managerial, and other socially useful functions. An important feature of state corporations is that their top executives are appointed by Russia's government or by the President himself. Importantly, state corporations received significant property contributions and direct government funds, without any obligation to pay them back.

Initially, the government established seven state corporations: the Deposit Insurance Agency, the Housing Fund, the Bank for Development, the State Corporation for Construction of Olympic Objects (Olympstroy), the Nanotechnologies State Corporation (Rusnano), the Russian Technologies State Corporation (Rostec), and the State Nuclear Corporation (Rosatom). In 2015, another state corporation, Roskosmos, was created in the space industry. These state corporations have a very broad array of functions ranging from national defense to innovation policy. Only two of them were organized as temporary entities. Olympstroy was liquidated after the closing of the 2014 Olympic Games in Sochi. Similarly, the Housing Fund is to be liquidated after the fulfillment of its mission. Other state corporations continue to function in the economy, with the only exception being Rusnano, which was transformed into an open stock company in 2011.

The specific legal status, obscure regulation, and insufficient economic justification for the establishment of state corporations provoked a strong wave of criticism among economists, legal scholars, and political scientists.[44] For example, according to Sergey Silvestrov and Alexei Zeldner, key problems of Russian state corporations include their nontransparent procurement, unaccountable management, and weak external control over their financial activities.[45] Another problem relates to protectionism that leads to market distortions, which negatively affect all other economic actors, in particular, microenterprises and small businesses. When the State Duma adopted the federal laws regarding the establishment of state corporations, they did not include any effective mechanisms to ensure accountability and transparency of their activities. Their establishment was a political decision, rather than an economically justified necessity, which is also confirmed by closed discussions about legislative drafting, the lack of the related public debates in the media, and a surprisingly unusual haste in their adoption.

Vague legislature regarding state corporations made them a very easy tool to siphon resources from the national economy into the pockets of their top executives. Specifically, Russia's legislature granted them a high level of financial flexibility and operational freedom, leaving their top managers with wide discretion in the use of public funds and resources. The lack of transparency and accountability resulted in excessive salaries received by top executives of state corporations. For example, inspections conducted by the Prosecutor General's Office in 2009 registered numerous cases of excessive compensation plans, unjustified bonuses, and other payments to executives of the Housing Fund, the Bank for Development, Rosatom, Olympstroy, and Rusnano.[46] Just to give one example, according to the income statement published on the official website, Sergey Kiriyenko received 41,878,279 rubles (equivalent to $1,395,943) in 2011 in his capacity as the Director General of the state corporation Rosatom.[47] In the same year, Steven Chu, the Nobel Prize-winning physicist who served as the United States Secretary of Energy, earned a salary of $199,700,[48] which was about sevenfold less. After his resignation as the Head of Rosatom in 2016, Sergey Kiriyenko was appointed the First Deputy Chief of Staff of the Presidential

Administration. Some analysts explain his close relations with Putin by their common interest in eastern martial arts, while others point to Kiriyenko's attempts to position himself as a loyal and disciplined subordinate in the Kremlin's circles.

Apart from excessive salaries, state corporations were characterized by nontransparent management. For example, the 2011 report by the Analytical Center under the Government of the Russian Federation indicated that in the case of Russian Technologies, all decisions were made by its Director General Sergey Chemezov.[49] Nontransparent procedures made it impossible to identify other decision-makers responsible for the development of the corporation's policy. Specifically, the report noted that "according to a widely accepted opinion, most decisions on Russian Technologies activities were based entirely on personal relations between Chemezov and Putin."[50] This finding was consistent with another analytical report published in 2011 by the Integrum group, an independent management consulting firm based in Moscow.[51] In particular, the report stated that "management and governance in the corporation were not based on market principles," instead, the defining factors in the process of making management decisions were the political and career-oriented motives of top executives.[52] An analysis of the decision-making process in other state corporations also points to an excessive role of individual and personal loyalties in their management systems.

There are three particular groups of challenges associated with the economic activities of Russian state corporations. First, weak oversight over their transactions leads to an increase in corruption risks associated with their access to financial resources and government contracts. Another group of challenges is related to the preferential treatment that state corporations receive from the government and regulatory authorities. This gives them an unfair competitive advantage over other economic actors, especially small and medium-sized enterprises in the private sector. Finally, state corporations control a large variety of enterprises in a number of strategically important sectors of the economy, such as energy, transport, technology, and defense. Moreover, their key strategy is aimed at further expansion by absorbing private competitors in the related industries. This process of industrial concentration parallels the centralization trend in the political sphere. In this respect, state corporations represent a special type of "market capture" by actors affiliated with the political elite.

The negative result of "market capture" is that the Russian economy became skewed between a group of large corporations and another group of small "kiosk-type businesses."[53] In addition to state corporations, many private companies are vertically integrated into large corporations. Large private corporations in Russia control economic activity in their regions. Such corporations often receive preferential treatment from both federal and regional administrations. Their monopolistic behavior constrains the development of the entire entrepreneurial sector. This institutional environment is not favorable for the growth of medium-sized businesses. A relatively high degree of industrial concentration in Russia and protectionism granted to large corporations constitute significant barriers to the entry of new firms in the market. In turn, a lack of medium-sized businesses leads to insufficient market competition, resulting in low competitiveness of Russian products on the international markets. The insufficient development of the entrepreneurial sector has been a pressing problem in Russia. This problem is especially noticeable in cross-country comparisons and international rankings.

Russia's Entrepreneurial Performance and Ecosystem

Cross-country comparisons allow for a better understanding of the dynamics of entrepreneurial activity. They also contribute to in-depth analysis of the relationship between entrepreneurship and various institutional factors that either facilitate or impede small business development. The study of Russia's entrepreneurial performance and institutional environment is based on several international rankings, including the Global Entrepreneurship Monitor, the Global Entrepreneurship Index, and the Female Entrepreneurship Index. There is strong evidence that Russia is lagging in terms of entrepreneurial development not only behind developed economies, but also behind other transition countries of the former Eastern Bloc. For example, Alessandro Kihlgren notes that after the collapse of the Soviet Union and the Eastern Bloc, small business growth was much slower in Russia compared to other post-communist countries, including Poland, the Czech Republic, and Hungary.[54]

Unlike in Russia, the rapidly developed private sector and small businesses in Poland, the Czech Republic, and Hungary became the main force behind their economic recovery in the transition period. In comparison with these countries, Russia's level of entrepreneurial activity remains much lower, even 25 years after the transition from a command economy to a market economy. Among the institutional factors that prevent entrepreneurial development in Russia, Kihlgren distinguishes a high level of corruption, strong income inequality, a business-unfriendly legislative framework, the general situation of instability caused by the lack of clear rules, insufficient financing for small businesses, the market domination of large industrial enterprises, and a high level of crime.[55] International datasets on entrepreneurship and composite indices confirm this finding.

The Global Entrepreneurship Monitor (GEM) is one of the most comprehensive datasets on entrepreneurship. GEM reports are based on a data collection process that provides high quality information on entrepreneurship across the world. Cross-country comparisons help researchers better understand both individual country profiles and global trends in entrepreneurial development. GEM reports allow for the identification of specific institutional factors that impede the development and growth of businesses in Russia. The first GEM report was published in 1999 as a joint project between Babson College (in the USA) and the London Business School (in the UK). This report addressed the question of why some countries are more entrepreneurial than others. Only ten developed countries participated in the GEM pilot project, including eight member countries of the Organisation for Economic Co-operation and Development (OECD), Japan, and the United States. In

2016, the GEM report covered over 100 economies.[56] Currently, the GEM consortium includes over 400 experts on entrepreneurship from over 100 research and academic institutions.[57] GEM reports represent a valuable resource for entrepreneurship scholars and development experts worldwide. Their validity is confirmed by a number of prominent international organizations, such as the United Nations, the World Economic Forum, the World Bank Group, and the OECD.

One of the most important advantages of GEM reports is that they provide comparable data across a large variety of countries on different aspects of entrepreneurship, including its gender dimension. The data for the 2016 GEM report were collected through an adult population survey distributed in 64 world economies and a national experts survey distributed in 65 world economies.[58] In GEM reports, all countries are placed into three groups according to their economic development: factor-driven, efficiency-driven, and innovation-driven economies. This classification is adapted from the World Economic Forum (WEF). According to the WEF, factor-driven economies are dominated by agriculture and resource extraction businesses, with a heavy reliance on unskilled labor and natural resources.[59] Efficiency-driven economies are more competitive and have more effective production processes characterized by a relatively high product quality.[60] Finally, innovation-driven economies are dominated by knowledge-intensive businesses and are characterized by the rapidly expanding service sector.[61]

The 2016 GEM report includes 12 post-communist countries from the former Eastern Bloc. Among them, only Russia (RUS) and Kazakhstan (KAZ) are classified as factor-driven economies. Eight countries are placed in the efficiency-driven group, namely, Bulgaria (BGR), Croatia (HRV), Georgia (GEO), Hungary (HUN), Latvia (LVA), Macedonia (MKD), Poland (POL), and Slovakia (SVK). Finally, Estonia (EST) and Slovenia (SVN) have the most advanced innovation-driven economies in comparison with other post-communist countries. Table 2.1 compares indicators of entrepreneurial activity in Russia and other post-communist countries that participated in the 2016 GEM report.

Table 2.1 demonstrates that in Russia, small and medium-sized businesses produce only 21 percent of Gross Domestic Product (GDP), which is the lowest indicator among post-communist transition economies. Furthermore, Russia's scores on perceived opportunities and perceived capabilities are significantly lower than the related average indicators for the entire GEM sample of the post-communist economies. The first indicator of perceived opportunities measures the percentage of the adult population (between the ages of 18 and 64 years) who see good opportunities to start a company. In Russia, this indicator is 17.9 percent, while an average indicator in the post-communist countries is estimated at 31.5 percent. The second indicator of perceived capabilities measures the percentage of the adult population who believe they have the required skills and knowledge to start a new business. In Russia, this indicator is 28.4 percent, which is significantly lower than an average indicator of 46.0 percent in the post-communist countries. In addition, Russia has the lowest entrepreneurial intentions indicator (2.1 percent), which measures the percentage of the adult

Table 2.1 Russia's scores on indicators of entrepreneurial activity in comparison with other post-communist countries, 2016

	RUS	KAZ	BGR	HRV	HUN	LVA	MKD	POL	GEO	SVK	SVN	EST	Average
SME contribution to GDP (%)	21.0	26.0	66.0	56.0	52.0	72.0	64.0	52.0	n/a	57.0	63.0	75.0	54.9
Perceived opportunities (%)	17.9	44.2	21.0	24.6	30.1	31.9	38.4	39.5	29.5	23.0	25.3	52.3	31.5
Perceived capabilities (%)	28.4	50.0	39.7	50.2	38.4	49.9	54.5	60.2	41.6	44.0	51.8	43.7	46.0
Entrepreneurial intentions (%)	2.1	16.8	7.1	18.2	15.1	18.9	24.9	20.8	12.8	8.0	11.4	16.4	14.4
Early-stage entrepreneurship activity (%)	6.3	10.2	4.8	8.4	7.9	14.2	6.5	10.7	8.6	9.5	8.0	16.2	9.3
Established business ownership rate (%)	5.3	2.4	6.2	4.2	5.5	9.5	7.2	7.1	8.6	6.1	6.7	7.8	6.4
Entrepreneurial employee activity (%)	0.7	0.7	0.9	5.3	3.0	4.5	1.4	5.2	0.5	2.2	4.7	6.3	3.0
Job expectations (6+) (%)	18.7	33.1	13.4	30.4	35.8	31.3	19.0	28.3	20.6	22.2	26.4	27.0	25.5
Innovation (%)	5.4	19.6	17.5	23.3	20.4	29.4	15.5	27.7	20.1	25.9	33.2	34.5	22.7

Source: These data were derived from the Global Entrepreneurship Research Association (2017) The 2015/2016 Global Entrepreneurship Monitor, www.gemconsortium.org/report

population who intend to start a business within the following three years. Russia's scores reflect low perceptions of entrepreneurs about opportunities to start a new business.

One key indicator, the total early-stage entrepreneurship activity (TEA), measures the percentage of the adult population either in the process of starting a business or who have recently started a business.[62] Table 2.1 demonstrates that there is a substantial variation on this indicator among the post-communist economies, ranging from 4.8 percent in Bulgaria to 16.2 percent in Estonia. Russia's TEA indicator of 6.3 percent is the second lowest after Bulgaria. Another indicator of the established business ownership rate shows the percentage of the adult population who own businesses older than 42 months. In Russia, this indicator is the third lowest (5.3 percent) after Kazakhstan (2.4 percent) and Croatia (4.2 percent).

Table 2.1 also contains the indicator of entrepreneurial employee activity that measures the percentage of employees involved in developing new products or setting up a new business unit or subsidiary. It is also relatively low in Russia (0.7 percent) in comparison with an average indicator of 3 percent among the post-communist economies. Finally, Russia has the lowest job expectation indicator of 18.7 percent and the lowest innovation rate of 5.4 percent in this group. The former shows the potential of entrepreneurs to create job opportunities in the coming five years, while the latter measures the potential of entrepreneurs to introduce new goods or services, identify new market niches, and develop innovative methods to distribute their products. The fact that Russia receives the worst scores on these indicators among the post-communist countries provides evidence of the failure of domestic policies and institutions to ensure sustainable and inclusive economic development in the entrepreneurial sector.

In addition to these indicators, GEM reports measure the perceived quality of the entrepreneurial ecosystem. This indicator is estimated as an average value of experts' perceptions on a 9-point scale from 1 (highly insufficient) to 9 (highly sufficient). The perceived quality of the entrepreneurial ecosystem includes several components: entrepreneurial finance, government policy (support and relevance), entrepreneurship programs, entrepreneurship education (at the school and post-school stages), research and development (R&D) transfer, commercial and legal infrastructure, entry regulation, physical infrastructure, and cultural and social norms. Table 2.2 compares the perceived quality of the Russian entrepreneurial ecosystem with other post-communist countries that participated in the 2016 GEM report.

In Table 2.2, education at the post-school stage and internal market dynamics in Russia are the only two indicators with above-average scores among the post-communist countries that participated in the 2016 GEM survey. Russia's weakest conditions of the entrepreneurial ecosystem, with the lowest scores, include entrepreneurial finance, government programs, R&D transfer, market burdens, and entry regulation. This suggests that Russian policy-makers should prioritize the introduction of regulatory reforms to make it easier for entrepreneurs to open and operate new businesses, gain access to finance and government support

Table 2.2 Scores on the perceived quality of the Russian entrepreneurial ecosystem in comparison with other post-communist countries, 2016

	RUS	KAZ	BGR	HRV	HUN	LVA	MKD	POL	GEO	SVK	SVN	EST	Average
Entrepreneurial finance	3.1	4.9	4.4	3.8	4.5	4.6	3.6	4.7	4.0	4.9	3.9	4.9	4.3
Government policies	3.3	5.3	2.6	2.8	3.0	3.9	3.4	4.3	5.6	2.9	4.1	5.0	3.8
Taxes and bureaucracy	3.0	4.3	4.8	2.2	2.8	3.2	4.4	3.2	6.6	3.1	3.0	6.3	3.9
Government programs	2.9	4.6	3.1	3.5	3.4	4.1	4.0	4.0	5.3	3.3	4.3	5.3	4.0
Education at the school stage	3.1	3.0	2.5	2.5	2.2	3.8	3.8	2.6	3.6	3.4	2.7	4.6	3.2
Education at the post-school stage	4.7	4.2	3.7	3.8	4.3	4.8	4.5	3.3	4.8	4.6	4.4	5.5	4.4
R&D transfer	2.7	3.1	3.2	2.7	3.8	3.6	3.5	3.6	3.5	3.3	3.8	4.7	3.5
Commercial and legal infrastructure	4.9	5.2	5.1	4.2	4.9	6.1	5.1	4.6	4.7	4.8	5.0	5.7	5.0
Internal market dynamics	5.8	4.7	4.9	5.5	5.2	4.5	5.6	6.3	5.2	4.5	5.3	4.8	5.2
Market burdens or entry regulation	3.3	4.1	3.8	3.3	4.2	4.1	3.5	4.5	5.1	4.1	4.1	5.6	4.1
Physical infrastructure	5.6	4.1	6.9	6.2	6.9	7.2	6.2	7.0	7.1	6.9	7.0	8.0	6.6
Cultural and social norms	3.4	5.1	3.7	3.0	3.4	4.6	3.7	3.9	5.6	3.7	3.2	6.4	4.1

Source: These data were derived from the Global Entrepreneurship Research Association (2017), The 2015/2016 Global Entrepreneurship Monitor, www.gemconsortium.org/report

programs, as well as facilitate R&D transfers between various sectors in the economy. In addition, Russia has unfavorable conditions (with below-average ratings) in such areas as government policies, taxes and bureaucracy, commercial and legal infrastructure, physical infrastructure, and socio-cultural norms. These conditions represent other critical areas constraining the development of entrepreneurship in Russia that also require urgent attention from policy-makers.

Overall, the 2016 GEM report points to a need to build a more supportive entrepreneurial ecosystem in Russia. The Global Entrepreneurship Index (GEI) could serve as another source of information about obstacles to effective entrepreneurial development in Russia. The GEI is a composite index that was developed by the Global Entrepreneurship and Development Institute (GEDI) in 2011. It defines entrepreneurs as people "with the vision to see an innovation and the ability to bring it to market."[63] The GEI is made up of 24 individual and institutional indicators that are combined into three sub-indices: attitudes, abilities, and aspirations.[64] Attitudes contain such indicators as opportunity perceptions about entrepreneurial potential, startup skills, risk acceptance, networking abilities of entrepreneurs, and cultural support, among others. Abilities consist of such indicators as the prevalence of opportunity-driven versus necessity-driven start-ups, the technological intensity of start-up activity, the quality of human capital, and competition. Aspirations include such indicators as product innovation, process innovation, high growth of businesses, an internalization degree of the exporting potential, and risk capital. In addition, the GEI index measures the impact on entrepreneurship of both individual indicators of entrepreneurial behavior and institutional indicators in the national context. They allow for a deep understanding of the business environment and provide valuable insights into the nature of entrepreneurship. Table 2.3 shows the GEI index and three sub-indices of attitudes, abilities, and aspirations in Russia in the period between 2006 and 2017.

As Table 2.3 demonstrates, despite certain fluctuations in annual values of the GEI index and the three sub-indices of attitudes, abilities, and aspirations, Russia's scores on these indicators remain low. In addition, Russia demonstrates unsatisfactory results on the development of female entrepreneurship. In 2015, Russia received the lowest score of 25.4 on the Female Entrepreneurship Index (FEI) among 14 post-communist countries that participated in the GEDI study of women-owned businesses. The group of post-communist countries included the Czech Republic, Lithuania, Latvia, Poland, Slovenia, Slovakia, Estonia, Hungary, Croatia, Romania, Macedonia, Montenegro, Russia, and Bosnia and Herzegovina. The FEI index was introduced by the GEDI at the 2013 annual meeting of the Dell Women Entrepreneurs Network (DWEN). The FEI index measures the global development of high potential female entrepreneurs, who are defined as "women who own and operate businesses that are innovative, market expanding, and export-oriented."[65] It includes 23 gender-specific variables that characterize three sub-indices of the entrepreneurial environment, such as equal rights and market size, secondary education, business risk, and access to childcare; the entrepreneurial eco-system, such as SME support and training and

Table 2.3 Russia's scores on the Global Entrepreneurship Index and three sub-indices of attitudes, abilities, and aspirations from 2006 to 2017

	2006	2007	2008	2009	2010	2011	2012	2013	2014	2015	2016	2017
Attitudes (ATT)	26.4	21.4	20.8	25.0	24.7	29.2	31.3	31.0	34	31.6	33.9	24.1
Abilities (ABT)	40.0	41.1	39.5	36.2	33.7	35.9	36.1	37.0	36.4	37.3	36.7	29.5
Aspirations (ASP)	29.9	28.9	28.3	28.5	26.1	25.1	24.9	25.8	26.2	26.2	26.1	22.7
GEI	32.1	30.5	29.5	29.9	28.2	30.1	30.8	31.3	32.2	31.7	32.2	25.4

Source: These data were derived from annual reports on the Global Entrepreneurship Index (2006–2017) developed by the Global Entrepreneurship and Development Institute, https://thegedi.org/downloads/

labor force parity; and entrepreneurial aspirations, such as R&D expenditure and external financing.[66]

An analysis of recent reports on entrepreneurship developed by the GEM consortium and the Global Entrepreneurship and Development Institute shows that administrative corruption, burdensome taxation, inefficient regulations, government bureaucracy, and political instability remain significant barriers to doing business in Russia. These persistent problems contributed to a low level of entrepreneurial performance, which is reflected in both the Global Entrepreneurship Index and the Female Entrepreneurship Index. These indices point to the fact that the Russian entrepreneurial ecosystem is significantly hampered by unnecessary barriers and bottlenecks. As the 2017 GEI report states, Russia is held back by poor institutional conditions and government policies that are not favorable to entrepreneurs.[67] As a result, the country remains a factor-driven economy highly dependent on energy and raw materials.

The 2017 GEI report points out that the abundance of natural resources "allowed Russian politicians to fail to introduce the political and economic reforms needed to facilitate innovation and the diversification of the Russian industrial base."[68] In economics, the causal relationship between the abundance of natural resources and a decline in other sectors is often referred to as the Dutch disease[69] or the resource curse. The negative effect of the resource curse goes much further than the decline in production in such sectors as manufacturing and agriculture. Michael Ross' study of countries rich in oil and other mineral resources finds that the resource curse has detrimental effects on democratic development.[70] Unrestrained opportunities for the redistribution of resource rent diminish the incentives of the political elites to create conditions for sustainable economic growth. Consequently, Russian entrepreneurs suffer from a hostile business environment, characterized by political instability, a lack of the rule of law, insufficient business infrastructure, and the domination of large private and state corporations in the market.

Notes

1 Shelley, L. I. Crime and Corruption: Enduring Problems of Post-Soviet Development. *Demokratizatsiya*, *11*(1) (2003), 111.
2 See, for example, Shelley, L. I. Post-Soviet Organized Crime, *Demokratizatsiya*, *2*(31) (1994), 341–358; Wedel, J. R. Clique-Run Organizations and US Economic Aid: An Institutional Analysis, *Demokratizatsiya*, *4*(4) (1996), 571–602; Jaffe, E. D., & Tsimerman, A. Business Ethics in a Transition Economy: Will the Next Russian Generation Be Any Better? *Journal of Business Ethics*, *62*(1) (2005), 87–97; Nichols, P. M. The Fit between Changes to the International Corruption Regime and Indigenous Perceptions of Corruption in Kazakhstan, *University of Pennsylvania Journal of International Law*, *22*(4) (2001), 863–973; Timofeev, L. *Institutsional'naya korruptsiya* [in Russian] (Moscow: RGGU, 2000); Satarov, G. *Diagnostika rossiiskoi korruptsii* [in Russian] (Moscow: INDEM, 2002); Oleinik, A. Biznes po ponyatiiham: ob institutsional'noi modeli rossiiskogo kapitalisma [in Russian], *Voprosy Ekonomiki*, *5* (2001), 4–25; Klyamkin, I., & Timofeev, L. *Tenevaya Rossiya* [in Russian] (Moscow: Russian State University for the Humanities, 2004).

3 Ledeneva, A. V. *Russia's Economy of Favours: Blat, Networking and Informal Exchange* (Cambridge: Cambridge University Press, 1998), p. 81.
4 Shelley, L. I. Corruption in the Post-Yeltsin Era. *East European Constitutional Review, 9* (2000), 72.
5 See, for example, Holmes, L. *The End of Communist Power: Anti-corruption Campaigns and Legitimation Crisis* (Oxford: Oxford University Press, 1993), pp. 143–144; Karklins, R. *The System Made Me Do It: Corruption in Post-Communist Societies* (New York: M.E. Sharpe, 2005), p. 76.
6 Boutillier, S. The Russian Entrepreneur Today: Elements of Analysis of the Socialized Entrepreneur. *Journal of Innovation Economics & Management, 1,* (2008), 145.
7 Ibid.
8 Cited in Holmes, op. cit., p. 175.
9 Ledeneva, op. cit., pp. 1–2.
10 Ibid.
11 Ibid., p. 2.
12 Shleifer, A., & Vishny, R. Corruption. *The Quarterly Journal of Economics, 108*(3) (1993), 605.
13 Blackwell, W. The Russian Entrepreneur in the Tsarist Period: An Overview. In G. Guroff & F. V. Carstensen (Eds.), *Entrepreneurship in Imperial Russia and the Soviet Union* (pp. 13–26) (Princeton, NJ: Princeton University Press, 1983), p. 21.
14 Zhuplev, A., & Shein, V. Small and Medium Size Enterprises in Russia. In L. P. Dana, I. Welpe, M. Han, & V. Ratten (Eds.), *Handbook of Research on European Business and Entrepreneurship: Towards a Theory of Internationalization* (pp. 544–563) (Cheltenham: Edward Elgar, 2008), p. 559.
15 Blackwell, op. cit., p. 13.
16 Ibid., p. 17.
17 Gréen, O. S. *Entrepreneurship in Russia: Western Ideas in Russian Translation* (Gothenburg: University of Gothenburg, 2009), p. 244.
18 Lobyzenkova, V. Istoriya predprinimatel'stva v Rossii: traditsii i sovremennost' [in Russian]. *Vestnik Volgogradskogo Gosudarstvennogo Universiteta, 9*(6) (2007), 208.
19 Yudanov, A. USSR: Large Enterprises in the USSR: The Functional Disorder. In A. D. Chandler, F. Amatori, & T. Hikino (Eds.), *Big Business and the Wealth of Nations* (Cambridge: Cambridge University Press, 1997), p. 398.
20 Boettke, P., & Butkevich, B. Entry and Entrepreneurship: The Case of Post-Communist Russia. *Journal des Economistes et des Etudes Humaines, 11*(1) (2001), 92.
21 Kroll, H. Monopoly and Transition to the Market. *Soviet Economy, 7* (1991), 167–168.
22 Cited in Nelson, L. D., Babaeva, L. V., & Babaev, R. O. Perspectives on Entrepreneurship and Privatization in Russia: Policy and Public Opinion. *Slavic Review, 51*(2) (1992), 275.
23 Cited in Boettke & Butkevich, op. cit., p. 107.
24 Ibid.
25 Freedom House. *Freedom in the World: Russia* (Washington, DC: Freedom House 2017).
26 De Carbonnel, A. Putin Signs Law to Allow Him to Pick Russian Governors. *Reuters*, April 2, 2013. Available at: www.reuters.com/article/us-russia-elections-idUSBRE 9310GR20130402
27 *BBC News*. Russia Levada Centre Pollsters Targeted as "Foreign Agents." May 20, 2013. Available at: www.bbc.com/news/world-europe-22599321
28 Human Rights Watch. Russia: Government vs. Rights Groups (2017). Available at: www.hrw.org/russia-government-against-rights-groups-battle-chronicle
29 Council of Europe Commissioner for Human Rights. The Russian Federation's Law on Foreign Agents Contravenes Human Rights. (2017). Available at: www.coe.int/en/web/commissioner/-/the-russian-federation-s-law-on-foreign-agents-contravenes-human-rights

30 Ibid.
31 Monaghan, A. The Vertikal: Power and Authority in Russia. *International Affairs*, 88(1) (2012), 1–16.
32 Ivanitskaya, N., & Sedakov, P. Kak drug Putina Sergey Chemezov "otzhimal" u aktsionerov VSMPO-Avisma [in Russian]. *Forbes*, May 20, 2013.
33 Goble, P. Putin's Destruction of Entrepreneurs Hurting Russia More than Stalin's Destruction of Peasants Did, Bitkov Says. *The Interpreter*, October 26, 2015. Available at: www.interpretermag.com/putins-destruction-of-entrepreneurs-hurting-russia-more-than-stalins-destruction-of-peasants-did-bitkov-says/
34 Malkin, E., & Nechepurenko, I. For a Russian Couple, Safe Haven in Guatemala is Fleeting. *New York Times*, May 30, 2016.
35 Ibid.
36 Cited in Goble, op. cit.
37 World Bank. *Anticorruption in Transition: A Contribution to the Policy Debate* (Washington, DC: World Bank, 2000).
38 Hellman, J., Jones, G., & Kaufmann, D. *Seize the State, Seize the Day: State Capture, Corruption and Influence in Transition* (Washington, DC: World Bank, 2000), p. 2.
39 Dawisha, K. *Putin's Kleptocracy: Who Owns Russia?* (New York: Simon & Schuster, 2014).
40 Murtazaev, E. Gvardiya Putina: kak rabotaet vertikal' vlasti [in Russian]. *Forbes*, August 27, 2012. Available at: www.forbes.ru/sobytiya/vlast/102436-gvardiya-putina-desyat-klyuchevyh-biznes-figur-putinskoi-vertikali
41 Ibid.
42 Ibid.
43 Bogdanov E. Pravovoi rezhim imushchestva gosudarstvennoi korporatsii [in Russian]. *Khozyaistvo y pravo*, 5 (2008), 111–115.
44 See, for example, Tsimmerman, J. Gosudarstvennaya korporatsiya – spetsifika pravovogo regulirovaniya [in Russian], *Pravo i ekonomika*, 10 (2008), 4–12; Stepanov, B. Gosudarstvennaya korporatsiya kak institut rynochnoi ekonomiki [in Russian] (doctoral dissertation) (Moscow: Moscow State University, 2010).
45 Silvestrov, S., & Zeldner, A. *Gosudarstvennye korporatsii v ekonomicheskom razvitii Rossii* [in Russian] (Moscow: The Institute of Economics, 2009), p. 12.
46 President of the Russian Federation. Novosti [in Russian]. (2009). Available at: http://kremlin.ru/news/5965
47 Rosatom. Svedeniya o dokhodakh general'nogo directora 'Rosatom' za 2011 [in Russian]. (2011). Available at: www.rosatom.ru/wps/wcm/connect/rosatom/rosatom-site/resources/91cabf004b0cb5719dcbfd13f7f719e3/dohody_direktor_2011.pdf
48 Paywizard. Steven Chu. (2011). Available at: www.paywizard.org/main/VIPPaycheck/salaries-president-obamas-administration/president-obamas-administration-salaries/vip_details?id=steven-chu
49 Savitskii, K., Markin, K., Mogrycheva, V., & Pappe, J. *Gosudarstvennye korporatsii kak element modernizatsii rossiiskoy ekonomiki* [in Russian] (Moscow: Analytical Center under the Government of the Russian Federation, 2011).
50 Ibid.
51 Integrum. *Evolyutsiya gosudarstvennykh korporatsii: informatsionno-analiticheskii obzor* [in Russian] (Moscow: Integrum, 2010).
52 Ibid.
53 Boutillier, op. cit., p. 147.
54 Kihlgren, A. Small Business in Russia: A Case Study of St. Petersburg. (2002). Available at: https://papers.ssrn.com/sol3/papers.cfm?abstract_id=307091
55 Ibid.
56 Global Entrepreneurship Research Association. *The 2015/2016 Global Entrepreneurship Monitor*. (2017). Available at: www.gemconsortium.org/report
57 Ibid.

58 Ibid., p. 8.
59 Schwab, K. *The Global Competitiveness Report 2016–2017: Insight Report* (Geneva: World Economic Forum, 2016), p. 37.
60 Ibid.
61 Ibid.
62 Ibid., p. 17.
63 Ibid., p. 2.
64 Ács, Z. J., Szerb, L., Autio, E., & Lloyd, A. *Global Entrepreneurship Index 2017* (Washington, DC: The Global Entrepreneurship and Development Institute, 2017), p. 7.
65 Terjesen, S. A., & Lloyd, A. The 2015 Female Entrepreneurship Index (SSRN Scholarly Paper No. ID 2625254) (Rochester, NY: Social Science Research Network, 2015), p. 4.
66 Ibid., p. 7.
67 Ács et al., op. cit., p. 58.
68 Ibid., p. 59.
69 The term "Dutch disease" was coined by *The Economist* in 1977 to describe the decrease in the Netherland's manufacturing sector after the discovery of the large Groningen natural gas field. *The Economist*, "The Dutch Disease," November 26, 1977, pp. 82–83.
70 Ross, M. Does Oil Hinder Democracy? *World Politics, 53* (2001), 326–361.

References

Ács, Z. J., Szerb, L., Autio, E., & Lloyd, A. (2017). *Global Entrepreneurship Index 2017*. Washington, DC: The Global Entrepreneurship and Development Institute.
BBC News. (2013, May 20). Russia Levada Centre Pollsters Targeted as "Foreign Agents." Available at: www.bbc.com/news/world-europe-22599321
Blackwell, W. (1983). The Russian Entrepreneur in the Tsarist Period: An Overview. In G. Guroff & F. V. Carstensen (Eds.), *Entrepreneurship in Imperial Russia and the Soviet Union* (pp. 13–26). Princeton, NJ: Princeton University Press.
Boettke, P., & Butkevich, B. (2001). Entry and Entrepreneurship: The Case of Post-Communist Russia. *Journal des Economistes et des Etudes Humaines, 11*(1), 91–114.
Bogdanov, E. (2008). Pravovoi rezhim imushchestva gosudarstvennoi korporatsii [in Russian]. *Khozyaistvo y pravo, 5,* 111–115.
Boutillier, S. (2008). The Russian Entrepreneur Today: Elements of Analysis of the Socialized Entrepreneur. *Journal of Innovation Economics & Management, 1,* 131–154.
Council of Europe Commissioner for Human Rights. (2017). The Russian Federation's Law on Foreign Agents Contravenes Human Rights. Available at: www.coe.int/en/web/commissioner/-/the-russian-federation-s-law-on-foreign-agents-contravenes-human-rights
Dawisha, K. (2014). *Putin's Kleptocracy: Who Owns Russia?* New York: Simon & Schuster.
De Carbonnel, A. (2013, April 2). Putin Signs Law to Allow Him to Pick Russian Governors. *Reuters*. Available at: www.reuters.com/article/us-russia-elections-idUSBRE9310GR20130402
Freedom House. (2017). *Freedom in the World: Russia*. Washington, DC: Freedom House.
Global Entrepreneurship Research Association. (2017). *The 2015/2016 Global Entrepreneurship Monitor*. Available at: www.gemconsortium.org/report
Goble, P. (2015, October 26). Putin's Destruction of Entrepreneurs Hurting Russia More than Stalin's Destruction of Peasants Did, Bitkov Says. *The Interpreter*. Available at:

www.interpretermag.com/putins-destruction-of-entrepreneurs-hurting-russia-more-than-stalins-destruction-of-peasants-did-bitkov-says/
Gréen, O. S. (2009). *Entrepreneurship in Russia: Western Ideas in Russian Translation*. Gothenburg: University of Gothenburg.
Hellman, J., Jones, G., & Kaufmann, D. (2000). *Seize the State, Seize the Day: State Capture, Corruption and Influence in Transition*. Washington, DC: The World Bank.
Holmes, L. (1993). *The End of Communist Power: Anti-corruption Campaigns and Legitimation Crisis*. Oxford: Oxford University Press.
Human Rights Watch. (2017). Russia: Government vs. Rights Groups. Available at: www.hrw.org/russia-government-against-rights-groups-battle-chronicle.
Integrum. (2010). *Evolyutsiya gosudarstvennykh korporatsii: informatsionno-analiticheskii obzor* [in Russian]. Moscow: Integrum.
Ivanitskaya, N., & Sedakov, P. (2013, May 20). Kak drug Putina Sergey Chemezov "otzhimal" u aktsionerov VSMPO-Avisma [in Russian]. *Forbes*.
Jaffe, E. D., & Tsimerman, A. (2005). Business Ethics in a Transition Economy: Will the Next Russian Generation Be Any Better? *Journal of Business Ethics*, 62(1), 87–97.
Karklins, R. (2005). *The System Made Me Do It: Corruption in Post-Communist Societies*. New York: M.E. Sharpe.
Kihlgren, A. (2002). Small Business in Russia: A Case Study of St. Petersburg. Available at: https://papers.ssrn.com/sol3/papers.cfm?abstract_id=307091
Klyamkin, I., & Timofeev, L. (2004). *Tenevaya Rossiya* [in Russian]. Moscow: Russian State University for the Humanities.
Kroll, H. (1991). Monopoly and Transition to the Market. *Soviet Economy*, 7(2), 143–174.
Ledeneva, A. V. (1998). *Russia's Economy of Favours: Blat, Networking and Informal Exchange*. Cambridge: Cambridge University Press.
Lobyzenkova, V. (2007). Istoriya predprinimatel'stva v Rossii: traditsii i sovremennost' [in Russian]. *Vestnik Volgogradskogo Gosudarstvennogo Universiteta*, 9(6), 207–208.
Malkin, E., & Nechepurenko, I. (2016, May 30). For a Russian Couple, Safe Haven in Guatemala is Fleeting. *New York Times*.
Monaghan, A. (2012). The Vertikal: Power and Authority in Russia. *International Affairs*, 88(1), 1–16.
Murtazaev, E. (2012, August 27). Gvardiya Putina: kak rabotaet vertikal' vlasti [in Russian]. *Forbes*.
Nelson, L. D., Babaeva, L. V., & Babaev, R. O. (1992). Perspectives on Entrepreneurship and Privatization in Russia: Policy and Public Opinion. *Slavic Review*, 51(2), 271–286.
Nichols, P. M. (2001). The Fit between Changes to the International Corruption Regime and Indigenous Perceptions of Corruption in Kazakhstan. *University of Pennsylvania Journal of International Law*, 22(4), 863–973.
Oleinik, A. (2001). Biznes po ponyatiiham: ob institutsional'noi modeli rossiiskogo kapitalisma [in Russian]. *Voprosy Ekonomiki*, 5, 4–25.
Paywizard. (2011). *Steven Chu*. Available at: www.paywizard.org/main/VIPPaycheck/salaries-president-obamas-administration/president-obamas-administration-salaries/vip_details?id=steven-chu
President of the Russian Federation. (2009). Novosti [in Russian]. Moscow. Available at: http://kremlin.ru/news/5965.
Rosatom. (2011). Svedeniya o dokhodakh general'nogo directora 'Rosatom' za 2011 [in Russian]. Available at: www.rosatom.ru/wps/wcm/connect/rosatom/rosatomsite/resources/91cabf004b0cb5719dcbfd13f7f719e3/dohody_direktor_2011.pdf
Ross, M. (2001). Does Oil Hinder Democracy? *World Politics*, 53, 326–361.

Satarov, G. (2002). *Diagnostika rossiiskoi korruptsii* [in Russian]. Moscow: INDEM.
Savitskii, K., Markin, K., Mogrycheva, V., & Pappe, J. (2011). *Gosudarstvennye korporatsii kak element modernizatsii rossiiskoy ekonomiki* [in Russian]. Moscow: Analytical Center under the Government of the Russian Federation.
Schwab, K. (2016). *The Global Competitiveness Report 2016–2017: Insight Report.* Geneva: World Economic Forum.
Shelley, L. I. (1994). Post-Soviet Organized Crime. *Demokratizatsiya, 2*(31), 341–358.
Shelley, L. I. (2000). Corruption in the Post-Yeltsin Era. *East European Constitutional Review, 9*, 70–74.
Shelley, L. I. (2003). Crime and Corruption: Enduring Problems of Post-Soviet Development. *Demokratizatsiya, 11*(1), 110–114.
Shleifer, A., & Vishny, R. (1993). Corruption. *The Quarterly Journal of Economics, 108*(3), 599–617.
Silvestrov, S., & Zeldner, A. (2009). *Gosudarstvennye korporatsii v ekonomicheskom razvitii Rossii* [in Russian]. Moscow: The Institute of Economics.
Stepanov, B. (2010). Gosudarstvennaya korporatsiya kak institut rynochnoi ekonomiki [in Russian] (doctoral dissertation). Moscow: Moscow State University.
Terjesen, S. A., & Lloyd, A. (2015). The 2015 Female Entrepreneurship Index (SSRN Scholarly Paper No. ID 2625254). Rochester, NY: Social Science Research Network. Available at: https://papers.ssrn.com/abstract=2625254
The Economist. (1977). The Dutch Disease. *53*, 82–83.
Timofeev, L. (2000). *Institutsional'naya korruptsiya* [in Russian]. Moscow: RGGU.
Tsimmerman, J. (2008). Gosudarstvennaya korporatsiya – spetsifika pravovogo regulirovaniya [in Russian]. *Pravo i ekonomika, 10*, 4–12.
Wedel, J. R. (1996). Clique-Run Organizations and US Economic Aid: An Institutional Analysis. *Democratizatsiya, 4*(4), 571–602.
World Bank. (2000). *Anticorruption in Transition: A Contribution to the Policy Debate.* Washington, DC: The World Bank.
Yudanov, A. (1997). USSR: Large Enterprises in the USSR – The Functional Disorder. In A. D. Chandler, F. Amatori, & T. Hikino (Eds.), *Big Business and the Wealth of Nations* (pp. 397–431). Cambridge: Cambridge University Press.
Zhuplev, A., & Shein, V. (2008). Small and Medium Size Enterprises in Russia. In L. P. Dana, I. Welpe, M. Han, & V. Ratten (Eds.), *Handbook of Research on European Business and Entrepreneurship: Towards a Theory of Internationalization* (pp. 544–563). Cheltenham: Edward Elgar.

3 From Kleptocracy to "Regulocracy"

Administrative Barriers to Doing Business in Russia

Surveys of businessmen conducted in Russia demonstrate that administrative corruption is one of the most significant obstacles to developing the entrepreneurial sector.[1] In 2015, Russia's economy lost more than 50 percent of the 5.6 million entrepreneurs registered in the country.[2] The economic crisis and sanctions against Russia played a critical role in this process. Yet another important factor behind the decline in the number of entrepreneurs is the administrative barriers to doing business. They are often introduced by regulatory agencies to extort informal payments from businesses. The rise of rent-seeking activities by the police, the tax authorities, customs, antimonopoly administration, registration organizations, and labor and social services agencies represents a disturbing trend in Russia.

This chapter moves from a macro-level analysis of corruption in Russia toward the assessment of its regional impact on entrepreneurial activity and employment. The chapter's objective is to bring together what we know about the relationship between administrative corruption and entrepreneurship and to turn attention to what we still have to learn in order to develop and implement business-friendly policies. This objective requires looking more carefully at the negative consequences of corrupt practices in the public administration system at the regional level. In this context, drawing on recent research into administrative corruption, this chapter analyzes the system of corrupt regulatory agencies ("regulocracy") that blocks deregulation reforms in Russia. Empirical evidence comes from case studies of administrative barriers in three regions: Moscow, Saint Petersburg, and Karelia. In addition, the chapter uses spatial regression analysis to explore the impact of administrative corruption on entrepreneurial employment in 83 Russian regions.

Literature Review

Research into the impact of administrative corruption on entrepreneurship represents a specific area within a broader body of anti-corruption literature. For the purposes of this research, administrative corruption is defined as the abuse of office for personal gain by regulatory agencies that perform oversight and maintain control over economic activities of various business entities. This definition of administrative corruption is closely related to rent seeking. Administrative corruption can be considered a specific form of rent seeking in the entrepreneurial sector, where access to property rights is organized with little transparency, limited competition, and is directed toward promoting private ends of government agencies. The understanding of rent-seeking behavior has changed and become more sophisticated in the last four decades.

In 1974, Anne Krueger coined the term "rent seeking" to describe bureaucrats' attempts to gain access to informal payments through overregulation.[3] Using the example of quantitative trade restrictions, she demonstrated that rent seeking is socially unproductive. According to her estimates, rent-seeking activities were responsible for India's loss of 7.3 percent of national income in 1964 and Turkey's loss of 15 percent of GNP in 1968.[4] In Russia, a systematic study aimed at calculating the aggravated loss associated with overregulation and rent seeking was conducted by Aleksander Auzan and Polina Kruchkova in 2001. According to their estimates, Russia's loss due to rent seeking represents about 5–7 percent of GDP annually.[5]

Jagdish Bhagwati coined a broader term "directly unproductive, profit-seeking activities" (DUP) to describe situations where public officials are responsible for overregulation that provides opportunities to extort illegal payments.[6] These activities, according to Bhagwati, "yield pecuniary returns but do not produce goods or services that enter a utility function directly or indirectly via increased production or availability to the economy of goods."[7] Examples of DUP activities include excessive bureaucratic procedures related to starting a business, acquiring licenses, employing workers, registering property, securing credit, protecting investors, paying taxes, enforcing contracts, and closing a business. To circumvent excessive administrative regulations, economic actors often have to provide informal payments to expedite the performance of routine governmental actions.

To study the problem of overregulation and promote administrative reforms in developing countries, the Peruvian economist, Hernando de Soto founded the Institute for Liberty and Democracy (ILD) in 1981. The establishment of this institute was inspired by de Soto's personal experience in running several small mining companies in Peru in the 1970s. De Soto quickly realized that administrative regulations had a negative impact on productivity and efficiency of his businesses. He lost too much management time due to the excessive red tape. De Soto's experience was no exception. He discovered that many other businessmen in Peru suffered from burdensome regulations and were similarly frustrated with excessive administrative requirements. This frustration gave de Soto a strong impetus to dedicate his research efforts to studying possible ways to mitigate this problem in the economy.

The researchers from the Institute for Liberty and Democracy found that overregulation was one of the main factors leading to the expansion of the informal economy in Latin American countries. To measure quantitative effects of overregulation, de Soto and his team used experiments that allowed them to calculate transaction costs of meeting legal requirements for starting and operating businesses in Latin America. For instance, in Lima, they opened a small garment workshop. It took 289 days to register the workshop, despite the fact that it was organized to operate with only one worker.[8] According to another example, it took about seven years and 207 administrative procedures in 52 governmental agencies to obtain legal authority to build houses on state-owned land in Peru.[9] It is not surprising that these administrative obstacles to doing business led to the expansion of the illegal system of property rights in the Peruvian national economy.

De Soto and other researchers from the Institute for Liberty and Democracy observed similar processes in other developing countries. Since 1981, the Institute has dedicated significant efforts to introducing reforms decreasing administrative burdens on businesses worldwide. The Institute's impressive record includes projects in more than 25 developing countries and consultations provided to over 40 national governments on administrative, legal, and property rights reforms.[10] Among many other successful projects, the Institute performed an in-depth real estate and business diagnostics in Tanzania, implemented land reforms in El Salvador, and helped streamline legal requirements for property and business registration in Egypt. The Institute also deserves credit for conducting four programs in cooperation with international development organizations, including the Doing Business Project (the International Financial Corporation), Titling and Anti-corruption (the World Bank), Legal Empowerment for the Poor (the United Nations), and Opportunities for the Majority (the Inter-American Development Bank).[11]

The negative effects of administrative corruption and overregulation on economic growth and social development are well documented in the literature.[12] According to Pak Hung Mo's estimates, a 1 percent increase in the corruption level reduces economic growth by 0.72 percent.[13] His study shows that the most important channel through which corruption influences economic growth is political instability, which accounts for about 53 percent of its total effect, followed by private investment (20 percent) and human capital (15 percent).[14] Adverse consequences of corruption also include reduced investment, particularly foreign direct investment (FDI), decreased government revenues due to tax evasion, and an inefficient public spending structure, with preference given to government projects which provide opportunities to extort illegal payments and kickbacks. Vito Tanzi and Hamid Davoodi suggest that higher corruption is associated with poor conditions of the existing infrastructure, including roads, buildings, and industrial facilities.[15] Numerous empirical studies show that the higher the corruption, the less attractive the country is to foreign investors. For instance, Shang-Jin Wei and Yi Wu argue that "an increase in corruption from the level of Singapore to that of Mexico would have the same negative effect on inward foreign investment as raising the marginal corporate tax by fifty percentage points."[16] These are only a few examples of how corruption contributes to the creation of an anti-investment climate characterized by the insecurity of property rights and high risks for businesses.

An increasing number of studies analyze the negative consequences of administrative corruption for entrepreneurship and economic opportunities in the private sector in Russia.[17] Caroline Humphrey shows how overregulation pushed businesses toward the informal economy in the mid-1990s.[18] For example, traders who drove trucks to move their goods from one region to another within Russia were required to have licenses not only to drive a truck, but also to travel to other regions. Excessive bureaucratic requirements made it extremely difficult for entrepreneurs to get licenses to move their goods even to neighboring regions. As a result, traders had to bribe public officials to circumvent these excessive regulations. It was the frustration of truck drivers with administrative barriers at the regional level that made them move their businesses into the informal sector. Similar processes were observed in other industries and sectors of the economy.

In Russia, an in-depth study of the impact of administrative overregulation on the economy demonstrates that the rent seeking by regulatory agencies is responsible for the creation of "administrative barriers."[19] Aleksander Auzan and Polina Kruchkova define them as "a set of rules adopted by state agencies to collect charges for bureaucratic procedures related to doing business in markets."[20] Another definition of administrative barriers was formulated by Alexander Degtyarev and Rustam Malikov, who consider them as "obstacles to starting and doing business that result from the introduction of excessive bureaucratic procedures and rules set by federal, regional, and municipal regulatory agencies in order to receive additional payments."[21] Recent studies demonstrate a significant negative relationship between the level of cost, time, and procedures required to start a business and new firm registration.[22]

In a broad sense, administrative barriers can be divided into two groups. The first group is related to bureaucratic procedures that are necessary to start a new business, such as registering a business, acquiring licenses and permits, and getting electricity into new buildings. The second group is related to bureaucratic procedures that emerge in the process of operational activities of the already existing businesses. For example, they can include inspections by regulatory agencies, getting access to credit and procurement contracts, and reporting to government authorities. In the 2000s, the Centre for Economic and Financial Research (CEFIR), an independent research center in Moscow, conducted a special project to monitor administrative barriers to small business development in Russia. This project was implemented in collaboration with the World Bank and with the financial support of the U.S. Agency for International Development (USAID). Its key objective was to evaluate the results of the deregulation reform implemented by Russia's federal government. The researchers from CEFIR found that administrative barriers significantly diminish economic opportunities in Russia's entrepreneurial sector and divert substantial resources from the business community. The first round of the monitoring project, which took place in 2001, showed that the administrative burden on small businesses was very heavy.[23]

In 2007, the final round of the CEFIR monitoring project demonstrated that the new laws on inspections, registration, and entrepreneurial rights adopted after 2001 induced positive changes for small businesses, simplifications in registration procedures, and a decrease in the frequency of inspections by regulatory agencies.[24] For example, the time required to get licenses dropped from 50 to 32 days.[25] Nevertheless, administrative barriers in Russia remained high in comparison with the advanced economies.

International experiences provide strong evidence of the positive socio-economic effects of public policies that improve the regulatory environment and reduce administrative barriers to doing business.[26] For instance, a study conducted in 40 industrialized countries by Luís Costa and Miguel Aubyn shows that simplification programs and streamlined regulations led to a 0.6 percent increase in total factor productivity.[27] Case studies of good governance in the developed countries demonstrate that eliminating ineffective regulatory burdens boosts economic opportunities and entrepreneurship.[28] This is why policymakers in the advanced economies systematically consult businesses and entrepreneurs regarding proposed regulations before their adoption and implementation.[29] Conversely, initiatives proposed by Russian businesses to improve public policies in the entrepreneurial sector are often blocked by rent-seeking bureaucrats who are interested in keeping the current status quo.

"Regulocracy" and Administrative Barriers

Institutional reforms in Russia's entrepreneurial sector are undermined by the dominance of status quo-oriented bureaucrats engaged in predations on businesses. Deregulation laws are often bypassed by corrupt officials. The most significant challenge in this area is the wide discretion of public officials in bending policies in the entrepreneurial sector to their own interests. Predatory behavior is so widespread among Russian regulatory agencies that some scholars refer to them as the "grabbing hand." This term was coined by Andrei Shleifer and Robert Vishny to describe "a large number of substantially independent bureaucrats pursuing their own agendas, including taking bribes."[30] This book offers another term – "regulocracy" – to refer to widespread predatory behavior among government agencies that perform oversight and maintain control over various business entities. In a broad sense, "regulocracy" means a system of government agencies at the federal, regional, and local levels that abuse their authority over market actors for their personal enrichment. This term is closely related to kleptocracy, which means a government regime where corrupt rulers (kleptocrats) seize public assets and exploit the population. In the same vein, "regulocrats" are engaged in extortion and unlawful seizures of valuable assets from businesses.

The famous Russian expression "the fish rots from the head" turns attention to the negative consequences of corruption among kleptocratic rulers. It means that in weak and failed states, the root cause of corruption is attributed to its leadership. For example, Louise Shelley indicates that "criminalization thrives at the bottom of society because the top offers the worst examples of entrenched crime and corruption."[31] In this respect, kleptocracy and "regulocracy" represent interdependent parts integrated into the same system of informal capital flows within the state. In Russia's highly hierarchical public administration, informal payments collected by street-level bureaucrats who are directly involved in everyday administrative corruption are distributed in certain proportions to higher-level public officials. In such a system, it is difficult, if not impossible, for honest public officials to receive a promotion since they cannot contribute a share of informal payments to their superiors. In "regulocracy," loyalty is measured by the amount of "annuities" from illegal proceeds distributed by civil servants to their superiors. Importantly, loyalty is valued much more than experience and professional qualifications.

An analysis of regulations regarding inspections of businesses by federal, regional, and local agencies explains why administrative barriers persist in the Russian entrepreneurial sector, even after several deregulation reforms. According to Boris Titov, Russia's business ombudsman, "in 2013, only 12 percent of inspections ended with warnings, while in the remaining 88 percent, large fines were imposed on businesses."[32] Russian regulatory agencies often use unrealistic and conflicting requirements, outdated regulations, and arbitrary interpretations of legislative acts. A survey of 2,000 entrepreneurs conducted by Russia's business ombudsman in 2014 showed that "94 percent of businesses are not aware of all requirements set by the related regulatory agencies. In one case, a regulatory agency used outdated legal standards and official guidelines which were developed in the 1930s."[33] In turn, the reluctance of regulatory agencies to modernize their standards and improve their requirements is related to their focus on collecting fines and informal payments from businesses.

Systematic failures to improve laws regarding the inspection regime in Russia stem from the resistance of the "regulocracy" to deregulation reforms. Corrupt officials sabotage deregulation reforms by taking advantage of loopholes and gaps in new laws. For example, in 2001, the State Duma adopted Federal Law #134 on "Protection of the Rights of Legal Entities and Individual Entrepreneurs During State Control (Inspections)." This law allowed a regulatory agency to inspect a business only once within a two-year period. However, a survey conducted by the Association of Entrepreneurs OPORA Russia in 2003 showed that "nearly 75 percent of respondents complained that they were still inspected more than once a year, and among them 30 percent were even inspected once a month or more."[34] The key reason was that the law made an exception for unscheduled (unplanned) inspections, and regulatory agencies took advantage of this loophole.

The same happened with Federal Law #294 of 2008 that replaced Federal Law #134. Federal Law #294 further reduced the number of inspections per each agency from one every two years to one every three years. It also decreased the time period for inspections from 30 to 20 days and prohibited duplicating inspections by different agencies. However, enforcement of the new law was also ineffective. In 2009, "small businesses had to deal with inspections from more than forty different agencies."[35] As a result, Russian entrepreneurs continued to complain about burdensome inspections in the post-reform period. Table 3.1 presents an average number of inspections of entrepreneurs and small businesses in 2011

Table 3.1 Average numbers of inspections of businesses by federal regulatory agencies in 2011 and 2012

Inspections by agencies	2011	2012	Change by %
Customs Service	1.89	3.05	61.4
Police	1.7	2.0	21.4
Antimonopoly Service	1.1	1.9	80.2
Biomedical Agency	1.5	1.6	8.0
Ministry of Culture	1.4	1.5	13.2
Supervision of Transport	1.6	1.4	−10.0
Ecological, Technological, and Nuclear Supervision	1.2	1.4	14.8
Financial Supervision	1.7	1.4	−15.8
Consumer Protection Service	1.3	1.4	9.5
Ministry of Finance	1.0	1.3	33.0
Technical Regulation and Metrology	1.4	1.3	−6.3
Supervision of Natural Resources and Ecology	0.9	1.3	47.7
Supervision of Health Care	1.4	1.3	−9.4
Veterinary Supervision	1.2	1.2	0.8
State Registration	1.1	1.1	3.7
Emergency Ministry	1.0	1.1	12.0
Labor and Employment Service	1.1	1.1	0.9

Source: Ministry of Economic Development of the Russian Federation (2013). *Svodnyi doklad ob osushchestvlenii gosudarstvennogo kontrolya (nadzora) za 2012 god* [in Russian]. Moscow: Ministry of Economic Development, p. 72.

and 2012 by different governmental agencies. Only four of the 17 federal regulatory agencies decreased the number of inspections in 2012 in comparison with the previous year.

On average, small businesses and individual entrepreneurs were subject to 1.3 inspections by federal regulatory agencies in 2011 and 1.5 in 2012.[36] According to Alexander Litvak, the average score of the administrative burden of such inspections on entrepreneurs was estimated at 2.8 on a 4-point scale (1 – extremely burdensome, 4 – not burdensome at all).[37] Litvak found that entrepreneurs use informal relationships and bribes more frequently during fire safety and veterinary inspections.[38] In 2015, Russia's Governmental Commission adopted amendments to Federal Law #294, "On the Protection of the Rights of Legal Entities and Individual Entrepreneurs During State Control (Supervision) and Municipal Control." These amendments introduced a three-year moratorium on planned inspections of small businesses and individual entrepreneurs beginning from January 1, 2016 until December 31, 2018.[39] However, similarly to previous deregulation reforms, this three-year moratorium was not very successful in removing excessive inspections in the entrepreneurial sector.

The existence of numerous loopholes in the three-year moratorium on inspections of small businesses explains its inefficient implementation. First, the amendments to Federal Law #294 allowed regulatory agencies to inspect those entrepreneurs who had received an administrative penalty of disqualification, suspension or the cancellation of their licenses within the previous three years. Second, the moratorium did not cover regular inspections of individual entrepreneurs who work in the spheres of health, education, social services, heating, electricity, and energy conservation. Third, the moratorium was not related to inspections of industrial safety, radiation safety, and facilities that might have a negative impact on the environment. Finally, the moratorium covered only planned inspections, that is, inspections scheduled in the official plan that is published in advance (usually in September–October of the previous year) on the website of the regional public prosecutor's office. Therefore, regulatory agencies preserved their right to conduct unannounced (also known as "unplanned") inspections that do not require any advance notice.

Table 3.2 shows the percentage of unannounced inspections conducted by different regulatory agencies in 2011–2012. In most regulatory agencies, the percentage of unannounced inspections outnumbers the percentage of planned inspections. This explains why the three-year moratorium on planned inspections did not have a significant impact on the administrative burden of monitoring activities performed by regulatory agencies.

The problem of inspections is further fueled by the lack of external public and legal control over discretionary abuses by public officials. The most severe problems in this sphere are limited public access to information about the regulatory activities of agencies, insufficient coverage of corruption in the media, inadequate judicial review of agencies' actions, and lack of ombudsman programs in

Table 3.2 Percentage of unannounced inspections in 2011 and 2012

Agency	2011	2012
Accreditation Service	–	100
Antimonopoly Service	91	92
Customs Service	48	90
Migration Service	60	75
Ministry of Finance	66	75
Labor and Employment Service	77	74
Service for Financial Supervision	71	62
Ecological, Technological, and Nuclear Supervision	68	62
Agency for Supervision of Health Care	63	62
Consumer Protection Service	66	59
Biomedical Agency	70	58
Emergency Ministry	62	56
Agency for Technical Regulation and Metrology	52	53
Supervision of Transport	68	48
Ministry of Culture	45	43
Veterinary Supervision	48	42
State Registration	31	35

Source: Ministry of Economic Development of the Russian Federation (2013). *Svodnyi doklad ob osushchestvlenii gosudarstvennogo kontrolya (nadzora) za 2012 god* [in Russian]. Moscow: Ministry of Economic Development, p. 73.

the entrepreneurial sector. The reluctance of public authorities to decrease administrative barriers to doing business explains systematic failures to improve the inspections regime in Russia. The existence of a powerful "regulocracy" makes the implementation of administrative and institutional reforms ineffective and often blocks their development at the early design stage. In this regard, business associations can provide additional control over inspecting agencies. For example, in 2009, the Association of Entrepreneurs OPORA Russia received the right to be present during inspections of their members.[40] Monitoring activities by business associations provide mechanisms of collective defense against violations of entrepreneurial rights.

A Case Study of Administrative Barriers and Governance in Moscow, Saint Petersburg, and Karelia

The case study conducted in 2015 in three Russian regions provides in-depth information about administrative corruption. The interviews with Russian entrepreneurs in Moscow, Saint Petersburg, and Karelia help identify key problems that businesses face while dealing with regulatory agencies at the regional level. Figure 3.1 shows key spheres where administrative problems are especially burdensome for entrepreneurs in these regions. At the stage of starting a new business, the most burdensome administrative barriers include getting electricity, licenses, and permits. Also, entrepreneurs in Moscow, Saint Petersburg, and

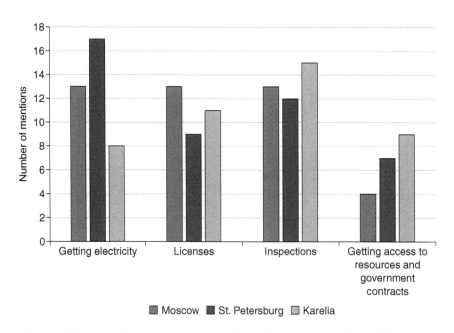

Figure 3.1 Spheres where entrepreneurs are facing the severest problems while dealing with regulatory agencies (the number of mentions in the interviews).

Karelia indicate that in the process of their operational activities, they face severe problems during inspections by regulatory agencies and while obtaining access to resources and government contracts.

Getting electricity is one of the most severe problems in all regions. A story told by one of the interviewed entrepreneurs from Saint Petersburg is illustrative of the seriousness of the situation in this sphere:

> I am an owner of a furniture business, with nine employees under my supervision. During my first years, I rented a shop in one of the largest commercial centers in the city. However, taking into account annual increases of my rent payments and my plans to expand my business, I decided to take out a loan in a local bank to buy my own small building. The only thing that I did not take into account was the problem of getting electricity in my new building located in one of the city suburbs. An official from the state electrical agency informed me that the necessary administrative procedures might take over a year. I could not wait for such a long time. The official told me that he could speed up the administrative process in return for additional money above the appropriate legal fees and formal payments. I did not want to pay extra but I feared I could lose my business if I did not get electricity.

Overregulation in the sphere of getting electricity in Saint Petersburg is typical for Russia. For instance, the 2015 World Bank's *Doing Business* report ranked Russia 143rd among 189 countries on the ease of getting electricity for small businesses.[41] According to this report, to get electricity, Russian businesses were required to go through six administrative procedures which took 189 days on average, with an estimated cost of 321 percent of income per capita.[42] Another 2015 report completed by the World Bank showed that Saint Petersburg, Moscow, and the Karelian capital city of Petrozavodsk are among the worst regions in terms of the ease to get electricity.[43] As a result, many businesses try to overcome excessive regulation through corrupt methods.[44] The same phenomenon can be observed in the sphere of issuing licenses and permits that also remain burdensome in comparison with other countries.

Another problem for entrepreneurs is access to financial resources and procurement. According to a 2015 OECD report, Russian banks' "rejection rates remain high, and it is widely believed that SMEs [small and medium-sized enterprises] face more severe problems with access to external capital than large enterprises."[45] The OECD report explains high rejection rates by three factors: (1) the uneven level of Russia's banking industry that is still underrepresented outside of the biggest cities, such as Moscow and Saint Petersburg; (2) insufficient use of new lending technologies; and (3) the lack of financial transparency of small businesses and individual entrepreneurs.[46] These factors make this type of lending risky for financial institutions. A survey of small businesses conducted by the Association of Entrepreneurs OPORA Russia demonstrates that limited access to financial resources is a major obstacle to their growth and development. According to the survey, 44 percent of small businesses face severe problems in accessing long-term financing.[47] The survey also points to very high interest rates for entrepreneurs (typically ranging from 14–17 percent) and their uneven regional distribution, with increased interest rates in remote regions.[48] This explains why entrepreneurs in Karelia consider access to financial resources more challenging than entrepreneurs in Moscow.

As far as government contracts are concerned, entrepreneurs in Moscow have much better access to public procurement than those in other regions. There are two key factors explaining this situation. First, the majority of federal agencies are located in Moscow and, therefore, there are more opportunities for businesses to use their connections with procurement officers in the capital. Second, the main offices of national entrepreneurial organizations (such as the Russian Union of Industrialists and Entrepreneurs, the Association of Entrepreneurs OPORA Russia, the Russian Chamber of Commerce and Industry, and the Russian Public Organization *Delovaya Rossiya*) are located in Moscow. They make significant efforts to help their members obtain access to government contracts. However, even in Moscow, individual entrepreneurs complain that they are systematically underrepresented in public procurement. For example, an entrepreneur from Moscow illustrates the existence of unfair disparities in procurement in the following way:

> In the area of public procurement, most contracts are signed either with affiliated companies or with large companies that pay enormous kickbacks. In Moscow, kickbacks can be as high as 70 percent. This is why for an individual entrepreneur like me, it is hardly possible to get a government contract, despite the fact that, in accordance with Federal Law #44, at least 15 percent of the annual volume of government purchases should be placed among small businesses and socially-oriented non-profit organizations. However, you will never find any public agency that follows this rule. I think that the key problem is low fines for public officials. For example, the Administrative Code states that if an agency buys less than 15 percent of the total annual volume of their purchases from small businesses and socially-oriented non-profit organizations, they will receive an administrative penalty in the amount of 50,000 rubles [about $715]. However, this amount is nothing in comparison with the amount of government contracts and the related amount of kickbacks. Therefore, for public officials, it is more profitable to violate the legislation and then pay administrative fines than to follow the abovementioned procurement rule.

Finally, as far as inspections by regulatory agencies are concerned, they remain burdensome in all Russian regions. In Moscow, Saint Petersburg, and Karelia, entrepreneurs complain that their regional public authorities fail to resolve this problem. In most cases, regulatory agencies use reactive responses to irregularities in the operational activities of businesses by imposing large fines, instead of proactive measures aimed at preventing such irregularities.

An analysis of the quality of local governance helps explain variations in entrepreneurial activity at the regional level. According to the Federal Statistics

Service of the Russian Federation, the worst results are observed in Karelia, where the number of entrepreneurs decreased by almost 44 percent between 2008 and 2015.[49] One of the key reasons behind this negative trend is the failure of the Karelian Administration to create a favorable entrepreneurial climate in the region. Russian ratings of the effectiveness of economic development at the regional level provide a relative measure of the quality of local governance in Moscow, Saint Petersburg, and Karelia. Table 3.3 summarizes their regional ranks on the development of a competitive environment, public–private partnerships, and innovation activities.

The regional ratings reveal that Karelia's ranks on the development of a competitive environment, public–private partnerships, and innovation policies are among the lowest in Russia. Not surprisingly, the former Head of the Karelian Administration Aleksandr Khudilainen was ranked among the least effective governors in Russia in 2014 and 2015 by the Center for Information and Communications Research.[50] The Foundation for the Development of Civil Society also included the Karelian head in the group of the worst governors at the regional level in 2014 and 2015.[51] Khudilainen received the worst rankings not only because of low socio-economic indicators of the region's development, but also because of negative assessments of his governance by Karelian residents due to his involvement in corruption scandals. For example, Khudilainen was personally involved in the case of an illegal sale of the Siversky forest in the Gatchina district of the Leningrad region. In 2005, in his capacity as the Head of the Administration of the Gatchina district, Khudilainen issued a decree to transfer the forest land to a private company that later sold it at a tenfold profit for the construction of individual luxury cottages.[52] At that time, Khudilainen remained only a witness. In 2013, the case of the illegal sale of the Siversky forest in the Gatchina district was reopened.

Table 3.3 Ratings of the effectiveness of regional policies in Moscow, Saint Petersburg, and Karelia

Rating	Year	Moscow	Saint Petersburg	Karelia
Development of a competitive environment (of 82 regions)	2014	2nd–3rd	4th	67th–68th
Innovation development (of 82 regions)	2015	1st	3rd	71st
Development of public-private partnerships (of 85 regions)	2014–2015	3rd	1st	63rd

Sources: These data were derived from the Federal Anti-Monopoly Service of the Russian Federation (2015) *Reiting konkurentsii v regionakh* [in Russian], Moscow: FAS; National Research University Higher School of Economics (2014) *Reiting innovatsionnogo razvitiya sub''ektov RF* [in Russian], Moscow: NIU VSHE; The Center for the Development of Public-Private Partnership (2015) *Razvitie GCHP v sub''ektakh RF: Reiting regionov GCHP 2014–2015* [in Russian], Moscow, pp. 25–28.

In 2015, residents of Karelia signed an Internet petition, requesting to change the regional governor by stating that "in the three-year period since his appointment, he [Khudilainen] was not able to earn citizens' trust, failed to improve the socio-economic situation in Karelia, and is responsible for a tremendous growth of regional debt."[53] The previous Karelian governor Andrei Nelidov, who headed the Republic's Administration from 2010 to 2012, was also unpopular with local residents.[54] His Administration was tainted by corruption. In September 2015, Nelidov was arrested on charges of bribe taking (Article 290 of the Criminal Code of the Russian Federation). According to the Investigative Committee of the Russian Federation, Nelidov received a bribe to the amount of 500,000 rubles (equivalent to $8,065) from an entrepreneur for the right to carry out his trade and commercial activities on the territory of the Kizhi national park.[55]

The corruption of the Karelian Administration demoralizes low-ranking officials in the lower-level regulatory agencies. Regional administrations and regulatory agencies are highly hierarchical. In these centralized bureaucratic systems, the number of bribes received by heads of regional administrations depends on the number of civil servants who work under their direct supervision. This leads to an uncontrolled expansion of public-sector employment, without any corresponding social benefit. For instance, in 2015, Karelia had a high number of bureaucrats per 10,000 citizens (204.1), which significantly exceeded an average indicator in Russia of 148.5 bureaucrats per 10,000 people.[56] In Moscow and Saint Petersburg, these indicators were 99.2 and 118.8 bureaucrats per 10,000 citizens, respectively.[57]

The negative effect of excessive bureaucratization manifests itself in competition between numerous public officials for informal payments, which increases the uncertainty of doing business in the related region. Moscow, Saint Petersburg, and Karelia have different levels of corruption. According to the Annual Report on Corruption in Russia's Regions developed by the Association of Russian Lawyers for Human Rights, Moscow and the Moscow region have the highest level of corruption.[58] In 2015, they received 28.9 and 5.6 percent of the total number of complaints about corruption, respectively.[59] In other regions, including Saint Petersburg and Karelia, levels of corruption did not exceed 4 percent.[60] However, regional indicators of corruption that are based on the number of citizens' complaints might be distorted in those regions where citizens are not willing or not ready to file complaints about officials. Such distortions in perceptions of corruption might be caused by state-controlled media or by fear of repression on the part of corrupt officials. This is evident from an interview with a Karelian entrepreneur who describes the situation with media censorship in his region as follows:

> In Karelia, the media is controlled by the Administration. I cannot name a single newspaper or journal that could help us disseminate information about violations of rights of entrepreneurs by public officials and regulatory agencies. It is just impossible to publish any article about corruption. No media source raises issues of corruption in Karelia. It all depends on the

Karelian Administration. In Petrozavodsk, with its population of 300,000 people, the situation is much worse than in larger regions and cities, such as Moscow and Saint Petersburg. In Karelia, the Administration has a strong influence not only on the media, but also on business organizations. In fact, the Administration provides support and protection to affiliated organizations that are loyal to local high-ranking officials in return for informal payments or benefits. Other businesses do not have any opportunities to receive government contracts.

Furthermore, entrepreneurs from Karelia demonstrate a very low level of trust in the enforcement system. As a result, Karelian entrepreneurs are less likely to file legal complaints about administrative harassment in comparison with Moscow and Saint Petersburg. Importantly, interviews with Karelian entrepreneurs in 2015 showed that in some cases, enforcement officers acted in the same way as criminals offering their protection in return for informal payments for their services. For example, in his interview, a bar owner in Karelia told the following story of his acquaintance with local police officers:

> One year after I opened my bar, I received a phone call from the police department and they asked me to pay them money for protection services to the amount of one million rubles [about $14,286]. I did not have the money and refused to pay. After all, why should I pay? One week later, they [policemen] came with a search warrant, they made a big mess in my bar, and confiscated all the alcohol. Eventually, I did what they asked. I did not have another option. Whom could I complain to?

Similar cases were registered in other Russian regions. In the Saratov region, policemen seized nearly 90 bottles of vodka from a local entrepreneur.[61] Interestingly, as Nadezhda Andreyeva notes, "there was no official information about the whereabouts of the seized bottles ... whether they became the property of the state or were destroyed, despite the fact that the law requires such information to be documented."[62] In the same vein, alcohol seized in three more stores by policemen disappeared without any trace.[63]

The negative consequences of a corrupt enforcement system can be attributed to the effect of dual taxation. In addition to taxes paid to the state, entrepreneurs also have to make informal payments to the police in order to secure and protect their property. Under such conditions, entrepreneurs do not know exactly what proportion of their output will be taken in the form of informal payments. This has a negative impact on their investment incentives and production efficiency. The uncertainty of doing business has a disastrous impact on the economic development of the region. As Mancur Olson points out, "the victims of violence and theft lose not only what is taken from them but also the incentive to produce any goods that would be taken by others."[64] Most importantly, entrepreneurs who face illegal activities by enforcement authorities lose their trust in public institutions in general.

Police corruption explains why entrepreneurs prefer to solve their problems with regulatory agencies on their own, instead of filing legal complaints to law enforcement organizations. Furthermore, individual entrepreneurs are not actively involved in business associations and chambers of commerce that can protect them in situations of violations of their rights by corrupt officials. To a large extent, this can be explained by insufficient information about collective entrepreneurial organizations and their anti-corruption activities. An analysis of regional agencies responsible for small business development shows that they do not pay sufficient attention to the dissemination of such information. Table 3.4 compares the contents of the official websites of the regional committees for small business development in Moscow, Saint Petersburg, and Karelia.

Only the website of the Moscow Committee for Small Business Development contains some information about administrative barriers at the regional level and publishes online links to a hotline and bureau where entrepreneurs can complain about violations of their rights by public officials. Furthermore, only the Moscow Committee provides analytical information about changes in regulations and laws concerning entrepreneurs. The Karelian and Saint Petersburg committees publish mainly information about state support programs for entrepreneurs. However, they do not provide any assessments of the effectiveness of these

Table 3.4 Comparative analysis of information published on official websites of the regional committees for small businesses development, 2016

	Moscow Committee for Small Business Development	Saint Petersburg Committee for Entrepreneurial Development	Karelia's Portal of Small and Medium-Sized Entrepreneurship
Programs of support	Yes	Yes	Yes
Information about administrative barriers	Yes	No	No
Anti-corruption policies	Yes	No	No
Information about regional self-regulatory organizations	No	No	No
Hotline to complain about violations of entrepreneurial rights	Yes	No	Yes

Source: These data were derived in 2016 from the official websites of the Moscow Committee for Small Business Development (www.mbm.ru), the Saint Petersburg Committee for the Development of Entrepreneurship and the Consumer Market (http://gov.spb.ru/gov/otrasl/c_business), and Karelia's Portal of Small and Medium-Sized Entrepreneurship (http://smb10.ru).

programs at the regional level. In all regions, the Committees for Small Business Development do not provide directories where individual entrepreneurs can find out about self-regulatory organizations that help in situations of administrative barriers and corruption.

The Impact of Administrative Corruption on Entrepreneurial Employment at the Regional Level

The study of the impact of administrative corruption on entrepreneurial employment at the regional level extends the country-level anti-corruption research.[65] This study focuses on regional differences in rent-seeking behavior of public officials. It is based on spatial regression analysis of the relationship between administrative corruption and entrepreneurial employment in 83 Russian regions. It is aimed at checking the hypothesis of whether Russian regions with a higher level of administrative corruption are more likely to have lower levels of entrepreneurial employment in comparison with other regions.

This study is based on the premise that regional locations are critically important for entrepreneurial activities. Historical studies of Russian entrepreneurship point to the importance of a spatial dimension for business formation across regions. For example, William Blackwell argues that "the spatial and locational aspects of enterprise during the several periods of Russian history form a subject that ... assumes crucial importance."[66] In Kievan Rus', major entrepreneurial centers were located on river-trading routes. During the Kievan era, trade with the Vikings, the Byzantine Greeks and the countries of Central Asia depended to a great extent on networks of rivers and portages. In Tsarist Russia, industrial enterprise concentrated in Moscow and steadily expanded its activities to other cities in the central region.[67]

Throughout Russian history, the central region has played an important role in economic development. For example, Dmitry Mendeleev noted in his report on the 1893 World International Exposition held in Chicago: "Moscow ... now concentrates so many enterprising people and forms such an advanced economic center that it will long remain at the head of the extensive manufacturing development destined for Russia."[68] Saint Petersburg became Russia's political and manufacturing capital during the era of Peter the Great and Catherine the Second. Due to the city's geographical position on the Gulf of Finland, entrepreneurs there were mostly engaged in international trade, shipbuilding, and industrial manufacturing. Later, another group of banking entrepreneurs emerged in Saint Petersburg, transforming it into Russia's major financial center.

In the seventeenth century, the Ural region, located between the East European and West Siberian plains, became another important industrial center in Russia. After the discovery of rich mineral deposits in the Urals, the Russian government recognized the region as a strategic source of natural resources. In the first half of the eighteenth century, over 60 factories were built in the Urals. In the nineteenth century, the industrial importance of the Ural region slowly declined despite some growth of the largest economic and commercial centers of

Perm, Yekaterinburg, Orenburg, Ufa, and Irbit. During the last decades of the Russian Empire, the economic role of the Ural region was mostly transferred to the south-western part of Russia, which became a new industrial center. The south-western industrial center extended from the eastern part of Ukraine to Rostov on the Don. The construction of the railroads in this region facilitated the rapid development of the iron, coal, and steel industries.

An analysis of entrepreneurial employment in contemporary Russia demonstrates both the historical continuity in spatial locations of their activities and the emergence of new industrial centers. The data on entrepreneurial employment are derived from the Federal Statistics Service of the Russian Federation that annually estimates the number of entrepreneurs per 1,000 employed at the regional level. The sample includes 83 regions characterized by various levels of entrepreneurial employment. At the present time, Russia includes 85 federal subjects that are constituent members of the Federation. However, since two federal subjects, namely the Republic of Crimea and the city of Sevastopol, are not recognized internationally, they are not included in this analysis. Figure 3.2 presents a preliminary visual spatial analysis which maps the number of entrepreneurs per 1,000 employed at the regional level in Russia. It shows that the central, north-western and south-western regions continue to generate a high level of entrepreneurial employment. In addition, we can note a large concentration of entrepreneurs in the north-eastern part of Russia.

A visual examination of the number of entrepreneurs per 1,000 employed at the regional level reveals interesting patterns. The highest levels of entrepreneurial employment can be observed in the south-western part of the country (the Adygey, Astrakhan, Belgorod, Chechnya, Ingush, Kalmyk, Krasnodar, Karachay-Cherkess,

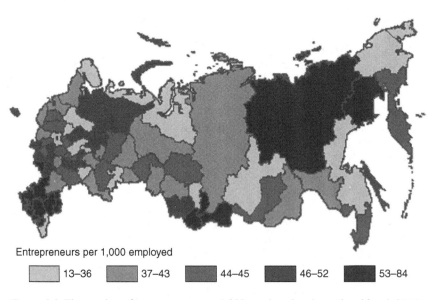

Figure 3.2 The number of entrepreneurs per 1,000 employed at the regional level, 2015.

Kabardin-Balkar, Stavropol', and Rostov regions), the central-southern part (the Gorno-Altay, Khakass, and Tuva regions), and the north-eastern part (Sakha and Magadan). The data on corruption in Russia's regions are derived from an annual regional rating calculated by the Association of Russian Lawyers for Human Rights based on the number of complaints about administrative abuses they received in 2015. The highest level of corruption is observed in the central European part of Russia, particularly in Moscow City, the Moscow, Saratov, Tatarstan, Leningrad, and Samara regions.[69] Importantly, these regions are characterized by relatively low indicators of entrepreneurial employment.

Other variables include three composite indices derived from the 2015 regional ratings related to small business development calculated by the Agency of Strategic Initiatives.[70] These indicators measure the quality of the regulatory environment, business infrastructure, and small business programs. The composite index of the quality of the regulatory environment is calculated based on five indicators: (1) the effectiveness of procedures for starting new businesses; (2) issuing construction permits; (3) registering ownership rights; (4) issuing licenses; (5) and connecting electricity. The composite index of the quality of the regulatory environment represents an average of the total scores calculated for each of these five indicators. The composite index of infrastructure includes the following indicators: the ease of obtaining state and municipal orders for small businesses, availability of real estate for doing business, and financing. The composite index of small business programs includes the following indicators: availability of financial resources (government investment and funding), regional infrastructure (roads, telecommunications, and industrial facilities), innovation centers (incubators, technological and industrial parks), and human capital (the quality of labor resources).

In accordance with these composite indices, the Agency of Strategic Initiatives places Russian regions into six groups, ranging from F (the worst) to A (the best). For regression analysis, these groups are coded on a 6-point scale, ranging from 1 (F) to 6 (A). The collected data were imported into the ArcGIS suite of geospatial processing programs, including ArcMap and GeoDa. ArcMap was used primarily to view geospatial data and create maps. GeoDa was used for running spatial regression models. The dependent variable of entrepreneurial employment is represented by the number of entrepreneurs per 1,000 employed, which illuminates interpretation problems inherent in the comparison of regions characterized by different levels of population density and unemployment. Apart from administrative corruption, the quality of the regulatory environment, infrastructure, and small business programs, the analysis includes the number of bureaucrats per 1,000 employed to check whether the size of bureaucracy impacts entrepreneurial employment at the regional level. In addition, the relationship between the number of entrepreneurs per 1,000 employed and administrative corruption is controlled for gross regional product per capita.[71] Table 3.5 provides descriptive statistics for these variables.

The Moran's I test is a common tool to check spatial autocorrelation of the residuals. It helps determine if entrepreneurial employment at the regional level

Table 3.5 Descriptive statistics

Variable	Number of observations	Mean	Standard deviation	Min	Max
Entrepreneurs per 1,000 employed	83	45.1	12.5	13.1	84.5
Administrative corruption	83	2.8	3.0	1.8	28.9
Regulatory environment	83	3.0	1.1	1	5
Infrastructure	83	2.8	0.9	1	5
Small business programs	83	3.2	1.2	1	5
Bureaucrats per 1,000 employed	83	39.7	15.8	18.1	104.7
Gross regional product per capita (rubles)	83	506,350	700,445	116,008	4,990,260

is both significant and clustered. The calculated Moran's I score of 0.38, with $p<0.01$, indicates a strong spatial autocorrelation of the residuals. After identifying the presence of spatial autocorrelation, the spatial error models improve the ordinary least squares (OLS) regression. The number of entrepreneurs per 1,000 employed is regressed on administrative corruption, the quality of the regulatory environment, infrastructure, small business programs, the number of bureaucrats per 1,000 employed, and gross regional product per capita. The results are summarized in Table 3.6.

The classic OLS regression model indicates a negative correlation between the number of entrepreneurs per 1,000 employed and administrative corruption, with an estimated coefficient of −1.0 at the 5 percent level of significance. This result provides evidence that regions with a higher level of administrative corruption are more likely to have lower levels of entrepreneurial employment in comparison with other regions. In addition, the results of the OLS regression model show that regions with more developed infrastructure and small business programs are more likely to have higher levels of entrepreneurial employment in comparison with other regions. Finally, the OLS regression model demonstrates a positive relationship between entrepreneurial employment and the quality of the regulatory environment; however, the related coefficient is not significant at the 5 percent level.

Since the Moran's I test identified the existence of spatial autocorrelation, the spatial error regression models re-estimate the coefficients to improve the model's fit. After introducing the spatial error, the coefficients for administrative corruption, infrastructure, and small business programs are still significant. The spatial error models include an additional indicator that represents spatially correlated errors (LAMBDA in Table 3.6). It also has a positive effect and is highly significant. In the spatial error models, the effects of other independent

Table 3.6 Results of the OLS and spatial error regression models

Entrepreneurs per 1,000 employed	Model 1 OLS		Model 2 spatial error		Model 3 spatial error	
	Coefficient	Standard error	Coefficient	Standard error	Coefficient	Standard error
Administrative corruption	−1.0**	0.4	−0.9***	0.4	−0.9***	0.4
Regulatory environment	0.8	1.2	0.8	1.0	0.9	1.0
Infrastructure	3.2***	1.3	2.1*	1.1	2.1*	1.1
Small business programs	2.2*	1.1	2.9***	0.9	3.2***	0.9
Bureaucrats per 1,000 employed	0.3***	0.08	0.3***	0.1	0.3***	0.1
Gross regional product per capita					−2.0	1.3
Constant	15.6**	7.5	17.7***	6.9	17.7***	6.7
LAMBDA			0.5***	0.1	0.5***	0.1

Notes
*** $p < 0.01$;
** $p < 0.05$;
* $p < 0.1$.

variables remain similar, while the coefficients are estimated at −0.9 for administrative corruption, 2.1 for infrastructure, and 3.2 for small business programs, and they are significant. The spatial regression analysis emphasizes the regional nature of determinants of entrepreneurial activity. It points to the importance of incorporating a spatial dimension into regression models that explore relationships between entrepreneurial development and institutional factors at the regional level. Two important aspects emerge from this analysis. First, levels of corruption, regional infrastructure, and access to capital through small business programs are important determinants of entrepreneurship. Second, local public policies related to administrative regulation and governance play a strong role in business formation at the regional level.

The results of the regression models that include 83 regions confirm the finding of the interviews with Russian entrepreneurs in Moscow, Saint Petersburg, and Karelia. The spatial regression models demonstrate that administrative corruption is negatively related to entrepreneurial employment at the regional level in Russia. This finding confirms theoretical assumptions about the relationship between corruption and the development of the entrepreneurial sector.[72] Similarly to a recent study of Brazilian municipalities,[73] the research on Russian regions demonstrates that higher levels of corruption at the regional level are associated with reductions in the number of entrepreneurs. Furthermore, the interviews with entrepreneurs show that not only does corruption increase cost of doing business; it also discourages investment in productive and innovative activities. Corruption also increases the uncertainty of doing business, which has a negative impact on national and regional entrepreneurial development.

The analysis presented in this chapter shows that although corruption is significant in all Russian regions, some regions suffer from it more than others. The regression models also demonstrate that regional policies that improve the regulatory environment through a decrease in administrative barriers to doing business have a positive impact on entrepreneurship. This result is highly consistent with previous studies conducted in Russia.[74] The regression analysis demonstrates that entrepreneurs in Russian regions suffer from rent-seeking practices of regulatory agencies. This discourages them from opening new businesses and contributing their innovative ideas, creativity, talents, and vibrant interest in making better lives for themselves and their communities. Uncertainty of doing business has a disastrous impact on regional economic development. The examination of administrative barriers to doing business at the regional level suggests a need for further deregulation reforms to mitigate corruption. The importance of such reforms stems from the finding that excessive administrative burden and overregulation contribute to a decrease in the entrepreneurial population in Russia.

Notes

1 See, for example, Besstremyannaya, G., Bondarenko, O., & Kartseva, M. *Analiz administrativnykh bar'erov v sfere obshchestvennogo pitaniya* [in Russian], (Moscow:

CEFIR, 2014); OECD. Regulatory Reform in the Russian Federation (OECD), available at: www.oecd.org/gov/regulatory-policy/2724142.pdf; OPORA. *Opora Indeks 2010–2011* [in Russian], (Moscow: OPORA, 2012); World Bank. *Administrativnaya reforma i reforma gosudarstvennogo regulirovaniya v Rossii* [in Russian] (Washington, DC: The World Bank, 2006).
2 Federal Statistics Service of the Russian Federation. Individual'nye predrinimateli [in Russian]. (2017). Available at: www.gks.ru/wps/wcm/connect/rosstat_main/rosstat/ru/statistics/enterprise/reform/
3 Krueger, A. O. The Political Economy of the Rent-Seeking Society. *The American Economic Review*, *64*(3) (1974), 291–303.
4 Ibid., p. 294.
5 Auzan, A., & Kruchkova, P. Administrativnye bar'ery v ekonomike: zadachi deregulirovaniya [in Russian]. *Voprosy Economiki*, *5* (2001), 77.
6 Bhagwati, J. N. Directly Unproductive, Profit-Seeking (DUP) Activities. *The Journal of Political Economy*, *90*(5) (1982), 988–1002.
7 Ibid., p. 989.
8 de Soto, H. *The Other Path: The Economic Answer to Terrorism* (New York: Basic Books, 1989), pp. 18–19.
9 Ibid., pp. 19–20.
10 Institute of Liberty and Democracy. ILD Projects. (2017). Available at: www.ild.org.pe/our-work/ild-projects
11 Ibid.
12 Numerous studies provide evidence that corruption has a significant negative impact on GDP growth, see, for example, Knack, S., & Keefer, P. Institutions and Economic Performance: Cross-Country Tests Using Alternative Institutional Measures, *Economics & Politics*, *7*(3) (1995), 207–227; Mauro, P. Corruption and Growth, *The Quarterly Journal of Economics*, *110*(3) (1995), 681–712.
13 Mo, P. H. Corruption and Economic Growth. *Journal of Comparative Economics*, *29*(1) (2001), 66–79.
14 Ibid.
15 Tanzi, V., & Davoodi, H. Corruption, Public Investment, and Growth, IMF Working Paper 97/139 (Washington, DC: IMF, 1997).
16 Wei, S.-J., & Wu, Y. Negative Alchemy? Corruption, Composition of Capital Flows, and Currency Crises, Working Paper No. 8187 (Cambridge, MA: National Bureau of Economic Research, 2001), pp. 3–4.
17 See, for example, Argandoña, A. Corruption and Companies: The Use of Facilitating Payments, *Journal of Business Ethics*, *60*(3) (2005), 251–264; Krylova, Y. The Nature of Corruption and Multilateral System of Anti-Corruption Regulation in the Transition Economy of Russia, *European Journal of Scientific Research*, *65*(1) (2011), 79–92; Lambsdorff, J. How Corruption Affects Productivity, *Kyklos*, *56* (2003), 457–474; Méon, P.-G., & Sekkat, K. Does Corruption Grease or Sand the Wheels of Growth? *Public Choice*, *122*(1/2) (2005), 69–97.
18 Humphrey, C. Russian Protection Rackets and the Appropriation of Law and Order. In J. Heyman (Ed.), *States and Illegal Practices* (pp. 199–232) (New York: Berg, 1999).
19 Auzan & Kruchkova, op. cit., pp. 291–303.
20 Ibid., p. 73.
21 Degtyarev, A., & Malikov, R. Institutsional'nye faktory sozdaniya mekhanizmov preodoleniya administrativnykh bar'erov v razvitii predprinimatel'stva [in Russian]. *Vestnik Moskovskogo Universiteta*, *6*(6) (2003), 48.
22 See, for example, Klapper, L. F., Lewin, A., & Quesada Delgado, J. M. The Impact of the Business Environment on the Business Creation Process, Policy Research Working Paper 4937 (Washington, DC: The World Bank, 2009).
23 CEFIR. *Monitoring of the Administrative Barriers to the Development of Small Business in Russia*, Round 1 (Moscow: CEFIR, 2002).

24 CEFIR. *Monitoring of the Administrative Barriers to the Development of Small Business in Russia*, Round 6 (Moscow: CEFIR, 2007).
25 Ibid., p. 7.
26 See, for example, Narovlyanskaya, T., & Kartasheva, V. *Administrativnye bar'ery kak institut transformatsionnoi ekonomiki* [in Russian] (Orenburg: Litres, 2012); Krylova, Y. The Anti-Corruption Policies and Regulation: The Case of Nicaragua, *Economic Analysis of Law Review*, 7(1) (2016), 36–52.
27 Costa, L., & Aubyn, M. The Macroeconomic Effects of Legal-Simplification Programmes. UECE Working Paper No. 12/2012. (2012). Available at: https://papers.ssrn.com/sol3/papers.cfm?abstract_id=2294170
28 See, for example, Klapper, L. F., & Love, I. The Impact of Business Environment Reforms on New Firm Registration, Policy Research Working Paper 5493 (Washington, DC: The World Bank, 2010).
29 Diergarten, Y., and Krieger, T. Large-Scale Land Acquisitions, Commitment Problems and International Law. *Law and Development Review*, 8(1) (2015), 217–33.
30 Frye, T., & Shleifer, A. The Invisible Hand and the Grabbing Hand. *American Economic Review*, 87(2) (1997), 354.
31 Shelley, L. I. *Dirty Entanglements: Corruption, Crime, and Terrorism* (Cambridge: Cambridge University Press, 2014), p. 78.
32 Titov, B. Pora proverit' proverki [in Russian]. *Vegomosti*, October 2, 2014.
33 Ibid.
34 Cited in Aitchison, B. *Small Business Collective Action and its Effects on Administrative Modernization in Putin's Russia: From "Grabbing Hand" to "Helping Hand"?* (London: The London School of Economics and Political Science, (LSE), 2014), p. 71.
35 Ibid., p. 74.
36 Ministry of Economic Development of the Russian Federation. *Svodnyi doklad ob osushchestvlenii gosudarstvennogo kontrolya (nadzora) za 2012 god* [in Russian] (Moscow: Ministry of Economic Development, 2013), p. 72.
37 Litvak, A. *Rezul'taty monitoringa administrativnykh bar'erov* [in Russian] (Moscow: MCHS, 2010), p. 8.
38 Ibid.
39 Ministry of Economic Development of the Russian Federation. A Three-Year Ban on Planned Inspections of Small Businesses (Moscow, 2015). Available at: http://en.smb.gov.ru/sme/news/280.html
40 Aitchison, op. cit., p. 74.
41 World Bank. *Doing Business 2015: Going Beyond Efficiency* (Washington, DC: The World Bank, 2014), p. 213.
42 Ibid., p. 122.
43 World Bank. *Getting Electricity* (Washington, DC: The World Bank, 2015).
44 Even foreign companies with a zero-tolerance policy toward corruption might be forced to pay facilitation payments for electricity in Russia. For example, in 2010, the Swedish furniture giant Ikea was involved in a large corruption scandal when its executives allowed a contractor to bribe an electrical agency official in Saint Petersburg. As a result, Ikea dismissed the senior executives Per Kaufmann, General Director for Russia and Eastern Europe, and Stefan Gross, Director for Ikea's shopping mall business in Russia. According to Kirill Kabanov, a former Federal Security Service official, who now heads the National Anti-Corruption Committee, "For foreign companies, the corruption risks in Russia can outweigh their potential profits. Foreign companies are concerned that zero tolerance to corruption might get them into situations of unfair competition with those businesses that agree to pay bribes" (cited in Nikishenkov, O. Ikea Case Exposes Bribe Culture in Russia, *The Moscow News*, February 23, 2010). For this reason, "Ikea had probably contracted out the work of securing permits so they could avoid the appearance of paying bribes" (ibid.). In this way,

45 OECD. *Financing SMEs and Entrepreneurs 2015* (Geneva: OECD Publishing, 2015), p. 289.
46 Ibid.
47 OPORA. *Opora Indeks 2012* [in Russian] (Moscow: OPORA, 2013).
48 Ibid.
49 Federal Statistics Service of the Russian Federation, op. cit.
50 See, for example, ratings developed by the Center for Information and Communication Research "Raiting" (2014, 2015) published on their official website, available at: http://russia-rating.ru/info/category/gubernators
51 Ratings of Russian regional governors developed by the Foundation for the Development of Civil Society are published on their official website. Available at: http://civilfund.ru
52 Zotov, D. Nelidova "vzyali" [in Russian]. *The Moscow Post*, September 25, 2015.
53 Zhiteli Karelii podpisyvayut petitsiyu o smeshchenii s dolzhnosti gubernatora [in Russian]. (April 20, 2015). Available at: www.b-port.com/news/item/152016.html
54 Sokolov, M. Karelia pod upravleniem samogo nepopulyarnogo gubernatora Rossii [in Russian]. *Radio Free Europe/Radio Liberty*. November 14, 2011.
55 Zotov, op. cit.
56 Federal Statistics Service of the Russian Federation. Chislennost' rabotnikov gosudarstvennykh organov [in Russian]. (Moscow, 2017). Available at: www.gks.ru/wps/wcm/connect/rosstat_main/rosstat/ru/statistics/state/#
57 Ibid.
58 Association of Russian Lawyers for Human Rights. *Korruptsiya v Rossii: nezavisimyi godovoi doklad vserossiiskoi antikorruptsionnoi obshchestvennoi priemnoi Chistye Ruki 2015–2016* [in Russian] (Moscow: Association of Russian Lawyers for Human Rights, 2017).
59 Ibid., p. 18.
60 Ibid.
61 Andreyeva, N. Predprinimatelya kazhdyi obidet' mozhet [in Russian]. *Gazeta Nedeli v Saratove*, February 25, 2009.
62 Ibid.
63 Ibid.
64 Olson, M. Dictatorship, Democracy, and Development. *The American Political Science Review*, *87*(3) (1993), 567.
65 Krylova, Y. Administrative Corruption and its Effects on Russian Entrepreneurs: A Regional Aspect. *Journal of Small Business & Entrepreneurship*, *30*(2) (2018), 121–137.
66 Blackwell, W. The Russian Entrepreneur in the Tsarist Period: An Overview. In G. Guroff & F. V. Carstensen (Eds.), *Entrepreneurship in Imperial Russia and the Soviet Union* (pp. 13–26) (Princeton, NJ: Princeton University Press, 1983), p. 16.
67 Ibid.
68 Cited in Blackwell, op. cit., p. 16.
69 Association of Russian Lawyers for Human Rights, op. cit.
70 Agency for Strategic Initiatives. Natsional'nye reitingi v 2015 godu [in Russian]. (Moscow, 2016). Available at: http://asi.ru/investclimate/ratings
71 Federal Statistics Service of the Russian Federation. Regional'nyi valovyi produkt na dushu naseleniya [in Russian]. (2016). Available at: www.gks.ru/dbscripts/cbsd/dbinet.cgi
72 See, for example, Anokhin, S., & Schulze, W. S. Entrepreneurship, Innovation, and Corruption, *Journal of Business Venturing*, *24*(5) (2009), 465–476; Avnimelech, G., Zelekha, Y., & Sharabi, E. The Effect of Corruption on Entrepreneurship in Developed vs Non-Developed Countries, *International Journal of Entrepreneurial*

Behavior & Research, 20(3) (2014), 237–262; Bologna, J., & Ross, A. Corruption and Entrepreneurship: Evidence from Brazilian Municipalities, *Public Choice, 165*(1–2) (2015), 59–77; Chowdhury, F., Terjesen, S., & Audretsch, D. Varieties of Entrepreneurship: Institutional Drivers Across Entrepreneurial Activity and Country, *European Journal of Law and Economics, 40*(1) (2015), 121–148; Ovaska, T., & Sobel, R. S. Entrepreneurship in Post-Socialist Economies, *Journal of Private Enterprise, 21*(Fall) (2005), 8–28.

73 Bologna, & Ross, op. cit.

74 See, for example, Krylova, Y. "Grease" Payments in the Relations Between Regulatory Agencies and Individual Entrepreneurs: The Case of Russia (doctoral dissertation) (George Mason University, Fairfax, VA, 2017).

References

Agency for Strategic Initiatives. (2016). Natsional'nye reitingi v 2015 godu [in Russian]. Moscow. Available at: http://asi.ru/investclimate/ratings

Aitchison, B. (2014). *Small Business Collective Action and its Effects on Administrative Modernization in Putin's Russia: From "Grabbing Hand" to "Helping Hand"?* London: The London School of Economics and Political Science (LSE), Available at: http://etheses.lse.ac.uk/994/

Andreyeva, N. (2009, February 25). Predprinimatelya kazhdyi obidet' mozhet [in Russian]. *Gazeta Nedeli v Saratove*.

Anokhin, S., & Schulze, W. S. (2009). Entrepreneurship, Innovation, and Corruption. *Journal of Business Venturing, 24*(5), 465–476.

Argandoña, A. (2005). Corruption and Companies: The Use of Facilitating Payments. *Journal of Business Ethics, 60*(3), 251–264.

Association of Russian Lawyers for Human Rights. (2017). *Korruptsiya v Rossii: nezavisimyi godovoi doklad vserossiiskoi antikorruptsionnoi obshchestvennoi priemnoi Chistye Ruki 2015–2016* [in Russian]. Moscow: Association of Russian Lawyers for Human Rights.

Auzan, A., & Kruchkova, P. (2001). Administrativnye bar'ery v ekonomike: zadachi deregulirovaniya [in Russian]. *Voprosy Economiki, 5*, 73–88.

Avnimelech, G., Zelekha, Y., & Sharabi, E. (2014). The Effect of Corruption on Entrepreneurship in Developed vs Non-Developed Countries. *International Journal of Entrepreneurial Behavior & Research, 20*(3), 237–262.

Besstremyannaya, G., Bondarenko, O., & Kartseva, M. (2014). *Analiz administrativnykh bar'erov v sfere obshchestvennogo pitaniya* [in Russian]. Moscow: CEFIR.

Bhagwati, J. N. (1982). Directly Unproductive, Profit-Seeking (DUP) Activities. *The Journal of Political Economy, 90*(5), 988–1002.

Blackwell, W. (1983). The Russian Entrepreneur in the Tsarist Period: An Overview. In G. Guroff & F. V. Carstensen (Eds.), *Entrepreneurship in Imperial Russia and the Soviet Union* (pp. 13–26). Princeton, NJ: Princeton University Press.

Bologna, J., & Ross, A. (2015). Corruption and Entrepreneurship: Evidence from Brazilian Municipalities. *Public Choice, 165*(1–2), 59–77.

CEFIR. (2002). *Monitoring of the Administrative Barriers to the Development of Small Business in Russia, Round 1*. Moscow: CEFIR.

CEFIR. (2007). *Monitoring of the Administrative Barriers to the Development of Small Business in Russia, Round 6*. Moscow: CEFIR.

Center for Information and Communication Research "Rating." (2014). Reiting gubernatorov [in Russian]. Moscow. Available at: http://russia-rating.ru/info/4385.html

Center for Information and Communication Research "Rating." (2015). Reiting gubernatorov [in Russian]. Moscow. Available at: http://russia-rating.ru/info/4771.html

Center for the Development of Public–Private Partnership. (2015). *Razvitie GCHP v sub"ektakh RF: Reiting regionov GCHP 2014–2015* [in Russian]. Moscow: Center for the Development of Public–Private Partnership.

Chowdhury, F., Terjesen, S., & Audretsch, D. (2015). Varieties of Entrepreneurship: Institutional Drivers Across Entrepreneurial Activity and Country. *European Journal of Law and Economics, 40*(1), 121–148.

Costa, L., & Aubyn, M. (2012). The Macroeconomic Effects of Legal-Simplification Programmes. UECE Working Paper No. 12/2012. Available at: https://papers.ssrn.com/sol3/papers.cfm?abstract_id=2294170

Degtyarev, A., & Malikov, R. (2003). Institutsional'nye faktory sozdaniya mechanizmov preodoleniya administrativnykh bar'erov v razvitii predprinimatel'stva [in Russian]. *Vestnik Moskovskogo Universiteta, 6*(6), 42–58.

de Soto, H. (1989). *The Other Path: The Economic Answer to Terrorism*. New York: Basic Books.

Diergarten, Y., & Krieger, T. (2015). Large-Scale Land Acquisitions, Commitment Problems and International Law. *Law and Development Review, 8*(1), 217–233.

Federal Anti-Monopoly Service of the Russian Federation. (2015). *Reiting konkurentsii v regionakh* [in Russian]. Moscow: FAS.

Federal Statistics Service of the Russian Federation. (2016). Regional'nyi valovyi produkt na dushu naseleniya [in Russian]. Moscow. Available at: www.gks.ru/dbscripts/cbsd/dbinet.cgi

Federal Statistics Service of the Russian Federation. (2017a). Chislennost' rabotnikov gosudarstvennykh organov [in Russian]. Moscow. Available at: www.gks.ru/wps/wcm/connect/rosstat_main/rosstat/ru/statistics/state/#

Federal Statistics Service of the Russian Federation. (2017b). Individual'nye predrinimateli [in Russian]. Moscow. Available at: www.gks.ru/wps/wcm/connect/rosstat_main/rosstat/ru/statistics/enterprise/reform/

Foundation for the Development of Civil Society. (2015). Reiting effektivnosti gubernatorov [in Russian]. Moscow. Available at: http://civilfund.ru/mat/85

Frye, T., & Shleifer, A. (1997). The Invisible Hand and the Grabbing Hand. *American Economic Review, 87*(2), 354–358.

Humphrey, C. (1999). Russian Protection Rackets and the Appropriation of Law and Order. In J. Heyman (Ed.), *States and Illegal Practices* (pp. 199–232). New York: Berg.

Institute of Liberty and Democracy. (2017). *ILD Projects*. Available at: www.ild.org.pe/our-work/ild-projects

Klapper, L. F., Lewin, A., & Quesada Delgado, J. M. (2009). The Impact of the Business Environment on the Business Creation Process, Policy Research Working Paper 4937. Washington, DC: The World Bank.

Klapper, L. F., & Love, I. (2010). The Impact of Business Environment Reforms on New Firm Registration, Policy Research Working Paper 5493. Washington, DC: The World Bank.

Knack, S., & Keefer, P. (1995). Institutions and Economic Performance: Cross-Country Tests Using Alternative Institutional Measures. *Economics & Politics, 7*(3), 207–227.

Krueger, A. O. (1974). The Political Economy of the Rent-Seeking Society. *The American Economic Review, 64*(3), 291–303.

Krylova, Y. (2011). The Nature of Corruption and Multilateral System of Anti-Corruption Regulation in the Transition Economy of Russia. *European Journal of Scientific Research*, *65*(1), 79–92.

Krylova, Y. (2016). Corruption and Gender Inequality: The Case of Nicaragua. *International Journal of Ethics*, *12*(3), 273–289.

Krylova, Y. (2017). "Grease" Payments in the Relations Between Regulatory Agencies and Individual Entrepreneurs: The Case of Russia (doctoral dissertation). George Mason University, Fairfax, VA.

Krylova, Y. (2018). Administrative Corruption and its Effects on Russian Entrepreneurs: A Regional Aspect. *Journal of Small Business & Entrepreneurship. 30*(2), 121–137.

Lambsdorff, J. (2003). How Corruption Affects Productivity. *Kyklos*, *56*, 457–474.

Litvak, A. (2010). *Rezul'taty monitoringa administrativnykh bar'erov* [in Russian]. Moscow: MCHS.

Mauro, P. (1995). Corruption and Growth. *The Quarterly Journal of Economics*, *110*(3), 681–712.

Méon, P.-G., & Sekkat, K. (2005). Does Corruption Grease or Sand the Wheels of Growth? *Public Choice*, *122*(1/2), 69–97.

Ministry of Economic Development of the Russian Federation. (2013). *Svodnyi doklad ob osushchestvlenii gosudarstvennogo kontrolya (nadzora) za 2012 god* [in Russian]. Moscow: Ministry of Economic Development.

Ministry of Economic Development of the Russian Federation. (2015). *A Three-Year Ban on Planned Inspections of Small Businesses*. Moscow: Ministry of Economic Development.

Mo, P. H. (2001). Corruption and Economic Growth. *Journal of Comparative Economics*, *29*(1), 66–79.

Narovlianskaya, T., & Kartasheva, V. (2012). *Administrativnye bar'ery kak institut transformatsionnoi ekonomiki* [in Russian]. Orenburg: Litres.

National Research University Higher School of Economics. (2014). *Reiting innovatsionnogo razvitiya sub''ektov RF* [in Russian]. Moscow: NIU VSHE.

Nikishenkov, O. (2010, February 23). Ikea Case Exposes Bribe Culture in Russia. *The Moscow News*.

OECD. (2001). Regulatory Reform in the Russian Federation. Available at: www.oecd.org/gov/regulatory-policy/2724142.pdf

OECD. (2015). *Financing SMEs and Entrepreneurs 2015*. Geneva: OECD Publishing.

Olson, M. (1993). Dictatorship, Democracy, and Development. *American Political Science Review*, *87*(3), 567–576.

OPORA. (2012). *Opora Indeks 2010–2011* [in Russian]. Moscow: OPORA.

OPORA. (2013). *Opora Indeks 2012* [in Russian]. Moscow: OPORA.

Ovaska, T., & Sobel, R. S. (2005). Entrepreneurship in Post-Socialist Economies. *Journal of Private Enterprise*, *21*(Fall), 8–28.

Shelley, L. I. (2014). *Dirty Entanglements: Corruption, Crime, and Terrorism*. Cambridge: Cambridge University Press.

Sokolov, M. (2011, November 14). Karelia pod upravleniem samogo nepopulyarnogo gubernatora Rossii [in Russian]. *Radio Free Europe/Radio Liberty*. Available at: www.svoboda.org/content/transcript/24391147.html

Tanzi, V., & Davoodi, H. (1997). Corruption, Public Investment, and Growth. IMF Working Paper 97/139. Washington, DC: IMF.

Titov, B. (2014, October 2). Pora proverit' proverki [in Russian]. *Vegomosti*.

Wei, S.-J., & Wu, Y. (2001). *Negative Alchemy? Corruption, Composition of Capital Flows, and Currency Crises*, Working Paper No. 8187. Cambridge, MA: National Bureau of Economic Research. Available at: www.nber.org/papers/w8187

World Bank. (2006). *Administrativnaya reforma i reforma gosudarstvennogo regulirovaniya v Rossii* [in Russian]. Washington, DC: The World Bank.

World Bank. (2014). *Doing Business 2015: Going Beyond Efficiency*. Washington, DC: The World Bank.

World Bank. (2015). *Getting Electricity*. Washington, DC: The World Bank.

Zhiteli Karelii podpisyvayut petitsiyu o smeshchenii s dolzhnosti gubernatora [in Russian]. (2015, April 20). Available at: www.b-port.com/news/item/152016.html

Zotov, D. (2015, September 25). Nelidova "vziali" [in Russian]. *The Moscow Post*.

4 "No Grease, No Ride"
Facilitation Payments in the Relations Between Entrepreneurs and Regulatory Agencies

In recent decades, international development organizations have increasingly focused research on the relationship between administrative overregulation and informal payments. To decrease corruption and encourage entrepreneurship, the World Bank, for instance, developed comprehensive and detailed policy recommendations to assist the Russian authorities in structuring and implementing regulatory reforms in various spheres, including inspections, licensing, registration, and certification.[1] As a response, a deregulation reform was implemented in Russia and new laws on inspections, registration, and entrepreneurial rights were adopted in the 2000s. Contrary to the expected results, the deregulation reform did not have a significant impact on mitigating the problem of informal transactions between businesses and regulatory agencies. According to recent surveys of businesses and individual entrepreneurs, the frequency of "grease" payments, that is, facilitation payments for routine governmental actions, remains high in Russia.[2] They are also known as "expediting" payments.

In Russia, "grease" payments have existed since the very beginning of the public administration system. In the old Russian language, there were two different terms to refer to informal payments. The first term, *likhoimstvo* means activities associated with the extortion of informal payments by public officials for services that provide benefits to businesses in violation of the existing official regulations. The term *mzdoimstvo*, on the other hand, refers to situations where public officials accept "grease" payments in return for favors. These informal practices go back to the system of *kormlenie*, where the Russian tsar appointed local administrators who had no salary and instead received payments and presents from the local population.[3] In the fifteenth century, this system was abolished. Later, *likhoimstvo* and *mzdoimstvo* were replaced by a new legal term *vzyatochnichestvo* (bribery). Russia's first anti-bribery law was adopted in 1497.

The first people's rebellion against corruption occurred in Moscow in 1648. The Moscow uprising was provoked by widespread corruption among state administrators.[4] This rebellion eventually resulted in the adoption of the new legal code of 1649 (*Sobornoye Ulozheniye*), which introduced seizures of property as measures to punish public officials for bribery.[5] However, this law proved ineffective at eradicating informal payments. Russian history demonstrates that a top-down approach focusing exclusively on the legislative response to corruption is not always efficient because informal practices are deeply rooted in the institutional environment and public administration system. Numerous Russian sayings and proverbs related to the use of informal payments can serve as an illustration of their embeddedness in the socioeconomic and political systems: "no grease, no ride," "do not say a word, just show *groshi* [coins]," "it is the squeaky wheel that gets the grease," "a taking hand does not get tired," and "it's good fishing in troubled waters." This chapter presents an analysis of current factors that facilitate the prevalence of "grease" payments in the Russian economy.

Literature Review

Research into "grease" payments represents a specific area within a broader body of literature on corruption. It is situated at the intersection of three schools of thought: (1) the legal school; (2) rational choice theory; and (3) new institutional theory. Together, these schools of thought make it possible to understand the relationship between administrative overregulation and "grease" payments extorted by regulatory agencies. These schools do not, however, pay sufficient attention to how businesses and entrepreneurs perceive "grease" and other informal payments, nor do they adequately explore the factors that can potentially change entrepreneurs' attitudes toward corruption.

The legal school of thought analyzes legislative aspects of "grease" and other informal payments. In his study of transnational bribery, Philip Nichols distinguishes between "grease" payments that simply facilitate obtaining property rights that a business is legally entitled to receive and informal payments that provide illegal advantages.[6] The distinction between "grease" and other informal payments is important because the U.S. Foreign Corrupt Practices Act of 1977, 15 U.S.C. §§78dd-1, et seq (FCPA), which was the first law in the world prohibiting transnational bribery, makes exceptions for facilitating payments for routine governmental action. The FCPA defines facilitating payments as "expediting payments the purpose of which is to expedite or to secure the performance of a routine governmental action by a foreign official, political party, or party official."[7] The FCPA provides affirmative defenses as long as "grease" payments do not intend to encourage a foreign official or regulatory agency to award new business or to continue business with a particular party.

Similarly, the OECD Convention on Combating Bribery of Foreign Public Officials in International Business Transactions (also known as the OECD Anti-Bribery Convention) distinguishes between facilitation payments and bribes. This Convention was signed in 1997 and came into force in 1999. Paragraph 3 of Article 1 of the OECD Anti-Bribery Convention indicates that the criminalization of facilitation payments is not "a practical or effective action" because they are not aimed at obtaining or regaining business or other improper advantages.[8] The OECD Anti-Bribery Convention was adopted by 34 OECD member countries and seven non-member countries, including Argentina, Brazil, Bulgaria, Colombia, Latvia, Russia, and South Africa.

The FCPA and the OECD Anti-Bribery Convention recognize that businesses might be forced to make informal payments to avoid overregulation in developing countries. From this perspective, "grease" payments are distinguished from bribes. Nevertheless, many studies within the legal school still criticize "grease" payments. For example, Antonio Argadoña argues that facilitation payments are "the slippery slope to more serious forms of corruption."[9] Although petty unofficial payments are tolerated in many developing countries, they are prohibited by national legislation in most states. Specifically, Russia's legislature prohibits the use of "grease" payments in domestic and international transactions. Taking the negative consequences of facilitation payments into account, the OECD revisited their recommendations and introduced new provisions for combating corruption. In 2009, the OECD published its "Recommendation for Further Combating Bribery of Foreign Public Officials in International Business Transactions." This document recommends that signatory countries review their approach to facilitation payments.[10] It also encourages companies in these countries to prohibit or discourage the use of such payments in their ethics codes and internal programs. This recommendation is not binding, and it is up to a particular member country to decide whether to follow the OECD approach to facilitation payments or not.

Rational choice theory takes another approach to "grease" payments, by arguing that their benefits can exceed their costs in over-centralized administrative states.[11] It is necessary to note that this school had been the dominant approach to analysis of "grease" payments until the 1990s when new corruption studies based on cross-country comparisons disproved its key arguments. Rational choice theory proposes the "efficient grease" hypothesis, namely, that informal payments improve economic efficiency in situations of overregulation. As Nathaniel Leff puts it, "If the government has erred in its decision, the course made possible by corruption may well be the better one."[12] Samuel Huntington also suggests that "in terms of economic growth, the only thing worse than a society with a rigid, over-centralized, dishonest bureaucracy is one with a rigid, over-centralized, honest bureaucracy."[13]

Proponents of rational choice theory distinguish several mechanisms behind the "efficient grease" hypothesis. First, as indicated by Francis Lui, "grease" payments decrease the time spent in queues and give incentives to public officials to speed up bureaucratic procedures.[14] Samuel Huntington illustrates this phenomenon with the fast growth of industrial corporations and railroad construction in the United States in the 1870–1880s, which was fueled by corruption.[15] The second mechanism behind the "efficient grease" hypothesis is attributed to David Bailey's argument, according to which the low salaries of civil servants discourage highly qualified employees from seeking jobs in the public sector.[16] Consequently, "grease" payments might give them additional motivation and incentivize them to work in the public sector. The third mechanism is described by Paul Beck and Michael Maher who indicate that under the condition of high uncertainty and informational gaps, bureaucrats can effectively allocate resources when the highest "grease" payment is made by the most efficient firm.[17] In this case, corruption functions as a competitive auction.

Finally, a more recent study of corruption within the rational choice school conducted by Axel Dreher and Martin Gassebner shows that corruption increases entrepreneurial activity and facilitates firm entry in highly regulated economies.[18] However, this finding is compromised by the fact that it ignores potential long-term effects of overregulation, including a further increase in the number of entry regulations. Also, corruption makes market entry easier only for those businessmen who can afford and are prepared to bribe public officials. For a large number of individual entrepreneurs with limited economic resources, excessive bureaucratic procedures to start a business and large minimum capital requirements represent a significant barrier to market entry. The resulting negative consequence of overregulation is an increase in the number of businesses operating in the shadow market and the informal sector of the economy.

As such, one limitation of the rational choice school is that it ignores the negative impact of overregulation on doing business and economic growth in developing countries. Although "grease" payments can be rational from the perspective of individual businesses suffering from administrative corruption, they are not economically efficient for the entire entrepreneurial community in the long run. In this regard, Louise Shelley indicates that "although some analysts once suggested that corruption greases the wheels in overregulated and nonfunctional bureaucracies, the costs of corruption become so great in the global economy that this analytical perspective is now largely discredited."[19] Despite all these limitations, rational choice theory is useful in explaining how the perceived necessity of "grease" payments influences decisions of individual entrepreneurs.

Unlike rational choice theory, the institutional school of thought places a greater emphasis on the negative consequences of "grease" payments for the economy.[20] A significant number of studies developed within this school of thought find a positive correlation between bribery and administrative harassment, which disproves the "efficient grease" hypothesis.[21] For example, Daniel Kaufmann and Shang-Jin Wei demonstrate that informal payments lead to an increase in official harassment of businesses, as measured by management time wasted with bureaucracy, regulatory burden, and cost of capital.[22] To solve this problem, they propose removing excessive administrative procedures. Most studies within this school, however, focus on the demand side of informal payments (bureaucracy), rather than the supply side (businesses). Therefore, they do not take into account positive perceptions of businesses regarding informal payments. In response to this shortcoming, some scholars within sociological institutionalism point to a need to incorporate businesses' perceptions and attitudes toward informal practices into the research on administrative corruption.[23] The current "mainstream" focus on state agencies and public officials, who abuse their office for private gain, limits a set of potential anti-corruption strategies.

The depth to which "grease" payments are institutionally embedded in Russian society suggests the importance of research into both the demand and supply sides of corrupt practices. Studies conducted in other developing countries demonstrate that businesses' attitudes toward informal payments shape both corrupt practices and the related anti-corruption strategies. For instance, a recent study of Thailand's businesses finds that managers' attitudes toward corruption are directly related to the perceived necessity and perceived unethicality of bribing.[24] Another study of India's businesses demonstrates that executives' perceptions about corruption play a critical role in shaping informal practices. Importantly, the latter study finds that professional norms in particular industries significantly affect businesses' perceptions and attitudes toward corruption.[25] Specifically, the study suggests that "professional networks have developed more effective norms than those that exist in non-professionalized industries for discouraging engagement in corruption and guiding appropriate actions when confronted with corruption."[26]

In Russia, a study of managers' attitudes toward corruption was conducted by Stanislav Shekshnia, Alena Ledeneva, and Elena Denisova-Schmidt.[27] Based on interviews with CEOs in 20 companies, the researchers distinguish four positions related to informal practices: (1) toleration (perceptions about such practices as an inevitable state of affairs); (2) exploitation (their use as a legitimate instrument of doing business); (3) avoidance (abstaining from such practices within businesses); and (4) management of corruption (active involvement in anti-corruption efforts).[28] Interestingly, only a small minority of CEOs viewed corruption as a legitimate instrument of doing business, while the majority demonstrated tolerance toward informal practices.[29] In this respect, further research is needed to analyze factors that prevent Russian companies from active participation in anti-corruption efforts.

Recent literature on anti-corruption policies provides strong evidence of gender-specific attitudes toward corruption.[30] A previous attempt to determine differences in perceptions of male and female Russian managers regarding informal practices was conducted by Satish Deshpande, Jacob Joseph, and Vasily Maximov.[31] They find that in comparison with male managers, female managers consider the following informal activities more unethical: "doing personal business on company time, falsifying time/quality/quantity reports, padding an expense account more than 10 percent, calling in sick to take a day off, and pilfering organization materials and supplies."[32] Female managers also demonstrate more negative attitudes toward the acceptance of gifts and favors in exchange for preferential treatment.[33] Therefore, gender represents an important factor that impacts the effectiveness of anti-corruption policies and regulations.

In the case of individual entrepreneurs, another critical factor is the lack of resources to counteract officials who extort bribes. Self-regulatory organizations that provide legal and financial support for their members can be an effective solution to this problem. In this context, the analysis presented in this chapter pays particular attention to factors that are responsible for the formation of entrepreneurial attitudes toward corruption, including membership in self-regulatory organizations and gender. It also addresses the question of how these perceptions can be changed through professional networks and other forms of collective action by individual entrepreneurs. As such, this study moves beyond the dominant "mainstream" analysis of rent-seeking bureaucracy, focusing instead on entrepreneurs' perceptions about "grease" payments.

Analytical Framework of the Research into Attitudes of Entrepreneurs Toward "Grease" Payments

Drawing on the previous research into administrative corruption, this study analyzes how attitudes toward "grease" payments affect their use by Russian entrepreneurs. In this context, Hypothesis 1 proposes that the high frequency of "grease" payments made to regulatory agencies is related to positive attitudes and perceptions about such transactions among individual entrepreneurs, rather than to the problem of administrative overregulation alone. Expanding the research into the role of professional networks in anti-corruption efforts,[34] Hypothesis 2 proposes that individual entrepreneurs who belong to self-regulatory organizations, such as national or regional associations of entrepreneurs, are more likely to demonstrate negative attitudes toward informal payments than entrepreneurs who do not belong to any self-regulatory organization. In addition, Hypothesis 3 proposes that individual entrepreneurs who belong to self-regulatory organizations are less likely to be engaged in corrupt practices with regulatory agencies in comparison with entrepreneurs who do not belong to any self-regulatory organization. Expanding gender-specific studies of corruption,[35] Hypothesis 4 proposes that female entrepreneurs are more likely to demonstrate negative attitudes toward the use of "grease" payments in comparison with their male counterparts. Finally, Hypothesis 5 proposes that female entrepreneurs are less likely to pay "grease" money to regulatory agencies in comparison with their male counterparts.

The testing of these hypotheses is based on the 2015 survey conducted in three regions: Moscow, Saint Petersburg, and Karelia. Its objective was to obtain aggregate data on Russian entrepreneurs' attitudes toward "grease" payments and the frequency of their use. The survey used the probability sample technique according to which respondents are randomly chosen from the list of entrepreneurs registered in Russia's Unified State Register of Individual Entrepreneurs. The criteria to choose the respondents included their official registration as an individual entrepreneur in Russia's Tax Services and more than three years of business experience. The first criterion was used to distinguish individual entrepreneurs from other business entities. The second criterion relates to the fact that the formation of perceptions regarding "grease" payments is a process that requires time to develop.

As all subjects were Russians, the original survey was constructed in their native language, and then translated into English (see Appendix 2). The survey was based on a Likert scale, that is, a psychometric scale that specifies the level of respondents' agreement or disagreement on a symmetric agree-disagree scale for each of the statements: "strongly agree," "agree," "neither agree nor disagree," "disagree," and "strongly disagree." The advantage of this scale is that it allows researchers to explore the intensity of individual perceptions. To capture the intensity variation, the questionnaire used a 5-point scale, ranging from −2 to +2. For example, entrepreneurs received scores of −2 if they strongly disagreed and +2 if they strongly agreed with the following statement: "The use of "grease" payments is always justified in situations of excessive regulation." Similarly, the answers to the same question that indicate less certainty, such as "disagree" and "agree," received scores of −1 and +1. The midpoint of the scale 0 was reserved for neutral statements, such as "neither agree nor disagree." Clearly, points of +1 and +2 demonstrated positive attitudes about "grease" payments, while points of −1 and −2 showed that entrepreneurs had negative attitudes toward them. Then these scores were summed and a simple average was calculated for attitudes toward "grease" payments.

The answers on the frequency of "grease" payments included: "very often," "often," "rarely," "very rarely," and "never." To capture the frequency variation, the questionnaire used a 5-point scale, with a score range of 0 to 4. For example, entrepreneurs received scores of 4 if they made "grease" payments to regulatory agencies very often and 0 if they never used "grease" payments. Scores of 1–3 indicated less frequency: "very rarely," "rarely," and "often." This coding helped conduct regression analysis and run ordered logistic models generated in the Statistical Package for Social Scientists (SPSS).

The testing of the original questionnaire was based on purposeful sampling that relied on the personal contacts represented by three members of the Saint Petersburg Association of Individual Entrepreneurs. The purposeful technique for the test survey was chosen in order to receive respondents' feedback about the clarity of questions and their recommendations on possible improvements. To make the sample representative of the population of Russia's individual entrepreneurs, the survey was distributed to respondents from three regions characterized by various levels of entrepreneurial activities (Moscow, Saint Petersburg, and Karelia).[36] The questionnaire was administered by email. To avoid a bias related to the response order effect, the subsets of respondents, who were selected randomly, received the questionnaires with different question orders. The correlation between the subsets' results represented an inter-item estimate of reliability. In total, 91 usable questionnaires were collected.

Since the survey was not enough to obtain in-depth information about different methods to counteract "grease" payments, it was combined with follow-up expert interviews. Another reason for the combination of these methods is that anonymous surveys provide more honest answers to questions about informal transactions, while expert interviews are more useful for discussing anti-corruption methods and comparing views of individual entrepreneurs and representatives of self-regulatory organizations (regional chambers of commerce and associations of individual entrepreneurs). Although not a random sample, the persons interviewed for this research represented a broad spectrum of industries, such as cosmetics, education, food, furniture, and services. The contact data came from the directories of the Association of Entrepreneurs OPORA Russia, the Russian Association of Microenterprises, the Saint Petersburg Chamber of Commerce, and the Union of Entrepreneurs and Industrialists. In terms of ethics, the consent discussion and consent forms were provided to the participants with all necessary information related to the research before interviews took place.

Attitudes of Russian Entrepreneurs Toward "Grease" Payments

The survey provides evidence of the prevalence of "grease" payments in the entrepreneurial sector. Thus, 74 percent of respondents admitted to making "grease" payments on at least one occasion. The survey demonstrates that most entrepreneurs suffer from the rent-seeking practices of regulatory agencies and public officials who extort facilitation payments for issuing permits and licenses required for business activities, processing governmental documents, conducting inspections, and protecting property rights. The results of the survey allow for the testing of the hypotheses. Of the 91 respondents, 67 are male entrepreneurs, and 24 are female entrepreneurs. On average, they have three employees under their supervision. Only one-quarter of the respondents are members of business associations. Table 4.1 provides descriptive statistics for key variables.

The dependent variable of the frequency of "grease" payments is modeled in an ordinal logit framework, which illuminates interpretation problems inherent in Likert scales. The frequency is ordered from never (= 0) to very often (= 4). The model includes four independent variables: attitudes toward "grease" payments (estimated as an average of entrepreneurs' responses to the questions regarding their perceptions based on a Likert scale), gender, membership in business associations, and numbers of employees.

To test the hypotheses, the frequency of "grease" payments is regressed on entrepreneurs' attitudes toward these payments, their gender, and their membership in business associations. The number of employees is used as a control variable to check whether business size impacts the incidence of "grease" payments. For example, Claudia Trentini and Malinka Koparanova argue that large businesses have to interact more with government agencies, and, therefore, are subject to a severer administrative burden relative to small companies.[37] Furthermore, to check whether gender and membership in business associations combined together have an additional impact on the frequency of "grease" payments, the ordered logistic model includes the interaction term of female membership in business associations. The results are summarized in Table 4.2. It is important to note that in ordered logistic regression models, significantly positive coefficients indicate that marginal increases in the related independent variables will increase the probability of the highest frequency of "grease" payments and decrease the probability of their lowest frequency. Vice versa, significantly negative coefficients indicate that marginal increases in the related independent variables will

Table 4.1 Descriptive statistics

Variable	Number of observations	Mean	Standard deviation	Min	Max
Frequency of "grease" payments	91	2.25	1.53	0	4
Attitudes toward "grease" payments	91	0.28	0.74	−1.2	2
Number of employees	91	3.44	3.00	0	12

Table 4.2 Results of the ordered logistic regression

	Coefficients	Standard error
Female	−1.68***	0.58
Attitudes	1.11***	0.33
Membership	−1.86**	0.72
Number of employees	0.08	0.07
Female membership	0.15	1.38

Notes
Log likelihood = −106.68212.
Prob > χ^2 = 0.0000 Pseudo R squared = 0.1860 VIF = 1.35.
*** $p < 0.01$;
** $p < 0.05$;
* $p < 0.1$.

decrease the probability of the highest frequency of "grease" payments and increase the probability of their lowest frequency.

First, the results of the ordered logistic model support Hypothesis 1, according to which the high frequency of "grease" payments to regulatory agencies is related to positive attitudes toward such transactions, with an estimated coefficient of 1.11 significant at the 1 percent level. This suggests that a one-point increase in positive attitudes toward "grease" payments raises the log odds of moving one category up on the scale of the frequency of "grease" payments by 1.11. This result is consistent with empirical findings from previous studies.[38] Second, the results of the ordered logistic model support Hypothesis 3 related to a negative impact of membership in business associations on the frequency of "grease" payments. The regression coefficient is −1.86 and, it is significant at the 5 percent level. This suggests that being a member of a business association decreases the log odds of moving one category up on the scale of the frequency of "grease" payments by 1.86. The interaction term of female membership in business associations and the number of employees do not have significant coefficients at the 5 percent level.

Third, the results of the ordered logistic model confirm Hypothesis 5, by demonstrating that female entrepreneurs use "grease" payments less frequently than their male counterparts. The estimated coefficient is −1.68, and it is significant at the 1 percent level. This means that being a female entrepreneur decreases the log odds of moving one category up on the scale of the frequency of "grease" payments by 1.68. This result is consistent with previous studies of gender-specific attitudes toward corruption that provided evidence that women are less tolerant to corruption and are less likely to be involved in informal activities.[39]

To check if the model has the problem of multicollinearity (a correlation between predictors), the variance inflation factors (VIF) were estimated in order to measure how much the variance of the estimated regression coefficients is inflated as compared to when the predictor variables are not linearly related. The VIF is equal to 1.35 (VIF < 10), and multicollinearity is not problematic. Since logistic coefficients are in log-odds units and cannot be interpreted as regular

Table 4.3 Predicted probabilities of the frequency of "grease" payments for female and male entrepreneurs

Frequency of "grease" payments		Delta method	
	Gender	Margin	Standard error
0 = Never	Female	0.41***	0.08
	Male	0.16***	0.04
1 = Very rarely	Female	0.04*	0.02
	Male	0.02*	0.01
2 = Rarely	Female	0.18***	0.05
	Male	0.14***	0.04
3 = Often	Female	0.28***	0.06
	Male	0.41***	0.06
4 = Very often	Female	0.08*	0.04
	Male	0.27***	0.05

Notes
*** $p<0.01$;
** $p<0.05$;
* $p<0.1$.

OLS coefficients, it is useful to estimate predicted probabilities. Table 4.3 demonstrates the predicted probabilities of the frequency of "grease" payments for female and male entrepreneurs.

The predicted probability of the lack of "grease" payments for female entrepreneurs is 41 percent, while for male entrepreneurs, this probability is only 16 percent. In the same vein, the predicted probability of the highest frequency of "grease" payments for female entrepreneurs is 8 percent, while for male entrepreneurs, this probability is 27 percent. In addition, Table 4.4 demonstrates predicted probabilities of the frequency of "grease" payments for members and non-members of business associations. The predicted probability of the lack of "grease" payments for members of business associations is 46 percent, while for non-members, this probability is only 19 percent. In the same vein, the predicted probability of the highest frequency of "grease" payments for members of business associations is 7 percent, while for non-members this probability is 27 percent.

In addition, OLS regression models were run to check Hypothesis 2 and 4, with the dependent variable of attitudes toward "grease" payments and two independent variables of gender and membership in business associations. The results show that gender is predictive of different attitudes toward these payments, with a coefficient of −0.76 at the 5 percent level of significance. The results of the regression analysis support Hypothesis 4, according to which female entrepreneurs demonstrate more negative attitudes toward "grease" payments than their male counterparts. This finding is highly consistent with the previous research of gender-specific attitudes toward corruption.[40] However, the results of the OLS regression model do not confirm Hypothesis 2 regarding the

82 "No Grease, No Ride"

Table 4.4 Predicted probabilities of the frequency of "grease" payments for members and non-members of business associations

Frequency of "grease" payments		Delta method	
	Membership	Margin	Standard error
0 = Never	Member	0.46***	0.10
	Non-member	0.19***	0.04
1 = Very rarely	Member	0.04*	0.02
	Non-member	0.03*	0.01
2 = Rarely	Member	0.17***	0.05
	Non-member	0.13***	0.04
3 = Often	Member	0.26***	0.74
	Non-member	0.39***	0.05
4 = Very often	Member	0.07*	0.04
	Non-member	0.27***	0.04

Notes
*** $p < 0.01$;
** $p < 0.05$;
* $p < 0.1$.

impact of membership in business associations on attitudes toward "grease" payments. The estimated coefficient for membership in entrepreneurial organizations is −0.24, and it is not significant at the 5 percent level. This suggests that membership in business associations has no direct impact on attitudes toward "grease" payments; rather entrepreneurial organizations indirectly influence the frequency of informal transactions through their anti-corruption programs.

Factors Facilitating the Use of "Grease" Payments in Russia

In addition to the question about attitudes toward "grease" payments, the survey asked respondents about methods that they use in situations where regulatory agencies impose excessive administrative barriers to doing business. The most frequently used solutions in these situations included paying informal payments (36 percent) and using personal connections in regulatory agencies (24 percent). Only a small fraction of entrepreneurs file legal complaints with a court (7 percent of the respondents) or send a petition to public authorities (15 percent). As for self-regulatory organizations, some entrepreneurs prefer to ask for their help in situations of bribe extortion (18 percent).[41] Importantly, the survey identifies certain regional differences in the use of business associations as protectors of entrepreneurial rights. The interviews with entrepreneurs confirm this result. For example, entrepreneurs from Moscow consider entrepreneurial organizations more useful in resolving problems with regulatory agencies in comparison with entrepreneurs from Saint Petersburg and Karelia. As one interviewee from Moscow put it:

> Theoretically, entrepreneurs can take legal actions in courts or file a complaint to public authorities. In practice, it does not work. Nobody will listen

to an individual entrepreneur. Imagine that some Ivan Ivanovich filed a complaint. Most likely, he will receive *otpiska* [a runaround, that is, some formal explanation why his complaint is not valid], or his complaint will not be registered at all. The same happens in courts. That's why we need collective organizations of entrepreneurs. First, public authorities give more importance to complaints of collective organizations than to complaints of individual entrepreneurs. Second, collective organizations are more protected in cases of retaliations. If an individual entrepreneur criticizes state authorities, they can simply close his business or they can even open a criminal case against him. Collective organizations of entrepreneurs are a relatively safe way to convey entrepreneurial concerns to the authorities since it is more difficult to close them. In addition, they provide an opportunity for entrepreneurs to exchange ideas on how to mitigate corruption.

Interestingly, entrepreneurs from Saint Petersburg and Karelia expressed the opinion that it is necessary to create self-regulatory organizations in their regions. However, they did not have sufficient information about already existing business associations. This suggests that one of the problems of business associations in Saint Petersburg and Karelia is an inefficient system of information sharing about their activities. Since self-regulatory organizations are not very effective in defending entrepreneurial rights at the regional level, informal methods of solving administrative problems through "grease" payments and personal connections with public officials remain popular in all three regions. Positive attitudes of entrepreneurs toward "grease" payments are explained by the fact that they perceive such payments as the easiest and quickest way to solve administrative problems in comparison with legal alternatives.

The interviews conducted in Moscow, Saint Petersburg, and Karelia identified several reasons behind the unpopularity of legal solutions. They include distrust of courts, high levels of perceived corruption in the judicial system, and a lack of financial and human resources to take legal action. Also, certain regional differences were identified in the use of legal solutions. For example, Karelian entrepreneurs tend to file legal complaints with a court less frequently than their counterparts in Moscow and Saint Petersburg. One entrepreneur from Karelia explained it in the following way:

> Russia's laws have many loopholes that are often used by corrupt officials. For example, we filed an appeal to a local court about violations committed by Karelian procurement officers in an online auction. According to the federal law, we can appeal decisions of procurement officers at any time of placing the order in an online auction, but no later than ten days from the date of its posting on the official website. Courts are to make a decision on an appeal within five days. When we received a court refusal, we immediately submitted another appeal to the Arbitration court. Then we had to wait another five days. In total, we spent 11 days appealing violations in the online auction by the procurement officers. Therefore, we went beyond the

ten-day period established by the federal law. Another situation involves filing an application to terminate a government contract with affiliated private companies. It requires a lot of time – from three to six months. As a result, the whole process becomes useless because the contract might be executed within these three or six months. The court cannot nullify this contract after its termination, even though all violations are proven.

An entrepreneur from Moscow gave another example of inefficiencies in the court system:

> Courts may refuse to accept an application based on insufficient evidence in accordance with Articles 131 and 132 of the Code of Civil Procedure. In fact, this is a subjective decision of a particular court whether an entrepreneur has provided sufficient evidence of violations or not. And it is clear that virtually any complaint can be rejected on the basis of insufficient evidence. I do not recommend entrepreneurs spend their time solving problems with regulatory agencies in courts. There are many regulations that contradict each other. And there is almost always some legal act that will make a complaint invalid.

Therefore, insufficient legal protection in situations where public officials extort "grease" money affects entrepreneurs' decisions to use informal transactions. Weak enforcement of anti-corruption laws is one of the most important factors facilitating the use of "grease" payments in Russia. Respondents from Moscow, Saint Petersburg, and Karelia indicated that their second least favorable solution after taking legal actions in courts is filing complaints with public authorities. This finding relates to entrepreneurs' distrust in public authorities in Russia and their fear of retaliation for reporting corrupt regulatory agencies. Fear of revenge by officials was very strong in all regions. An interview with an entrepreneur from Moscow provides insights into why it is not very common for businesses to complain to public authorities about violations of their rights:

> If an entrepreneur complains about violations of his rights during an inspection organized by some regulatory agency, other regulatory agencies will immediately send their officials to inspect his business and they will definitely find some flaws in his activities. It is some kind of *krugovaya poruka* [shared responsibility/irresponsibility]. As a result, the entrepreneur will find himself in a situation where he might have to close his business. It is very difficult to resist regulatory agencies because of very controversial laws. Here is an example. Employees of security agencies require that business offices located on the ground floor install window bars. Officials from fire safety agencies require removing all bars from windows. In this case, entrepreneurs find themselves in situations where by following the prescriptions of one regulatory agency, they violate the requirements of another agency.

This explains why individual entrepreneurs prefer to solve their problems related to administrative overregulation on their own, instead of filing legal complaints against corrupt public officials and regulatory agencies. In fact, individual entrepreneurs act according to the Russian saying, "If you're drowning, you're on your own." This is why they often use informal practices, such as personal connections or "grease" payments to mitigate administrative barriers. In part, the unpopularity of legal solutions is related to the fact that entrepreneurs and other small business entities often lack experience and knowledge of how to defend their rights and publicly voice their concerns. Often regulatory agencies take advantage of this situation and create additional obstacles to doing business in their regions.

Elena Panfilova, the Chairperson of the Russian Chapter of Transparency International, distinguishes three strategies that companies can use in situations of extortion: "reject bribery, use a middleman or government relations specialist, or play by the [corrupt] rules. Only big companies can afford the first strategy as they have huge revenues and long-term plans."[42] This statement explains why entrepreneurs often choose to play by corrupt rules. To change this negative situation, it is necessary to introduce additional strategies to the arsenal of anti-corruption measures tailored to fit the needs of entrepreneurs and small businesses. In this context, research into perceptions of entrepreneurs toward "grease" payments helps in the search for strategies to increase their participation in anti-corruption efforts.

The findings of the survey and interviews with entrepreneurs suggest that their attitudes toward corruption are an important determinant of the frequency of informal payments. Besides, entrepreneurs who belong to self-regulatory organizations are less likely to participate in corrupt practices than entrepreneurs who are not members of any professional network. In the anti-corruption literature, numerous case studies give empirical support for a direct negative impact of self-regulatory organizations on the level of corruption.[43] This scholarship shows that collective entrepreneurial organizations mediate the effects of proactive and responsive anti-corruption efforts on the use of informal transactions. In this respect, the technical report commissioned by the Council of Europe entitled *Corruption Risks and Protection Mechanisms for Entrepreneurs in the Russian Federation* points to the importance of collective organizations for the development of anti-corruption policies:

> Business associations that bring together companies from certain regions or business sectors could be an important tool to increase the efficiency of anti-corruption initiatives. Collective action has the advantage of being more coordinated and cost-effective. Business associations could serve as platforms for companies' agreements and commitments to ethical standards and other joint anti-corruption actions. Trade chambers have been identified as another important player that could also assist companies in their anti-corruption efforts. Trade chambers could provide a platform for information exchange and discussions, as well as consulting and other services.[44]

In Russia, the mediating role of self-regulatory organizations in the relationship between businesses and authorities is not well documented. A certain limitation of the existing studies of anti-corruption policies in Russia is that they pay insufficient attention to an analysis of the potential of Russian business associations for collective action against administrative corruption. In this respect, it is imperative to find answers to the questions of how to increase the effectiveness of Russian regional self-regulatory organizations, how to intensify their activities aimed at discouraging their members from engaging in corruption, and how to increase their willingness to organize collective action against corruption.

Notes

1 World Bank. *Administrativnaya reforma i reforma gosudarstvennogo regulirovaniya v Rossii* [in Russian] (Washington, DC: The World Bank, 2006), pp. 53–55.
2 See, for example, Litvak, A. *Rezultaty monitoringa administrativnykh bar'erov* [in Russian] (Moscow: MCHS, 2010); Business Environment and Enterprise Performance Surveys (BEEPS) 2012–2014 (Washington, D.C.: World Bank, 2017), available at: http://ebrd-beeps.com/data/2012-2013/; Besstremyannaya, G., Bondarenko, O., & Kartseva, M. *Analiz administrativnykh bar'erov v sfere obshchestvennogo pitaniya* [in Russian], (Moscow: CEFIR, 2014); Krylova, Y. "Grease" Payments in the Relations Between Regulatory Agencies and Individual Entrepreneurs: The Case of Russia (doctoral dissertation) (George Mason University, Fairfax, VA, 2017).
3 Gilinskiy, Y. Corruption: Theory and Russian Reality. In R. Sarre, D. K. Das, & H.-J. Albrecht (Eds.), *Policing Corruption: International Perspectives* (pp. 157–168). Oxford: Lexington Books, 2005), p. 161.
4 Stepanov, S. *Politicheskaya istoriya Rossii* [in Russian] (Moscow: The Peoples' Friendship University, 2015).
5 Ibid.
6 Nichols, P. M. Regulating Transnational Bribery in Times of Globalization and Fragmentation. *Yale Journal of International Law, 24* (1999), 257–303.
7 See 15 U.S.C.§§78m(b), 78dd-1, 78dd-2, 78ff. (originally enacted as Pub. L No. 95–213, 91 Stat. 1494 (1977)) and amended by Foreign Corrupt Practices Act Amendments of 1988, Pub. L. No. 100–418, §§5001–5003, 102 Stat. 1107, 1415–1425.
8 OECD. OECD Convention on Combating Bribery of Foreign Public Officials in International Business Transactions. (OECD, 1997). Available at: www.oecd.org/corruption/oecdantibriberyconvention.htm
9 Argandoña, A. Corruption and Companies: The Use of Facilitating Payments. *Journal of Business Ethics, 60*(3) (2005), 251.
10 OECD. OECD Recommendation for Further Combating Bribery of Foreign Public Officials in International Business Transactions. (OECD, 2009). Available at: www.oecd.org/daf/anti-bribery/oecdantibriberyrecommendation2009.htm
11 See, for example, Sufrin, S. C. Graft: Grease for the Palm and Grease for the Wheels, *Challenge, 13*(1) (1964), 30–33; Myrdal, G. *Asian Drama: An Inquiry into the Poverty of Nations* (New York: Pantheon, 1968); Rashid, S. Public Utilities in Egalitarian LDCs: The Role of Bribery in Achieving Pareto Efficiency, *Kyklos, 34*(3) (1981), 448–460; Lien, D.-H. D. A Note on Competitive Bribery Games, *Economics Letters, 22*(4) (1986), 337–341; Li, S., & Wu, J. Why Some Countries Thrive Despite Corruption: The Role of Trust in the Corruption-Efficiency Relationship, *Review of International Political Economy, 17*(1) (2010), 129–154.
12 Leff, N. H. Economic Development Through Bureaucratic Corruption. *American Behavioral Scientist, 8*(3) (1964), 11.

13 Huntington, S. P. *Political Order in Changing Societies* (New Haven, CT: Yale University Press, 1968), p. 386.
14 Lui, F. T. An Equilibrium Queuing Model of Bribery. *Journal of Political Economy*, 93(4) (1985), 760–781.
15 Huntington, op. cit., p. 68.
16 Bayley, D. H. The Effects of Corruption in a Developing Nation. *Political Research Quarterly*, 19(4) (1966), 719–732.
17 Beck, P., & Maher, M. A Comparison of Bribery and Bidding in Thin Markets. *Economic Letters*, 20 (1986), 1–5.
18 Dreher, A., & Gassebner, M. Greasing the Wheels? The Impact of Regulations and Corruption on Firm Entry. *Public Choice*, 155(3/4) (2013), 413–432.
19 Shelley, L. I. *Dirty Entanglements: Corruption, Crime, and Terrorism*. (Cambridge: Cambridge University Press, 2014), p. 66.
20 See, for example, Krueger, A. O. The Political Economy of the Rent-Seeking Society, *The American Economic Review*, 64(3) (1974), 291–303; Bhagwati, J. N. Directly Unproductive, Profit-Seeking (DUP) Activities, *Journal of Political Economy*, 90(5) (1982), 988–1002; Wei, S.-J. Corruption in Economic Development: Beneficial Grease, Minor Annoyance, or Major Obstacle? SSRN Scholarly Paper No. ID 604923 (Rochester, NY: Social Science Research Network, 1999); Lambsdorff, J. How Corruption Affects Productivity, *Kyklos*, 56 (2003), 457–474.
21 See, for example, Kaufmann, D., & Wei, S.-J. Does "Grease Money" Speed up the Wheels of Commerce? (Cambridge, MA: National Bureau of Economic Research, 1999), available at: www.nber.org/papers/w7093; Méon, P.-G., & Sekkat, K. Does Corruption Grease or Sand the Wheels of Growth? *Public Choice*, 122(1/2) (2005), 69–97.
22 Kaufmann & Wei, op. cit., pp. 15–16.
23 Good examples of such studies include Powpaka, S. Factors Affecting Managers' Decision to Bribe: An Empirical Investigation, *Journal of Business Ethics*, 40(3) (2002), 227–246; Collins, J. D., Uhlenbruck, K., & Rodriguez, P. Why Firms Engage in Corruption: A Top Management Perspective, *Journal of Business Ethics*, 87(1) (2009), 89–108.
24 Ibid.
25 Collins, et al., op. cit., pp. 89–108.
26 Ibid., 94–95.
27 Shekshnia, S., Ledeneva, A., & Denisova-Schmidt, E. How to Mitigate Corruption in Emerging Markets: The Case of Russia. Edmond J. Safra Working Papers, (36). (2014). Available at: http://papers.ssrn.com/sol3/Papers.cfm?abstract_id=2391950
28 Ibid., p. 15.
29 Ibid.
30 See, for example, Dollar, D., Fisman, R., & Gatti, R. Are Women Really the "Fairer" Sex? Corruption and Women in Government, *Journal of Economic Behavior & Organization*, 46(4) (2001), 423–429; Swamy, A., Knack, S., Lee, Y., & Azfar, O. Gender and Corruption, *Journal of Development Economics*, 64(1) (2001), 25–55; Frank, B., Lambsdorff, J. G., & Boehm, F. Gender and Corruption: Lessons from Laboratory Corruption Experiments, *European Journal of Development Research*, 23(1) (2011), 59–71; Krylova, Y. Corruption and Gender Inequality: The Case of Nicaragua, *International Journal of Ethics*, 12(3) (2016), 273–289; Rivas, M. F. An Experiment on Corruption and Gender, *Bulletin of Economic Research*, 65(1) (2013), 10–42.
31 Deshpande, S. P., Joseph, J., & Maximov, V. V. Perceptions of Proper Ethical Conduct of Male and Female Russian Managers. *Journal of Business Ethics*, 24(2) (2000), 179–183.
32 Ibid., p. 179.
33 Ibid.
34 Collins, et al., op. cit., pp. 94–96.
35 Deshpande, et al., op. cit., pp. 179–183.

36 Federal Statistics Service of the Russian Federation. Individual'nye predrinimateli [in Russian]. (2017). Available at: www.gks.ru/wps/wcm/connect/rosstat_main/rosstat/ru/statistics/enterprise/reform/
37 Trentini, C., & Koparanova, M. *Corruption and Entrepreneurship: Does Gender Matter?* (Geneva: UNECE, 2013).
38 Powpaka, op. cit., p. 227; Shekshnia, et al., op. cit., p. 15.
39 For example, Alatas, V., Cameron, L., Chaudhuri, A., Erkal, N., & Gangadharan, L. Gender, Culture, and Corruption: Insights from an Experimental Analysis, *Southern Economic Journal*, 75(3) (2009), 663–680; Esarey, J., & Chirillo, G. "Fairer Sex" or Purity Myth? Corruption, Gender, and Institutional Context, *Politics & Gender*, 9(4) (2013), 361–389.
40 Deshpande, et al., op. cit., pp. 179–183.
41 Krylova, Y. The Role of Entrepreneurial Organizations in Organizing Collective Action against Administrative Corruption: Evidence from Russia. *Journal of Contemporary Central and Eastern Europe* (2017). Available at: www.tandfonline.com/doi/full/10.1080/25739638.2018.1419907
42 Cited in Nikishenkov, O. (2010, February 23). Ikea Case Exposes Bribe Culture in Russia. *The Moscow News*.
43 See, for example, Mantovani, M. The Business Case for Collective Action. In M. Pieth (Ed.), *Collective Action: Innovative Strategies to Prevent Corruption* (pp. 73–80) (Zürich: Dike Publishers, 2012); Mària, J. F., & Arenas, D. Societal Ethos and Economic Development Organizations in Nicaragua, *Journal of Business Ethics*, 88(S2) (2009), 231–244; Morell, J., & Bettcher, K. E. *Approaches to Collective Action: How Businesses Together Can Lead the Fight Against Corruption* (Washington, DC: Center for International Private Enterprise, 2013).
44 Rupchev, G., Moiny, Y., & Kudryashov, A. *Korruptsionnye riski i mekhanizmy zashchity prav predprinimatelei* [in Russian] (Brussels: Council of Europe, 2014), p. 52.

References

15 U.S.C.§§78m(b), 78dd-1, 78dd-2, 78ff. (originally enacted as Pub. L No. 95–213, 91 Stat. 1494 (1977)) and amended by Foreign Corrupt Practices Act Amendments of 1988, Pub. L. No. 100–418, §§5001–5003, 102 Stat. 1107, 1415–1425.

Alatas, V., Cameron, L., Chaudhuri, A., Erkal, N., & Gangadharan, L. (2009). Gender, Culture, and Corruption: Insights from an Experimental Analysis. *Southern Economic Journal*, 75(3), 663–680.

Argandoña, A. (2005). Corruption and Companies: The Use of Facilitating Payments. *Journal of Business Ethics*, 60(3), 251–264.

Bayley, D. H. (1966). The Effects of Corruption in a Developing Nation. *Political Research Quarterly*, 19(4), 719–732.

Beck, P., & Maher, M. (1986). A Comparison of Bribery and Bidding in Thin Markets. *Economic Letters*, 20, 1–5.

Besstremyannaya, G., Bondarenko, O., & Kartseva, M. (2014). *Analiz administrativnykh bar'erov v sfere obshchestvennogo pitaniya* [in Russian]. Moscow: CEFIR.

Bhagwati, J. N. (1982). Directly Unproductive, Profit-Seeking (DUP) Activities. *The Journal of Political Economy*, 90(5), 988–1002.

Collins, J. D., Uhlenbruck, K., & Rodriguez, P. (2009). Why Firms Engage in Corruption: A Top Management Perspective. *Journal of Business Ethics*, 87(1), 89–108.

Deshpande, S. P., Joseph, J., & Maximov, V. V. (2000). Perceptions of Proper Ethical Conduct of Male and Female Russian Managers. *Journal of Business Ethics*, 24(2), 179–183.

Dollar, D., Fisman, R., & Gatti, R. (2001). Are Women Really the "Fairer" Sex? Corruption and Women in Government. *Journal of Economic Behavior & Organization*, *46*(4), 423–429.

Dreher, A., & Gassebner, M. (2013). Greasing the Wheels? The Impact of Regulations and Corruption on Firm Entry. *Public Choice*, *155*(3/4), 413–432.

Esarey, J., & Chirillo, G. (2013). "Fairer Sex" or Purity Myth? Corruption, Gender, and Institutional Context. *Politics & Gender*, *9*(4), 361–389.

Federal Statistics Service of the Russian Federation. (2017). Individual'nye predrinimateli [in Russian]. Moscow. Available at: www.gks.ru/wps/wcm/connect/rosstat_main/rosstat/ru/statistics/enterprise/reform/.

Frank, B., Lambsdorff, J. G., & Boehm, F. (2011). Gender and Corruption: Lessons from Laboratory Corruption Experiments. *European Journal of Development Research*, *23*(1), 59–71.

Gilinskiy, Y. (2005). Corruption: Theory and Russian Reality. In R. Sarre, D. K. Das, & H.-J. Albrecht (Eds.), *Policing Corruption: International Perspectives* (pp. 157–168). Oxford: Lexington Books.

Huntington, S. P. (2006). *Political Order in Changing Societies*. New Haven, CT: Yale University Press.

Kaufmann, D., & Wei, S.-J. (1999). Does "Grease Money" Speed up the Wheels of Commerce? Cambridge, MA: National Bureau of Economic Research. Available at: www.nber.org/papers/w7093

Krueger, A. O. (1974). The Political Economy of the Rent-Seeking Society. *The American Economic Review*, *64*(3), 291–303.

Krylova, Y. (2016). Corruption and Gender Inequality: The Case of Nicaragua. *International Journal of Ethics*, *12*(3), 273–289.

Krylova, Y. (2017a). "Grease" Payments in the Relations Between Regulatory Agencies and Individual Entrepreneurs: The Case of Russia (doctoral dissertation). George Mason University, Fairfax, VA.

Krylova, Y. (2017b). The Role of Entrepreneurial Organizations in Organizing Collective Action against Administrative Corruption: Evidence from Russia. *Journal of Contemporary Central and Eastern Europe*. Available at: www.tandfonline.com/doi/full/10.1080/25739638.2018.1419907

Lambsdorff, J. (2003). How Corruption Affects Productivity. *Kyklos*, *56*, 457–474.

Leff, N. H. (1964). Economic Development Through Bureaucratic Corruption. *American Behavioral Scientist*, *8*(3), 6–14.

Li, S., & Wu, J. (2010). Why Some Countries Thrive Despite Corruption: The Role of Trust in the Corruption-Efficiency Relationship. *Review of International Political Economy*, *17*(1), 129–154.

Lien, D.-H. D. (1986). A Note on Competitive Bribery Games. *Economics Letters*, *22*(4), 337–341.

Litvak, A. (2010). *Rezul'taty monitoringa administrativnykh bar'erov* [in Russian]. Moscow: MCHS.

Lui, F. T. (1985). An Equilibrium Queuing Model of Bribery. *Journal of Political Economy*, *93*(4), 760–781.

Mantovani, M. (2012). The Business Case for Collective Action. In M. Pieth (Ed.), *Collective Action: Innovative Strategies to Prevent Corruption* (pp. 73–80). Zürich: Dike Publishers.

Mària, J. F., & Arenas, D. (2009). Societal Ethos and Economic Development Organizations in Nicaragua. *Journal of Business Ethics*, *88*(S2), 231–244.

Méon, P.-G., & Sekkat, K. (2005). Does Corruption Grease or Sand the Wheels of Growth? *Public Choice*, *122*(1/2), 69–97.

Morell, J., & Bettcher, K. E. (2013). *Approaches to Collective Action: How Businesses Together Can Lead the Fight Against Corruption.* Washington, DC: Center for International Private Enterprise.

Myrdal, G. (1968). *Asian Drama: An Inquiry into the Poverty of Nations.* New York: Pantheon.

Nichols, P. M. (1999). Regulating Transnational Bribery in Times of Globalization and Fragmentation. *Yale Journal of International Law*, *24*, 257–303.

Nikishenkov, O. (2010, February 23). Ikea Case Exposes Bribe Culture in Russia. *The Moscow News*.

OECD. (1997). OECD Convention on Combating Bribery of Foreign Public Officials in International Business Transactions. Available at: www.oecd.org/corruption/oecdantibriberyconvention.htm

OECD. (2009). OECD Recommendation for Further Combating Bribery of Foreign Public Officials in International Business Transactions. Available at: www.oecd.org/daf/anti-bribery/oecdantibriberyrecommendation2009.htm

Powpaka, S. (2002). Factors Affecting Managers' Decision to Bribe: An Empirical Investigation. *Journal of Business Ethics*, *40*(3), 227–246.

Rashid, S. (1981). Public Utilities in Egalitarian LDCs: The Role of Bribery in Achieving Pareto Efficiecy. *Kyklos*, *34*(3), 448–460.

Rivas, M. F. (2013). An Experiment on Corruption and Gender. *Bulletin of Economic Research*, *65*(1), 10–42.

Rupchev, G., Moiny, Y., & Kudryashov, A. (2014). *Korruptsionnye riski i mekhanizmy zashchity prav predprinimatelei* [in Russian]. Brussels: Council of Europe.

Shekshnia, S., Ledeneva, A., & Denisova-Schmidt, E. (2014). How to Mitigate Corruption in Emerging Markets: The Case of Russia. Edmond J. Safra Working Papers, (36). Available at: http://papers.ssrn.com/sol3/Papers.cfm?abstract_id=2391950

Shelley, L. I. (2014). *Dirty Entanglements: Corruption, Crime, and Terrorism.* Cambridge: Cambridge University Press.

Stepanov, S. (2015). *Politicheskaya istoriya Rossii* [in Russian]. Moscow: The Peoples' Friendship University.

Sufrin, S. C. (1964). Graft: Grease for the Palm and Grease for the Wheels. *Challenge*, *13*(1), 30–33.

Swamy, A., Knack, S., Lee, Y., & Azfar, O. (2001). Gender and Corruption. *Journal of Development Economics*, *64*(1), 25–55.

Trentini, C., & Koparanova, M. (2013). *Corruption and Entrepreneurship: Does Gender Matter?* Geneva: UNECE.

Wei, S.-J. (1999). Corruption in Economic Development: Beneficial Grease, Minor Annoyance, or Major Obstacle? (SSRN Scholarly Paper No. ID 604923). Rochester, NY: Social Science Research Network.

World Bank. (2006). *Administrativnaya reforma i reforma gosudarstvennogo regulirovaniya v Rossii* [in Russian]. Washington, DC: The World Bank.

World Bank. (2017). *Business Environment and Enterprise Performance Surveys (BEEPS) 2012–2014.* Washington, DC. Available at: http://ebrd-beeps.com/data/2012-2013/

5 "Stand and Deliver, Your Money or Your Life"

Illegal Raiding Against Businesses by Public Officials

Administrative corruption is responsible for the expansion of *reiderstvo* in Russia. *Reiderstvo* means the practice of illegal seizure of assets or businesses that involves the use of corrupt public officials, including policemen, security officers, judges, tax inspectors, and local or regional administrators. Unlike Western practices of hostile takeovers, *reiderstvo* has negative connotations in Russia. Due to its predatory nature, it is often compared with banditry and piracy. The use of corrupt and violent methods constitutes a key difference from legal corporate takeovers. Historically, the phenomenon of *reiderstvo* goes back to the 1990s. After the collapse of the Soviet Union, the weak public enforcement system and the absence of the rule of law facilitated the large-scale redistribution of property in the form of business seizures.

In the 1990s, raiders usually acted quickly and violently, using intimidation, physical force, seizures by armed groups, and even the outright murder of business owners. Over the last decade, the nature of raiding in Russia has transformed significantly. Contemporary raiders increasingly abuse the judicial and administrative systems and fabricate criminal cases against legal owners of targeted businesses. Some experts marked Putin's rise to power in 2000 as the end of private *reiderstvo* and the beginning of "state *reiderstvo*."[1] While in the 1990s, public officials and law enforcement officers mainly played the role of facilitators of illegal takeovers in exchange for bribes, they now increasingly act as initiators and beneficiaries of illegal raids. Recognizing the seriousness of this problem for Russia's entrepreneurial sector and business community, this chapter analyzes the roles of law enforcement, of the judiciary, and of regulatory agencies in the process of asset grabbing. Particular attention is paid to the abuse of international law enforcement and Interpol in illegal business raiding.

Literature Review

The phenomenon of *reiderstvo* has increasingly attracted attention from scholars, business analysts, the media, and civil society activists. To a large extent, this increasing interest is explained by the fact that the number of illegal raiding cases against owners of businesses and other valuable assets continues to rise in Russia.[2] The Presidential Council for Civil Society and Human Rights relates this trend to the economic crisis, which is responsible for the shrinking incomes of enforcement officers and public officials.[3] A long-term recession creates strong incentives for law enforcement officers to quickly regain their economic losses through the illegal raiding of property. One of the most common raiding techniques is the use of bogus criminal cases against legal owners of businesses. According to the alarming estimates of Russia's business ombudsman Boris Titov, "100,000 of such cases were opened against businessmen in the first half of 2016, which is 25 percent more than in the same period in 2015."[4]

Reiderstvo is a latent crime in Russia, meaning that the majority of illegal raids are not reflected in the official statistics and do not become the subject of judicial proceedings. The absence of exact official data makes an analysis of *reiderstvo* more difficult and adversely affects its prevention. According to various expert estimates, the number of illegal seizures amounts to several hundred thousand per year.[5] According to Gennady Gudkov, a Russian politician and businessman, working in Moscow City and in the Moscow region, his group registers thousands of raiding cases per year, but they are only the tip of the iceberg.[6] In 2008, the Center for Political Technologies conducted an in-depth study of business raiding in Russia based on expert interviews of entrepreneurs, lawyers, journalists, civil society activists, and members of the State Duma. The report states that the profitability of raider attacks might be as high as 1,000 percent.[7] In financial terms, Russia's Ministry of Internal Affairs (MVD) estimates that *reiderstvo* generates over 120 billion rubles (about $40 million) per year.[8] However, due to its latent nature, it is very difficult to assess the real damage caused by illegal takeovers of businesses.

Recent studies of *reiderstvo* demonstrate that most illegal seizures in Russia involve domestic businesses.[9] However, *reiderstvo* has also become a threat to foreign companies. High-profile cases of takeovers of foreign companies, such as the investment fund Hermitage Capital Management and TNK-BP, received broad coverage in the domestic and international media. At the same time, numerous low-profile cases of illegal raiding are not widely publicized in the media. A recent study of raiding cases in 2011–2013 showed that almost every second case was ignored by the media and was not covered in any print or electronic edition.[10] The geographical distribution of illegal seizures is affected by the regional industrial development. For example, Anton Kazun argues that illegal raiding is most frequent in regions with a small share in oil extraction and a relatively high share in construction and manufacturing production.[11] Small and medium-sized companies are especially vulnerable to illegal raiding because they do not have enough resources to protect themselves in comparison with large corporations.

An analysis of raiding cases shows that they involve a wide variety of different methods. According to one of the most systematic studies of *reiderstvo*, there are eight major raiding techniques:

1. Forgery and falsification of shareholder resolutions and other official documents.

2. Criminal malicious prosecutions against legal owners.
3. Harassment by regulatory agencies.
4. Misuse of shares and shareholder protections.
5. Misuse of the banking system.
6. Violence and armed seizures.
7. Psychological attacks and blackmailing.
8. Abuse of international enforcement mechanisms.[12]

This is not an exhaustive list of the methods used by raiders in illicit seizures of businesses; moreover, it is important to note that many of them are based on a combination of different techniques and the involvement of public officials. At the corporate level, illegal raiding often takes the form of so-called "velvet re-privatization." This is generally defined as the redistribution process based on the abuse of the legal and judicial systems by the politically connected officials from state corporations who drive out the current private owners.[13] The process of velvet re-privatization allows public officials to regain control over private businesses, such as the now notorious oil company YUKOS. Most raiding cases, however, are committed for speculative purposes, and the financial resources acquired through *reiderstvo* are hidden through offshore companies.

How Lawlessness Feeds State Predations on Russian Businesses

Heads of Russian government and law enforcement agencies have long recognized the role of public officials in *reiderstvo*. In 2010, Dmitry Medvedev, then President of Russia, noted:

> Raiding is a complex and very dangerous crime, in fact, it is strangling our economy. There is no way a raider could act on his own, he always has accomplices. Beware of those officials obligated to protect firms who join raider brigades.[14]

In 2008, Medvedev urged public officials to stop *koshmarit'* (literally, to cause nightmares or terrorize) businesses.[15] In 2010, he instructed the Minister of Interior that his duty was "to make sure that the people whose job is to protect companies from raiders do not join their gangs instead."[16] However, despite the recognition of the involvement of public officials in illegal raiding, few of them have been convicted.

The political elites do not show any intention to restrain *reiderstvo* and stop predations of public officials on businesses. The lack of political will is related to the institutional system introduced under President Putin, "where priority is given to securing political control, while economic objectives play only a secondary role."[17] In Russia's system of crony capitalism, high-ranking officials loyal to the political regime and businesses affiliated with the government can accumulate enormous wealth and are de facto immune from investigations into the legality of this wealth. It is the corruption of the law enforcement and the judicial system that allows illegal raiders to behave like this with impunity, undeterred by punishment. In this way, the state of lawlessness creates a fertile ground for *reiderstvo*.

Although the process of illegal raiding differs from case to case, it usually involves four critical stages: (1) the preparation stage, during which information about the object is gathered; (2) the negotiation stage, in which business owners are coerced into selling their company; (3) the execution stage, performed through various raiding techniques; and (4) the legalization stage, at which point the acquired property is laundered.[18] Raiders commit various illegal activities at each stage of this process. Table 5.1 illustrates the four stages of the raiding process with corresponding illegal activities under the Criminal Code of the Russian Federation.

The preparation stage of a takeover often involves an illegal receipt and disclosure of information classified as commercial, tax, or banking secrets (Article 183 of the Russian Criminal Code). Public officials who have access to such information can be bribed by illegal raiders or they can use this information themselves to organize raids against businesses. The second stage involves such crimes as extortion, compulsion to complete a deal, obstruction of lawful business activities, and abuse of authority (Articles 183, 179, 169, and 201 of the Russian Criminal Code). If legal owners refuse to negotiate, the third stage is the execution of takeovers. Among many options available to raiders are fraud, registration of illegal deals, lawless actions in the case of bankruptcy, abuse of authority by private notaries and auditors, official forgery, fabrication of criminal cases, and theft or damage of documents, stamps, or seals (Articles 159, 170, 195, 196, 197, 202, 292, 299, 305, and 325 of the Russian Criminal Code). This stage requires the direct or indirect involvement of a large number of public officials. Once a takeover is completed, raiders can begin the process of laundering illegally acquired funds and property (Articles 174 and 175 of the Russian Criminal Code). In many raiding cases, seizures occur with the help of state authorities and direct support of the city administration or regional administrative staff.[19] Even when initiators and key beneficiaries of raids are business rivals, law enforcement officers, judges, and officials of registration and regulatory agencies are often involved as accomplices.

Rent-Seeking Activities of Law Enforcement

The Russian law enforcement model is often described as "predatory policing." Theodore Gerber and Sarah Mendelson define it as police activities that are mostly "devoted to the personal enrichment and self-preservation of the police themselves rather than the protection of the public."[20] The key characteristics of "predatory policing" are widespread police violence and corruption. Predatory policing in Russia goes back to the 1990s, when the underfunding of the police, weak government oversight, and a lack of public control provided law enforcement officers with incentives for engaging in criminal activities. Some of these

Table 5.1 Stages of illegal raiding and the related crimes under the Russian Criminal Code

Stage	Actions	Articles of the Russian Criminal Code
Preparation	Identification of the object; assessment of risks and benefits; collection of information	Art. 183 Illegal receipt and disclosure of information classified as commercial, tax or banking secrets; Art. 272 Illegal accessing of computer information; Art. 290. Bribe-taking; Art. 291 Bribe-giving
Negotiation	Contact with legal owners; purchase of shares; pressure and intimidation of owners	Art. 179 Compulsion to complete a deal or to refuse to complete it; Art. 169 Obstruction of lawful business activities; Art. 201 Abuse of authority; Art. 290 Bribe-taking; Art. 291 Bribe-giving
Execution	Fraud and falsification of shareholder registers, resolutions of boards of directors, and securities depositories; intimidation of owners and violence, including armed seizures, arson attacks, physical violence, and police raids; abuse of the legal and judicial systems, such as malicious criminal prosecution of legal owners; misuse of the banking system	Art. 159 Fraud; Art. 170 Registration of illegal land deals; Art. 185 Abuse in the case of issuance of securities; Art. 195 Lawless actions in case of bankruptcy; Art. 196 Deliberate bankruptcy; Art. 197 Fictitious bankruptcy; Art. 202 Abuse of authority by private notaries and auditors; Art. 285 Abuse of official powers; Art. 292 Official forgery; Art. 299 Knowingly bringing an innocent person to criminal responsibility; Art. 301 Illegal detention, taking into custody; Art. 305 Knowingly giving an unjust judgment, decision, or any other juridical act; Art. 325 Theft or damage of documents, stamps, and seals; Art. 327 Forgery, manufacture, or sale of falsified documents; Art. 330 Arbitrariness
Legalization	Laundering of illegally acquired assets; laundering of funds resulted from sale or acquisition of raided objects	Art. 174 The legalization (laundering) of funds and other property acquired in an illegal way; Art. 175 Acquisition or sale of property, knowingly obtained in a criminal manner

activities precisely mirrored those of the criminals from whom the police were supposed to defend the public – for example, offering their protection (known as *krysha* in Russian) in return for illegal payments. Cases of rent-seeking behavior of the police are well documented in interviews with Russian entrepreneurs. For example, in an interview conducted by Igor Klyamkin and Lev Timofeev, a small shop owner told the story of his "friendship" with police officers:

> Two weeks after we opened our shop, they [policemen] came with an inspection. Ten armed people in camouflage and masks.... The police department is located in the nearby building and he [the police major] came to make "friendship".... The price for this "friendship" was to install three doors at the police department. We did it, as we did not have another option.... And now we are their "friends": one time we helped them to celebrate the promotion of their department head by donating $300, another time we repaired their flooring which cost us another $500. I do not know whether there is any sense for us in such "friendship."[21]

In 2008, Russia focused on curbing corruption and bribery by issuing new anti-corruption legislation. In 2011, then President Medvedev launched the Russian police reforms to decrease corruption and increase the effectiveness of law enforcement. These reforms, however, had little effect on corruption within the police. Even specialized anti-corruption units within law enforcement have been criticized for involvement in corruption scandals. In September 2016, Dmitry Zakharchenko, Deputy Head of the Interior Ministry's Committee for Economic Security and Combating Corruption, was arrested on charges of abuse of power, obstruction of justice, and accepting bribes. About $120 million were seized from his Moscow apartment, and over $300 million were found in his father's foreign bank accounts.[22] As Russia's business ombudsman Boris Titov suggests, "This money compiled from small amounts extorted from the business community is evidence of the corruption situation that has developed in the country."[23]

In 2011, the business association *Delovaya Rossiya* (Business Russia) created the Center for Public Procedures "Business Against Corruption" to receive and investigate businessmen's complaints about malicious criminal prosecutions and hostile takeovers of their property. Between 2011 and 2015, this Center received about 950 complaints. Geographically, they come from various Russian regions. Most complaints involve malicious criminal prosecutions by law enforcement agencies. Table 5.2 demonstrates the top ten regions according to the registered number of complaints from entrepreneurs. The city of Moscow and the Moscow region received the highest number of complaints about violations of entrepreneurial rights in 2014 and 2015. Together, these regions are responsible for about one-third of the total complaints registered by the Center for Public Procedures "Business Against Corruption" in this period. The percentage of complaints from other regions varies from 3.8 percent to 0.4 percent. The geographical distribution of illegal raiding is mostly determined by industrial development and protection of property rights in the related region.

Table 5.2 Top ten regions by count: victim complainants in 2014 and 2015

Region	Number of complaints	Percentage of the total number of complaints
Moscow City	75	28.3
Moscow region	19	7.2
Krasnodar region	10	3.8
Volgograd region	8	3.0
Nizhny Novgorod region	8	3.0
Chelyabinsk region	8	3.0
Novosibirsk region	7	2.6
Promorsky region	7	2.6
Chuvash Republic	7	2.6
Rostov region	7	2.6

Source: These numbers were calculated in 2015 based on the dataset of complaints published on the official website of the Center for Public Procedures "Business Against Corruption," www.nocorruption.biz/?cat=6

In many cases, raiders use their close connections and personal ties with the police and other law enforcement officers who can manipulate evidence, put pressure on legal owners, and open criminal cases against them. Often, the key objective of raiders is to neutralize anti-raid actions through malicious criminal prosecution on non-existent grounds. Such actions pave the way for illegal seizures because the imprisonment of legal owners makes it practically impossible to defend raided businesses. Raids on businesses by masked police officers armed with automatic rifles have become infamous in Russia. They were nicknamed "*maski* shows," after the post-Soviet sitcom featuring a clown troupe.[24] For example, in 2002, the former chief executive of the Russian oil company Slavneft hired the police to take over the corporation on the pretense of a criminal case against its new Director Yurii Sukhanov, who had been elected by shareholders.[25] The criminal case against Sukhanov was soon dropped because of the absence of a crime.

Russian enforcement officers increasingly abuse Interpol, the world's largest international police organization, with 190 member states, to request Red Notices on innocent victims of baseless criminal prosecution. Red Notices are international alerts used by the police to circulate information about criminals and crimes around the world through the Interpol system. Some countries treat them as international arrest warrants, although it is up to each Interpol member state to decide how to respond to them. Article 3 of the Interpol Constitution forbids this organization "from engaging in matters of political, military, religious, and racial character." Yet, a 2013 report of Fair Trials International, a UK-based NGO, provides evidence that Russia and other autocratic countries systematically exploit Interpol's system of Red Notices to prosecute political dissidents, refugees, civil society activists, and economic rivals.[26]

A serious cause for concern is the use of Red Notices in raiding cases. For example, the Russian police requested search notices on at least a dozen businessmen who had some connections or ties with the YUKOS oil company.[27] Among them, Ilya Katsnelson, a U.S. citizen residing in Denmark, was detained by the German police on a Red Notice that Interpol had issued on behalf of Russia in 2008. After his two-month imprisonment in a maximum-security prison, they recognized that Katsnelson was related to the politically motivated case of YUKOS. In fact, Katsnelson's shipping company had done some business with YUKOS. Both Denmark and Germany refused to extradite him to Russia.

Even if Red Notices do not lead to criminal arrests, they restrict the freedom of movement of the targeted individuals, as well as access to the banking and financial systems. This is why Russian authorities increasingly use allegations of fraud and money laundering against political and economic opponents to restrict their access to banks, financial institutions, and economic organizations that are subject to due diligence and know-your-customer requirements. The consequences include forced unemployment, frozen bank accounts and financial assets. This happened to Katsnelson when his account at Citibank was closed and his assets sold at significant loss.[28]

The Interpol General Secretariat reviews notices before their publication. If they are found to be politically motivated, Red Notices are not published. For example, in 2016, Interpol refused a Russian request for a search for Mikhail Khodorkovsky because it did not correspond with the organization's rules.[29] Interpol also refused all requests that Russia made for international assistance in locating Bill Browder, a co-founder of Hermitage Capital Management, stating that the case was political in nature.[30] However, Interpol itself recognizes that about 97 percent of notice requests are not reviewed in depth.[31] The number of notices requests has been rapidly increasingly in recent years. In 2014, Interpol published 10,718 Red Notices.[32] In 2016, their number increased to 12,878.[33] However, numbers of legal personnel of the Interpol General Secretariat remain limited, which explains why the organization often fails to react rapidly to many low-profile politically motivated requests sent by Russia and other autocratic countries. Unlike Khodorkovsky and Browder, less prominent individuals have serious difficulties in appealing already issued Red Notices since this process is extremely complicated and time-consuming. As Andrew Higgis indicates, "The only winners in most such cases are expensive lawyers, for whom pursuing Russia's foes in foreign courts has become a highly lucrative business."[34]

One of the most recent examples of Russia's abuse of the Interpol system in politically-motivated raiding cases is the Red Notice issued on Nikolay Koblyakov, a dual Russian and French citizen. In France, Koblyakov founded the NGO *Russie-Libertés* that organized several anti-Putin protests. In Russia, he had been running a profitable chain of nursery facilities, which were later seized by his competitors, who were backed by the regime.[35] After Koblyakov exposed large-scale corruption in public spending on the care and welfare of the elderly, a bogus criminal case was opened against him and he was forced to flee Russia. In 2014, he was detained in Bulgaria on an Interpol Red Notice. It took him more than a year to defeat the Red Notice by proving that the request of the Russian authorities violated Interpol's Constitution and legal rules. As Theodore Bromund notes, "The frightening thing about all of this is that it could happen to anyone Russia takes a dislike to.... When it happens, Interpol's processes are slow at best and useless at worst, and the Russians won't relent."[36]

A recent report published by Human Rights Watch suggests that in 2015, an increasing number of individuals were criminally prosecuted and harassed for criticizing the government in Russia.[37] As the Fair Trials International report states, it is "unrealistic to expect countries to refrain from abusing Interpol's tools when the rule of law is not observed at the national level."[38] Russia's abuse of Red Notices as an instrument of repression constitutes an international problem. It significantly damages Interpol's reputation and could jeopardize the utility of its global networks for law-abiding democratic countries.

Corruption of the Judiciary

Judges can facilitate raiding by blocking counteractions of legal owners, delaying the legal process, or making unjust decisions. In low-profile cases, favorable judgments can be bought through bribing or offering a share in illegal proceeds. Based on interviews with more than 100 businessmen and lawyers in Russia, the National Anti-Corruption Committee estimates that it costs between $5,000 and $10,000 to falsify companies' documents, $10,000 to secure a delay in court proceedings, and $50,000 to close a criminal investigation.[39] However, bribes vary by region. For example, while an improper judgment in Moscow costs between $50,000 and $200,000, the price at the regional level ranges from $10,000 to $20,000.[40] In high-profile politicized cases, decisions in courts are often made based on so-called "telephone justice," when public officials exert informal influence on the judiciary.[41]

One of the most infamous cases is the YUKOS oil company. In 2003, its top executives were arrested on charges of fraud by Russia's Prosecutor General's Office. According to the report of the Council of Europe Committee on Legal Affairs and Human Rights,

> the circumstances of the arrest and prosecution of leading YUKOS executives suggest that the interest of the State's action in these cases goes beyond the mere pursuit of criminal justice, to include such elements as the weakening of an outspoken political opponent, intimidation of other wealthy individuals and regaining control of strategic economic assets.[42]

After the YUKOS case, the Basmanny District Court became notoriously famous in Russia and abroad as an example of "a prosecution to order."[43] Now, the term "Basmanny justice" is widely used to denote the lack of independence and corruption of the judiciary.

Another example is the raiding case against TogliattiAzot (ToAZ), the largest ammonia producer in Russia. In this case, the judiciary took the misuse of the legal system to a new level by bringing criminal charges against a person who used his constitutional right not to testify against himself.[44] In 2006, the Investigative Committee opened a criminal case against the ToAZ press secretary Igor Bashunov, who refused to answer accusatory questions under Article 51 of the Russian Constitution. In 2007, a judge of the Presnensky District Court of Moscow ruled that the indictment violated the Criminal Procedure Code and returned the case to the prosecutor. In October 2008, the magistrate of the Presnensky district of Moscow terminated the criminal proceedings against Bashunov due to the statute of limitations.

There is evidence that "telephone justice" was systematically used in the ToAZ case. In 2008, Elena Valyavina, the first Deputy Chairwoman of the Highest Arbitrazh Court, gave evidence in a defamation case against the journalist Vladimir Solovyov brought by Valerii Boyev, an official from the Presidential Administration. Solovyov alleged that Boyev put pressure on judges in the interest of raiders. After Valyavina testified that she had been pressured to make a particular decision in the ToAZ case, Boyev dropped the defamation case.[45] According to Valyavina, when she refused to comply with Boyev's instructions to change her judicial rulings, he threatened that she would face serious problems with her reelection.[46] As Alena Ledeneva argues, "Valyavina took the case because none of the other judges at the Court were willing to oversee the hearing because, apparently, they were concerned about possible personal repercussions."[47] Earlier, Nadezhda Kostyuchenko, former Judge of the Samara Region Arbitrazh Court, was dismissed following her rulings in favor of ToAZ in 2005. Kostyuchenko also claimed that the Samara Court chairman made threats against her and her children.[48] In 2008, Kostyuchenko took her case to the European Court of Human Rights in Strasbourg.

These cases vividly demonstrate the lack of independence of Russia's judiciary. This conclusion is consistent with expert assessments of the current state of the judicial system in Russia. For example, Alexander Brod, a member of the Presidential Council for Civil Society and Human Rights, indicates that courts are part of the law enforcement system and judges are often pressured into making biased decisions in raiding cases.[49] Another issue is non-transparent procedures of judges' appointments. In 2011–2014, the Russian sociologist Vadim Volkov conducted an empirical study based on focus groups, expert interviews, and surveys of judges of magistrates courts and courts of general jurisdiction in 15 Russian regions. The results of Volkov's study demonstrate the lack of judicial independence. If a judge acquits a defendant, it means that a criminal case against him was opened by mistake and investigators might be reprimanded, while prosecutors will lose their bonuses.[50] In Russia, the work of judges is evaluated based on two criteria: the proportion of cases closed in a timely manner, and on the so-called "stability of judicial decisions," which measures the percentage of the judge's decisions overturned in the higher court over the total number of cases reviewed by this judge.[51] Bearing in mind that higher courts overturn acquittals more often than convictions, judges have more incentives to favor prosecutors. To do otherwise could put an entire judicial career in jeopardy.

The Council of Europe report on the *Comparative Analysis on Preventing Misuse of Public Authority in the Corporate Sector* lists a wide range of instances where raiders misuse courts.[52] For example, raiders often obtain court decisions that legalize counterfeited documents, arrest shares of the majority shareholder, freeze assets, and block sales of property. Raiding cases where interlocutory injunctions paralyzed the exercise of voting rights in shareholders' meetings are well documented in the literature.[53] As the Council of Europe report indicates, "even when it has proved possible to reverse an interlocutory injunction, its negative consequences have often already taken place and are not reversible, especially when an injunction has affected the voting rights of the targeted shareholder-defendant."[54]

Another issue of Russia's judiciary is the lack of common ethics within the profession of judges. Judges come from different organizations. Prosecutors, policemen, officers of the investigative bodies, attorneys, and even court assistants can become judges in Russia. Here, there are certain differences between the career ladders of Western and Russian courts. In Western practice, court clerks are managerial positions and they cannot automatically become judges due to the lack of specific competences. The peculiarity of the Russian judicial system is that an increasing proportion of judges come from the court staff. Between 1997 and 2013, their proportion increased from 11.4 to 30.3 percent of the judiciary.[55] According to an unspoken rule, court clerks and assistants need to work for six or seven years before their transition to the position of judges.[56] Decisions of those judges who came from the court hierarchy are guided more by formal aspects of the judicial process and the letter of the law, rather than by the spirit of the law and the notion of justice itself.[57] Such judges are more inclined to make decisions based on telephone justice or institutionalized informal practices within the court.

Rent-Seeking Activities of Regulatory and Registration Agencies

Raiding attacks increasingly involve the use of regulatory agencies that are authorized to receive legal and financial information about businesses and to conduct inspections of their activities. Raider attacks are often preceded by numerous inspections performed by regulatory agencies without sufficient reasons.[58] Officials from regulatory agencies can put significant pressure on raided enterprises through administrative harassment, extortion of bribes, and obstruction of business activities. Not surprisingly, an increasing number of books have been published recently to give instructions and recommendations to businessmen on dealing with inspections by regulatory agencies.[59] Regulatory agencies use a wide variety of different administrative tools to harass enterprises. For instance, in 2004, regulatory agencies tried to put pressure on the telecom company Vimpelcom by cancelling its licenses and submitting oversized tax bills to force its management to negotiate with raiders.[60] In 2006, fire inspectors cut off electricity to EkspoPUL, a lamp-making factory in Saratov, to pressure its legal owners to transfer control over the company to illegal raiders.[61] The abuse of regulatory authority is widespread in all Russian regions. Many illegal raids are committed through the use of administrative corruption that encompasses regulatory audits and inspections.

The Council of Europe report distinguishes between five types of possible misuse of inspections: (1) pirate inspections; (2) overlapping inspections due to rivalries between agencies; (3) poor self-management of inspectorates; (4) excessive inspections due to the lack of risk-based targeting; and (5) incentives for public officials to find violations.[62] Pirate inspections are carried out by public officials or other persons who are not authorized to conduct them. In some cases, public officials who have the authority to conduct inspections abuse their power through an arbitrary selection of businesses. Pirate inspections are pervasive in authoritarian regimes where businesses are afraid to question public authorities. A recent study shows that in post-communist countries it is very common for inspectors to visit more businesses and to do so with greater frequency than is officially required.[63] As a result, the number of unplanned inspections significantly outnumbers the number of officially planned inspections. There is evidence that this is the case in Russia.[64] Rivalries between regulatory agencies often lead to overlapping inspections, which are especially burdensome for businesses. In addition, poor self-management of inspectorates lacking transparent procedures and accountability leads to an increased risk of extortion by inspectors. The same effect is observed in situations where inspectorates provide incentives for their employees to find violations. The lack of transparent criteria for selection of businesses also facilitates excessive inspections in the companies targeted by illegal raiders.

The case of the Beirut café located in Saint Petersburg is illustrative of the abuse of power by regulatory agencies. After myriad inspections conducted in 2016 by the Investigative Committee, the Consumer Protection Service (Rospotrebnadzor), the Ministry of Emergency, and the police, the Beirut café's owner, Elizaveta Izvozchikova, had to suspend business activities due to the withdrawal of her cash register and legal documents. The official reason for these inspections was the low quality of rendering services. Yet, there might be other motives. The business owner describes the situation that led to the inspections as follows:

> In the fourth week of July, a man entered the café with the intention of using our bathroom facilities, yet, in accordance with our internal regulations, the administrator politely refused, indicating that the facilities can be used only by customers.[65]

According to Izvozchikova, after the incident, this man, who appeared to be an official from the Investigative Committee, threatened to close the café and open criminal proceedings against her personally.[66] Officially, the Investigative Committee can launch investigations into catering businesses only after the Consumer Protection Service finds violations of sanitary norms, while a criminal case can be opened only in the case of repeated violations. However, in the Beirut café, some inspections were allegedly carried out even without an official warrant.[67] As a result, the owner had to file a complaint to the Investigative Committee about the abuse of office by the inspectors.

Another cause for concern is the abuse of power by tax authorities. One of the most infamous examples is the raiding case against Hermitage Capital Management, founded by Bill Browder and Edmond Safra. In this case, the goal of the raiders was to secure a fraudulent tax refund to the amount of $230 million.[68] In 2008, Sergey Magnitsky, a lawyer of Hermitage Capital, testified against tax inspectors and enforcement officers involved in the tax fraud. In retaliation, he was accused of tax evasion and imprisoned for one year. After 11 months in pre-trial detention, Magnitsky died, while the corrupt tax inspectors did not face any legal consequences. In 2016, a team of investigators and lawyers tracked millions of dollars from this tax fraud in bank accounts of Russian public officials in Canada.[69]

The Council of Europe report points to the over-criminalization of tax violations of Russian businesses.[70] It is facilitated by weak coordination between investigative and tax authorities, as well as the lack of specific provisions defining tax fraud and value-added tax (VAT) fraud in the national legislature. In 2009, the Code of Criminal Procedures of the Russian Federation was amended to include a special provision, according to which investigations into tax violations could be initiated only by tax authorities. The introduction of this provision was explained by systematic allegations of arbitrary prosecutions of businessmen accused of tax violations. As expected, after 2009, the number of criminal cases related to tax violations decreased significantly in comparison with previous years. However, in 2014, this provision was removed from the Code of Criminal Procedures, which again led to an increase in criminal cases on charges of tax violations. Their rapid growth rates are fueled by the complexity of Russian tax legislature and its instability, with numerous changes introduced every year. At the same time, officials from the tax authorities do not provide sufficient information to entrepreneurs about the relevant legal changes on a systematic basis.

Apart from tax authorities, registration agencies are often involved in raiding cases, by entering false information in shareholder registries and securities depositories. In 2010, the Criminal Code of the Russian Federation was amended to increase the severity of punishment for falsifying and destroying registration documents. Article 170.1 of the Criminal Code provides liability for the falsification of unified state registries of legal entities, registries of security holders, and systems of depositary accounting. Furthermore, Article 285.3 of the Criminal Code provides liability of public officials for the intentional introduction of deliberately false information in unified public registries, as well as the deliberate destruction or forgery of registration documents. Despite these provisions, raiding attempts involving malicious actions by registration agencies persist in Russia. For example, in 2010, officials from the Interregional Tax Service of Saint Petersburg were found guilty of committing fraud by falsifying registration documents of several legal entities.[71]

In many cases, raiders try to reregister property through shell companies to establish a good faith purchaser exemption. Article 167 of the Civil Code states that each party must return property acquired through the transaction that was declared invalid. However, according to the decision of the Constitutional Court, Article 167 of the Civil Code cannot be extended to a good faith purchaser. For example, in 2013, the Investigative Department of the Ministry of Interior opened a case against a group of raiders who used employees of the state registry to forge legal documents and establish ownership over real estate in Moscow.[72] To abuse the good faith purchaser provision, the raiders together with some public officials, reregistered the property several times through various shell companies. As a result, the original owners were unable to recover their property through the court system.

This case is no exception. Business raiding schemes increasingly abuse the good faith purchaser provision to launder seized property and assets through multiple sales through shell companies. Even if legal owners can prove the fact of raiding, they are often unable to recover their assets and businesses. If courts recognize a third party, who acquired the stolen assets as a good faith purchaser, judicial practice limits the recovery of the assets. An analysis of numerous cases shows that laundering of raided property is often based on the collusion of criminal groups with registration agencies. The most effective way to restore the rights of legal business owners is through the identification of beneficial owners of shell companies, which is not required in Russia. Another measure against such violations is to increase the effectiveness of national financial institutions in reporting suspicious transactions.

Reiderstvo constitutes a significant part of Russia's illegal economy. It undermines the foundations of the state, harms citizens' trust in public authorities, destroys the rule of law, and prevents social and economic development of the country. The rise of raiding cases that involve malicious criminal prosecution of businessmen explains why entrepreneurship is considered one of the most dangerous occupations in Russia. One entrepreneur describes the current situation as follows: "The economy will be completely destroyed because businessmen are not safe in our country – anyone could be sent to jail."[73] According to Russia's business ombudsman Boris Titov, "It is hard to find another social group persecuted on such a large scale." Current provisions of the Criminal Procedure Code cannot effectively protect businessmen who are unjustly charged with economic crimes. Importantly, there are no clear criteria of classifying crimes in the entrepreneurial sphere. Chapter 22 of the Criminal Code provides a broad list of economic crimes that are subject to varying interpretations. In some cases, a simple failure to fulfill contractual obligations can be treated as fraud and lead to a criminal case.[74] The lack of a uniform legal approach to the classification of economic crimes gives wide discretion to the police and judges in applying Chapter 22 of the Criminal Code to business activities.[75] This suggests the need to establish clear criteria for classifying crimes in the entrepreneurial sector.

Collective organizations have an enormous potential for the organization of "anti-asset-grabbing" social movements. For example, the civil rights organization

Rus' Sidyashchaya (Jailed Russia) was founded by the Russian journalist Olga Romanova in an attempt to release her husband and help other businessmen who were imprisoned by raiders. In 2008, her husband, Alexei Kozlov, was arrested on charges of fraud and embezzlement, allegedly at the instigation of his business partner. In 2012, the charges against Kozlov were partially dropped and he was released from jail. While in prison, he began writing the *Butyrka Blog*, named after the infamous pretrial detention center in Russia. It became a vigorous platform for other businessmen who fell victim to malicious criminal prosecution. In 2010, his blog won an award at the world's largest international weblog competition founded by *Deutsche Welle*, the German International Broadcasting Service.

Another example is the civil society organization, *Solidarnost'* (Solidarity), founded by the Russian businesswoman Yana Yakovleva in 2011 to help victims of malicious criminal prosecution. In 2006, Yakovleva herself was jailed when illegal raiders attempted to seize her company.[76] Later, the charges against her were dropped and she could return to her business. Solidarity and Jailed Russia have helped many businessmen to recover assets stolen by raiders. Yet, these organizations have a severe disadvantage related to their limited membership.[77] In this respect, unions of industrialists, associations of entrepreneurs, and chambers of commerce that are based on wide membership can provide better support for businesses raided by public officials. Currently, they are not mobilized into an anti-asset-grabbing movement that can be incorporated into an official anti-corruption campaign.[78] The inability of entrepreneurs to organize collective action against *reiderstvo* leads to situations where their rights are systematically violated. This failure suggests that it is necessary to combine anti-corruption and anti-raid efforts of collective business organizations with other social groups. Judging from international experience, a partnership between civil society and business associations can be an effective tool for mobilizing isolated private actors and organizing a massive "anti-asset-grabbing" social movement.

Notes

1 See, for example, Center for Political Technologies, *Reiderstvo kak sotsial'no-ekonomicheskii i politicheskii fenomen sovremennoi Rossii* [in Russian], (Moscow: Center for Political Technologies, 2008); Gans-Morse, J. Threats to Property Rights in Russia: From Private Coercion to State Aggression, *Post-Soviet Affairs*, 28(3) (2012), 263–295; Sakwa, R. Systemic Stalemate: Reiderstvo and the Dual State. In N. Robinson (Ed.), *The Political Economy of Russia* (pp. 69–96) (Lanham, MD: Rowman & Littlefield, 2012); Yakovlev, A., Sobolev, A., & Kazun, A. Means of Production Versus Means of Coercion: Can Russian Business Limit the Violence of a Predatory State? *Post-Soviet Affairs*, 30(2–3) (2014), 171–194.
2 See, for example, Gridasov, A., & Evstifeev, D. Rederskikh zakhvatov stanovitsia vse bol'she [in Russian], *Izvestiya*, April 12, 2012; Kondrashov, N. Zakhvata ya i ne zametil [in Russian], *Rossiiskaya Biznes Gazeta*, May 20, 2014.
3 Chelishcheva, V. Rassledovanie: poprobui tut ne syad' [in Russian]. *Novaya Gazeta*, October 19, 2015.
4 Titov, B. Naidennye u polkovnika Zakharchenko den'gi po shchepotke sobiralis' s biznesa [in Russian]. *Vzglyad*, September 12, 2016.

5 Shelley, L., & Deane, J. *The Rise of Reiderstvo: Implications for Russia and the West* (Washington, DC: TraCCC, 2016).
6 Cited in Mereu, F. Corporate Raiders Use Cash, Friends. *The Moscow Times*, February 13, 2008.
7 Center for Political Technologies, op. cit., p. 6.
8 Cited in Firestone, T. Criminal Corporate Raiding in Russia. *The International Lawyer*, *42*(4) (2008), 1207.
9 See, for example, Rochlitz, M. Corporate Raiding and the Role of the State in Russia, *Post-Soviet Affairs*, *30*(2–3) (2014), 89–114; Viktorov, I. Corporate Raiding in Post-Soviet Russia, *Baltic Worlds*, *2* (2013), 4–8.
10 Kazun, A. *Intensivnost' silovogo davleniya na biznes v regionakh Rossii: indikatory i faktory* [in Russian] (Moscow: Higher School of Economics, 2014).
11 Kazun, A. Reiderstvo v regionakh Rossii: indikatory i faktory [in Russian]. *Mir Rossii*, *24*(3) (2015), 53.
12 Shelley & Deane, op. cit., pp. 13–17.
13 Settles, A. *Evolving Corruption: Hostile Takeovers, Corporate Raiding, and Company Capture in Russia* (Washington DC: Center for International Private Enterprise, 2008), p. 5.
14 Cited in Drobysh, E. Medvedev: reiderstvo dushit ekonomiku [in Russian]. *Komsomol'skaya Pravda*, July 1, 2010.
15 Cited in Latyshev, A. Khvatit koshmarit' biznes [in Russian]. *Izvestiya*, August 1, 2008.
16 President of the Russian Federation. Law on Improving the Effectiveness of Anti-Raiding Measures Has Been Signed. (2010). Available at: http://en.kremlin.ru/events/president/news/8223
17 Rochlitz, op. cit., p. 110.
18 Shelley & Deane, op. cit., p. 18.
19 Center for Political Technologies, op. cit., p. 33.
20 Gerber, T., & Mendelson, S. Public Experiences of Police Violence and Corruption in Contemporary Russia: A Case of Predatory Policing? *Law and Society Review*, *42*(1) (2008), 2.
21 Klyamkin, I., & Timofeev, L. *Tenevaya Rossiya* [in Russian]. (Moscow: Russian State University for the Humanities, 2000), p. 124.
22 Movchan, A. How Does the Head of an Anti-Corruption Agency Wind up with $120 Million in Cash? *The Moscow Times*, October 10, 2016.
23 Titov, op. cit.
24 See, for example, Barry, E. Russian Police Raid Billionaire's Bank, *New York Times*, November 2, 2010; Walker, S. Lebedev Blames Government for Police Raid on His Moscow Bank, *The Independent*, February 17, 2012.
25 Tavernise, S. Capitalist Tools: Police for Hire in Russia's Business Jungle. *New York Times*, July 28, 2002.
26 Fair Trials International. *Strengthening Respect for Human Rights, Strengthening Interpol* (London: Fair Trials International, 2013).
27 Lewis, L. Interpol's Red Flag (The International Consortium of Investigative Journalism, 2011). Available at: www.icij.org/project/interpols-red-flag/interpols-red-notices-used-some-pursue-political-dissenters-opponents
28 Bromund, T. Putin's Long Arm. *Weekly Standard*, March 2, 2015.
29 Winning, A. Interpol Refuses Russian Request for Khodorkovsky Search Notice: TASS. *Reuters*. February 12, 2016. Available at: http://in.reuters.com/article/russia-khodorkovsky-interpol-idINL8N15R4OG
30 Elia, D. How Russia Uses Interpol to Hit the Opposition. *East Online*, April 7, 2015. Available at: http://eastwest.eu/en/opinions/riding-the-russian-rollercoaster/how-russia-uses-interpol-to-hit-the-opposition
31 Bromund, T., & Kopel, D. Necessary Reforms Can Keep Interpol Working in the US Interest. *Heritage Foundation Backgrounder*, *2861* (2013), 12.

32 Interpol. *International Notices System, No. COM/FS/2015–02/GI-02* (Geneva: Interpol, 2015).
33 Interpol. *International Notices System, No. COM/FS/2017–02/GI-02* (Geneva: Interpol, 2017).
34 Higgins, A. How Moscow Uses Interpol to Pursue its Enemies. *New York Times*, November 6, 2016.
35 Estlund, M. The Effect of Russia's Court System(s) on Interpol. *Red Notice Law Journal*, September 12, 2014.
36 Bromund, op. cit.
37 Human Rights Watch. *The World Report 2016* (New York: Seven Stories Press, 2016), p. 478.
38 Fair Trials International, op. cit., p. 39.
39 Cited in Osadchuk, S. Bribe to Illegally Seize a Firm Put at $30,000. *The Moscow Times*, September 8, 2008.
40 Center for Political Technologies, op. cit., p. 64.
41 Shelley, L. Corruption in the Post-Yeltsin Era. *East European Constitutional Review*, 9 (2000), 70.
42 Council of Europe Committee on Legal Affairs and Human Rights. Report on the Circumstances Surrounding the Arrest and Prosecution of Leading Yukos Executives. (2004). Available at: http://assembly.coe.int/nw/xml/XRef/Xref-XML2HTML-en.asp?fileid=17293andlang=en
43 Sakwa, op. cit., p. 72.
44 Aleshin, A. Osnovnoi zakon ne pisan [in Russian]. *Izvestiya*, October 16, 2006.
45 Henderson, J. *The Constitution of the Russian Federation: A Contextual Analysis* (Oxford: Bloomsbury, 2011), p. 226.
46 Krainova, N. Judge Tells of Kremlin Threat. *The Moscow Times*, May 14, 2008.
47 Ledeneva, A. *Telephone Justice in Russia* (Brussels: EURUSSIA Center, 2011), p. 6.
48 Coalson, R. The Myth of Putin's Popularity. *Radio Free Europe/Radio Liberty*, December 30, 2008. Available at: www.rferl.org/a/1365202.html
49 Cited in Voronina, Y. Biznes ishchet zashchity [in Russian]. *Rossiyskaya Biznes Gazeta*, September 1, 2015.
50 Volkov, V. A sud'i kto? [in Russian]. *Ogonek*, October 5, 2015. Available at: http://kommersant.ru/doc/2820307
51 Ibid.
52 Kalnins, V., Visentin, M., & Sazonov, V. *Comparative Analysis on Preventing Misuse of Public Authority in the Corporate Sector* (Brussels: Council of Europe, 2014), p. 109.
53 Fedorov, A. *Reiderstvo i korporativnyi shantazh* [in Russian] (Moscow: Wolters Kluwer, 2010).
54 Kalnins, et al., op. cit., p. 109.
55 Volkov, op. cit.
56 Ibid.
57 Ibid.
58 Shmagina, Y., & Patsyuk, V. Raider Appears out of Nowhere, There's no Way to Escape. ULGroup Association. (2013). Available at: http://ulga.com.ua/en/cms/raiders_attack
59 See, for example, Barysheva, S. *Zashchita biznesa pri proverkakh* [in Russian] (Moscow: Eksmo, 2009); Kovalev, A., & Kovaleva, E. *Proverki nadzornykh organov* [in Russian] (Moscow: Feniks, 2015); Pichugin, V. *Bezopasnost' biznesa* [in Russian] (Moscow: Alpina, 2010); Selutin, A. *Proverka politsiei* [in Russian] (Moscow: Litres, 2014); Stepchenko, E. *Nalogovye proverki* [in Russian] (Moscow: Kinorus', 2013).
60 Markus, S. Secure Property as a Bottom-up Process: Firms, Stakeholders, and Predators in Weak States. *World Politics*, 64(2) (2012), 253–254.
61 Ibid., p. 252.

62 Kalnins, et al., op. cit., p. 144.
63 Blanc, F. *Inspection Reforms: Why, How, and With What Results* (Paris: OECD, 2012).
64 Ministry of Economic Development of the Russian Federation. *Svodnyi doklad ob osushchestvlenii gosudarstvennogo kontrolya (nadzora) za 2012 god* [in Russian] (Moscow: Ministry of Economic Development, 2013), p. 73.
65 Shcherbova, A. Kafe "Beirut" izvodyat proverkami i ugrozhaut ugolovnym delom [in Russian]. *Delovoi Peterburg*, October 5, 2016.
66 Ibid.
67 Ibid.
68 Shelley & Deane, op. cit., p. 14.
69 Leblanc, D. Investigators Track Millions of Dollars from Russian Tax Fraud Coming to Canada. *The Globe and Mail*, October 27, 2016.
70 Kalnins, et al., op. cit., p. 95.
71 Investigative Committee of the Russian Federation. V Sankt-Peterburge vynesen prigovor suda v otnoshenii gruppy lits, uchastvovavshikh v reiderskikh zakhvatakh [in Russian]. (2010). Available at: http://sledcom.ru/news/item/540987
72 Kalnins, et al., op. cit., p. 120.
73 Cited in Kesby, R. Why Russia Locks up so Many Entrepreneurs. *BBC News*, July 5, 2012. Available at: www.bbc.com/news/magazine-18706597
74 Kalnins, et al., op. cit., p. 82.
75 Cited in Shtykina, A., & Bikbov, A. V Rosssii stali chashche sazhat' biznesmenov za ekonomicheskie prestupleniya [in Russian]. *News Agency RBK*, April 15, 2015. Available at: http://top.rbc.ru/economics/15/04/2015/552e76599a794786fa57447e
76 Yakovlev, et al., op. cit., p. 176.
77 Ibid., p. 189.
78 Hanson, P. *Reiderstvo: Asset-Grabbing in Russia* (London: Chatham House, 2014), p. 11.

References

Aleshin, A. (2006, October 16). Osnovnoi zakon ne pisan [in Russian]. *Izvestiya*.
Barry, E. (2010, November 2). Russian Police Raid Billionaire's Bank. *New York Times*.
Barysheva, S. (2009). *Zashchita biznesa pri proverkakh* [in Russian]. Moscow: Eksmo.
Blanc, F. (2012). *Inspection Reforms: Why, How, and With What Results*. Paris: OECD.
Bromund, T. R. (2015, March 2). Putin's Long Arm. *The Weekly Standard*.
Bromund, T. R., & Kopel, D. (2013). *Necessary Reforms Can Keep Interpol Working in the U.S. Interest* (No. 2861). Washington, DC: Heritage Foundation.
Center for Political Technologies. (2008). *Reiderstvo kak sotsial'no-ekonomicheskii i politicheskii fenomen sovremennoi Rossii* [in Russian]. Moscow: Center for Political Technologies.
Chelishcheva, V. (2015, October 19). Rassledovanie: poprobui tut ne syad' [in Russian]. *Novaya Gazeta*.
Coalson, R. (2008, December 30). The Myth of Putin's Popularity. *Radio Free Europe/Radio Liberty*. Available at: www.rferl.org/a/1365202.html
Council of Europe Committee on Legal Affairs and Human Rights. (2004). Report on the Circumstances Surrounding the Arrest and Prosecution of Leading Yukos Executives. Available at: http://assembly.coe.int/nw/xml/XRef/Xref-XML2HTML-en.asp?fileid=17293andlang=en
Drobysh, E. (2010, July 1). Medvedev: reiderstvo dushit ekonomiku [in Russian]. *Komsomol'skaya Pravda*.

Elia, D. (2015, April 7). How Russia Uses Interpol to Hit the Opposition. *East Online*. Available at: http://eastwest.eu/en/opinions/riding-the-russian-rollercoaster/how-russia-uses-interpol-to-hit-the-opposition

Estlung, M. (2014, September 12). The Effect of Russia's Court System(s) on Interpol. *Red Notice Law Journal*.

Fair Trials International. (2013). *Strengthening Respect for Human Rights, Strengthening Interpol*. London: Fair Trials International.

Fedorov, A. (2010). *Reiderstvo i korporativnyi shantazh* [in Russian]. Moscow: Wolters Kluwer.

Firestone, T. (2008). Criminal Corporate Raiding in Russia. *The International Lawyer*, *42*(4), 1207–1229.

Gans-Morse, J. (2012). Threats to Property Rights in Russia: From Private Coercion to State Aggression. *Post-Soviet Affairs*, *28*(3), 263–295.

Gerber, T. P., & Mendelson, S. E. (2008). Public Experiences of Police Violence and Corruption in Contemporary Russia: A Case of Predatory Policing? *Law & Society Review*, *42*(1), 1–44.

Gridasov, A., & Evstifeev, D. (2012, April 12). Rederskikh zakhvatov stanovitsia vse bol'she [in Russian]. *Izvestiya*.

Hanson, P. (2014). *Reiderstvo: Asset-Grabbing in Russia*. London: Chatham House.

Henderson, J. (2011). *The Constitution of the Russian Federation: A Contextual Analysis*. Oxford: Bloomsbury.

Higgins, A. (2016, November 6). How Moscow Uses Interpol to Pursue its Enemies. *New York Times*.

Human Rights Watch. (2016). *The World Report 2016*. New York: Human Rights Watch.

Interpol. (2015). *International Notices System, No. COM/FS/2015–02/GI-02*. Geneva: Interpol.

Interpol. (2017). *International Notices System, No. COM/FS/2017–02/GI-02*. Geneva: Interpol.

Investigative Committee of the Russian Federation. (2010). V Sankt-Peterburge vynesen prigovor suda v otnoshenii gruppy lits, uchastvovavshikh v reiderskikh zakhvatakh [in Russian]. Available at: http://sledcom.ru/news/item/540987

Kalnins, V., Visentin, M., & Sazonov, V. (2014). *Comparative Analysis on Preventing Misuse of Public Authority in the Corporate Sector*. Brussels: Council of Europe.

Karklins, R. (2005). *The System Made Me Do It: Corruption in Post-Communist Societies*. New York: Sharpe.

Kazun, A. (2014). *Intensivnost' silovogo davleniya na biznes v regionakh Rossii: indikatory i faktory* [in Russian]. Moscow: Higher School of Economics.

Kazun, A. (2015). Reiderstvo v regionakh Rossii: indikatory i faktory [in Russian]. *Mir Rossii*, *24*(3), 33–59.

Kesby, R. (2012, July 5). Why Russia Locks up so Many Entrepreneurs. *BBC News*. Available at: www.bbc.com/news/magazine-18706597

Klyamkin, I., & Timofeev, L. (2004). *Tenevaya Rossiya* [in Russian]. Moscow: Russian State University for the Humanities.

Kondrashov, N. (2014, May 20). Zakhvata ya i ne zametil [in Russian]. *Rossiiaskaya Biznes Gazeta*.

Kovalev, A., & Kovaleva, E. (2015). *Proverki nadzornykh organov* [in Russian]. Moscow: Feniks.

Krainova, N. (2008, May 14). Judge Tells of Kremlin Threat. *The Moscow Times*.

Latyshev, A. (2008, August 1). Khvatit koshmarit' biznes [in Russian]. *Isvestiya*.

Leblanc, D. (2016, October 27). Investigators Track Millions of Dollars from Russian Tax Fraud Coming to Canada. *The Globe and Mail*.

Ledeneva, A. (2011). *Telephone Justice in Russia*. Brussels: EURUSSIA Centre.

Lewis, L. (2011, July 20). Interpol's Red Notices Used by Some to Pursue Political Dissenters, Opponents. Available at: www.icij.org/project/interpols-red-flag/interpols-red-notices-used-some-pursue-political-dissenters-opponents

Markus, S. (2012). Secure Property as a Bottom-up Process: Firms, Stakeholders, and Predators in Weak States. *World Politics*, *64*(2), 242–277.

Mereu, F. (2008, February 13). Corporate Raiders Use Cash, Friends. *The Moscow Times*.

Ministry of Economic Development of the Russian Federation. (2013). *Svodnyi doklad ob osushchestvlenii gosudarstvennogo kontrolya (nadzora) za 2012 god* [in Russian]. Moscow: Ministry of Economic Development.

Movchan, A. (2016, October 10). How Does the Head of an Anti-Corruption Agency Wind up with $120 Million in Cash? *The Moscow Times*.

Osadchuk, S. (2008, September 8). Bribe to Illegally Seize a Firm Put at $30,000. *The Moscow Times*.

Pichugin, V. (2010). *Bezopasnost' biznesa* [in Russian]. Moscow: Alpina.

President of the Russian Federation. (2010). Law on Improving the Effectiveness of Anti-Raiding Measures Has Been Signed. Available at: http://en.kremlin.ru/events/president/news/8223

Rochlitz, M. (2014). Corporate Raiding and the Role of the State in Russia. *Post-Soviet Affairs*, *30*(2–3), 89–114.

Sakwa, R. (2012). Systemic Stalemate: Reiderstvo and the Dual State. In N. Robinson (Ed.), *The Political Economy of Russia* (pp. 69–96). Lanham, MD: Rowman & Littlefield Publishers.

Selutin, A. (2014). *Proverka politsiei* [in Russian]. Moscow: Litres.

Settles, A. (2008). *Evolving Corruption: Hostile Takeovers, Corporate Raiding, and Company Capture in Russia*. Washington, DC: Center for International Private Enterprise.

Shcherbova, A. (2016, October 5). Kafe "Beirut" izvodyat proverkami i ugrozhaut ugolovnym delom [in Russian]. *Delovoi Peterburg*.

Shelley, L. I. (2000). Corruption in the Post-Yeltsin Era. *East European Constitutional Review*, *9*, 70–74.

Shelley, L., & Deane, J. (2016). *The Rise of Reiderstvo: Implications for Russia and the West*. Washington, DC: TraCCC.

Shmagina, Y., & Patsyuk, V. (2013). Raider Appears out of Nowhere, There's no Way to Escape. United Legal Group Association. Available at: http://ulga.com.ua/en/cms/raiders_attack

Shtykina, A., & Bikbov, A. (2015, April 15). V Rosssii stali chashche sazhat' biznesmenov za ekonomicheskie prestupleniya [in Russian]. *News Agency RBK*. Available at: http://top.rbc.ru/economics/15/04/2015/552e76599a794786fa57447e

Stepchenko, E. (2013). *Nalogovye proverki* [in Russian]. Moscow: Kinorus'.

Tavernise, S. (2002, July 28). Capitalist Tools: Police for Hire in Russia's Business Jungle. *New York Times*.

Tivov, B. (2016, September 12). Titov: naidennye u polkovnika Zakharchenko den'gi po shchepotke sobiralis' s biznesa [in Russian]. *Vzglyad*.

Viktorov, I. (2013). Corporate Raiding in Post-Soviet Russia. *Baltic Worlds*, *2*, 4–8.

Volkov, V. (2015, October 5). A sud'i kto? [in Russian]. *Ogonek*.

Voronina, Y. (2015, September 1). Biznes ishchet zashchity [in Russian]. *Rossiyskaya Biznes Gazeta*.

Walker, S. (2012, February 17). Lebedev Blames Government for Police Raid on his Moscow Bank. *The Independent*.

Winning, A. (2016, February 12). Interpol Refuses Russian Request for Khodorkovsky Search Notice: TASS. *Reuters*. Available at: www.reuters.com/article/us-russia-khodorkovsky-interpol-idUSKCN0VL202

Yakovlev, A., Sobolev, A., & Kazun, A. (2014). Means of Production Versus Means of Coercion: Can Russian Business Limit the Violence of a Predatory State? *Post-Soviet Affairs*, *30*(2–3), 171–194.

6 "Entrepreneurial Spring"
Collective Resistance to Administrative Corruption

International experiences provide strong evidence of the power of collective action against violations of human and entrepreneurial rights. Indeed, the Arab Spring revolutions began with popular mobilization sparked by an incident of administrative harassment against a self-employed vendor in Tunisia. On December 17, 2010, Tarek el-Tayeb Mohamed Bouazizi, a Tunisian street vendor, set himself on fire in response to the unjust confiscation of his wares by a municipal official.[1] Bouazizi's self-immolation served as a catalyst for social protests and riots against corrupt political regimes in Tunisia and other Arab-Spring countries.

In 2015, Guatemala experienced a similar popular mobilization sparked by an investigation into a corruption ring comprised of high-ranking officials from the government, customs, and tax authorities. The corruption ring was organized to bribe entrepreneurs and businesses in exchange for reduced import tariffs.[2] In response, over 35 civil society organizations, private-sector associations, human rights groups, and indigenous movements organized a public campaign called the Citizen Gathering.[3] For Guatemala, 2015 was a commemorative year because thousands of people took to the streets protesting against corrupt officials under the slogan "Justice now!" In the words of Guatemala's former Attorney General Claudia Paz y Paz, the protests were fueled by "a huge contrast between people who had yachts, planes, helicopters and mansions while there was no medicine in the hospitals."[4] The media called these protests "the Guatemalan Spring."[5] Eventually, they led to arrests of many high-ranking officials, including the former President Otto Pérez Molina.

Similarly, in Brazil, the epic scope of bribery by government officials and employees of state-controlled companies, including the oil corporation Petrobras, sparked a wave of public outcry. Popular mobilization in Brazil was a reaction to a series of corruption investigations (known as the Carwash case) that uncovered the bribery of high-ranking politicians and congressmen in exchange for lucrative construction and services contracts, including projects related to the 2016 Olympic Games in Rio de Janeiro.[6] In March 2015, former President Luiz Inácio Lula da Silva was arrested on charges of corruption. Although his successor President Dilma Rousseff denied any involvement in the Carwash case, she was the chairwoman on the Petrobras Board between 2003 and 2010. In 2015 and 2016, millions of Brazilians took to the streets demanding the resignation of President Rousseff. In August 2016, the Senate voted for her impeachment finding her guilty of breaking budgetary laws. In 2017, new accusations of corruption were raised against her successor, President Michel Temer.

In Russia, the 2015 and 2016 protests of entrepreneurs against administrative harassment failed to attract massive numbers of participants. One of the severest weaknesses of Russia's anti-corruption movement is the lack of cooperation between the general public and business communities. At the same time, entrepreneurs and their collective organizations represent an important part of civil society. Russian pre-revolutionary practices show that due to their representational role and economic leverage, self-regulatory organizations were powerful protectors of businesses against administrative harassment by public authorities. This chapter analyzes recent initiatives of business associations to promote anti-corruption programs and support broader human rights campaigns. The chapter also draws attention to critical factors that preclude Russian entrepreneurs from mobilizing against corruption.

Literature Review

Collective entrepreneurial organizations play an important role in holding public administration accountable. The concept of vertical and horizontal accountability serves as a theoretical background for interactions between state agencies and business organizations. Developed by Guillermo O'Donnell,[7] this concept distinguishes between two types of accountability. Horizontal accountability is provided by state agencies that are legally empowered to take actions against corrupt public officials and agencies, while vertical accountability is based on the electoral process.[8] Catalina Smulovitz and Enrique Peruzzotti distinguish another type of accountability: societal.[9] They define it as "a nonelectoral, yet vertical mechanism of control that rests on the actions of a multiple array of citizens' associations and movements and on the media."[10] The legitimacy of societal accountability is based on the right to petition. It is aimed at controlling political actors and regulatory agencies by exposing and denouncing their wrongdoing. Table 6.1 describes these types of accountability, with their key actors and activities.

Actors who provide horizontal accountability include the legislative, judicial, and executive branches, as well as enforcement agencies. They are ultimately responsible for prohibiting corruption legislatively and implementing appropriate enforcement procedures. Ordinary citizens and political organizations play a key role in providing vertical electoral accountability. Their main function is to hold politicians accountable through the electoral process. Finally, actors in charge of societal accountability include collective players, such as self-regulatory organizations, social movements, and the media. In the context of societal accountability, one of the most serious fallacies of anti-corruption initiatives in Russia is that they underestimate the role of self-regulatory organizations and their authority. These organizations have civil, legal, and human rights

Table 6.1 Types of accountability

Accountability	Key actors	Major activities
Horizontal accountability	The legislative, judicial, and executive branches, and enforcement agencies	Prohibiting corruption legislatively, enforcing anti-corruption laws, removing overregulation and administrative barriers
Vertical electoral accountability	Political organizations and citizens	Controlling political actors through the electoral process
Vertical societal accountability	Self-regulatory organizations, civil society, social movements, and the media	Whistleblowing, monitoring compliance with anti-corruption regulations, and organizing collective action against illegal activities

obligations to bring corruption and violations against entrepreneurs' rights to the attention of the appropriate authorities.

Self-regulatory organizations can play an active role in organizing anti-corruption campaigns, mobilizing different groups of businesses, and organizing their collective action. The World Bank defines collective action as "a collaborative and sustained process of cooperation amongst stakeholders," which "increases the impact and credibility of individual action, brings vulnerable individual players into an alliance of like-minded organizations and levels the playing field between competitors."[11] The importance of this approach to anti-corruption initiatives is explained by the fact that it "can complement or temporarily substitute for and strengthen weak local laws and anti-corruption practices."[12]

Another reason for the use of collective action is related to the inefficacy of the public system in mitigating the problem of corruption. In Russia, a continuing decline in trust in the government and enforcement institutions has led to an increasing skepticism and cynicism about anti-corruption campaigns organized by public authorities. According to the Global Competitiveness Report 2015–2016, public trust of politicians in Russia was ranked 70th out of 140 countries, with a score of 3.0 on a 7-point scale, with 1 meaning very low and 7 meaning very high.[13] The perceived reliability of police services was ranked 112nd (with a score of 3.2) and judicial independence 108th (with a score of 2.9).[14] These scores demonstrate the low confidence of the Russian population in these institutions, which in turn, explains why entrepreneurs often prefer not to object or respond to mistreatment by regulatory agencies. Indeed, under low levels of trust in political institutions, the police, and the judicial system, entrepreneurs do not feel such objections would be taken seriously by public authorities.

Collective initiatives organized by private companies, civil society, academia, NGOs, and the media help smooth the cyclical nature of anti-corruption reforms in the public sector and make them sustainable.[15] The adoption of anti-corruption laws is insufficient to eliminate corruption from society. As Ngoc Anh Tran argues, "Political will [to curb corruption] can hardly arise from the government itself but instead is the result of the demand from a population that is equipped with sufficient capabilities."[16] Numerous studies give empirical support to the negative impact of entrepreneurial organizations on the level of corruption, whether this impact transmits through changing attitudes of entrepreneurs toward informal practices[17] or through organizing their collective action against corrupt officials and agencies.[18] In other words, entrepreneurial organizations can decrease the frequency of corrupt practices indirectly through codes of conduct and education programs about anti-corruption compliance or directly through collective action campaigns against informal transactions.

Corruption is a collective action problem: although the business community as a whole is better off when corruption does not exist, individual firms have incentives to use informal transactions to their advantage. After all, there are no guarantees that other firms will act honestly. Thomas Dunfee and David Hess refer to this situation as a "paradox of corruption": "corruption is universally disproved, yet universally present."[19] Corruption is similar to another collective action problem known as the tragedy of the commons. The latter describes situations where unrestricted open access to common-pool resources leads to their overexploitation by actors who take only their own costs and benefits into account and ignore the social costs of their actions.

In her seminal book, *Governing the Commons*, Elinor Ostrom, the Nobel Prize-winner in Economics, demonstrates that in the long run, individuals can create institutional arrangements based on shared norms and patterns of reciprocity to resolve the tragedy of the commons.[20] This book contributes to the theory of collective action, by illustrating the diversity of possible solutions to the tragedy of the commons that do not require government enforcement. Continuing this tradition, Thomas Dunfee and David Hess propose using self-governance mechanisms to resolve the corruption paradox.[21] Based on this approach, economic communities of businesses and entrepreneurs are called on to develop and implement their own norms of ethical behavior to combat corruption.

The ability of entrepreneurs to mobilize themselves against corruption differs significantly across various countries. Countries' institutional environments have a strong impact on "either rewarding or discouraging the choice to engage in cooperative self-governance."[22] However, self-regulatory organizations can improve this ability through learning from best practices and successful cases of collective action initiatives. Indeed, "self-governance is a skill that can either atrophy or strengthen."[23] For example, many countries of the former Eastern Bloc prove that entrepreneurs can learn the "art and science of association." Self-regulatory organizations in these countries draw up their own anti-corruption regulations, develop enforcement procedures, and internally monitor compliance with them.[24] The advantage of self-regulatory organizations is that they represent collective players who can be very effective due to their shared values and common interests. National and regional associations of individual entrepreneurs and chambers of commerce can contribute to this process by developing codes of conduct, compliance programs, and initiatives to improve ethical behavior and culture at all levels of organizations.

Role of Entrepreneurial Organizations in Anti-Corruption Efforts: International Experiences

Successful experiences of international business associations in the fight against corruption can be used as role models for the development of Russian practices of collective action. In the long term, self-regulatory organizations can contribute to the creation of preconditions for the transition from a current model of state corporatism to societal corporatism based on mutual consultations between the government, business communities, and civil society. A collective action approach is widely used by different international development organizations, such as the World Bank Group, the United States Agency for International Development (USAID), the World Economic Forum (WEF), and the Center for International Private Enterprise (CIPE). As the World Economic Forum Report on *Combating Human Trafficking* demonstrates, the private sector can be very efficient in fighting against organized crime and corruption.[25] For instance, this report indicates that "public–private partnerships are the wave of the future and will link business, government and civil society together in entrepreneurial collaborations and resource sharing."[26]

Massimo Mantovani distinguishes four types of collective action initiatives.[27] The first type is anti-corruption declarations that represent short-term initiatives for specific projects or agreements. The second type is principle-based initiatives that involve long-term joint anti-corruption programs developed by multiple stakeholders. The third type includes integrity pacts that represent formal written agreements against bribery between customers and companies. Finally, the fourth type entails multi-stakeholder, certifying business coalitions that promote standards of business conduct within a certain industry or country. These collective action initiatives can be divided into two groups according to their short-term or long-term nature. Transparency and integrity pacts represent short-term initiatives. A good example is the development of the commercial ethics pacts in Georgia, Nicaragua, Panama, and Paraguay by a coalition of businesses, public authorities, and civil society.[28] These pacts are based on ethical principles and a set of actions taken by stakeholders to promote transparency and accountability in the relations between private and public organizations. For example, in Paraguay, the Commercial Ethics Pact requires businesses to attend special training sessions and provide records that show compliance with legal and tax requirements. In cooperation with the Inter-American Development Bank, the Paraguay Commercial Ethics Pact also implemented a certification system for businesses based on their transparency.

Longer-term collective action includes principle-based initiatives and multi-stakeholder business coalitions. The World-Economic Forum Partnering Against Corruption Initiative (PACI) is a good example of international principle-based initiatives. It represents a multinational and multi-sector task force intended to help businesses eliminate corruption, enhance their commitment to counter bribing, and improve their ethical standards. The PACI Principles "serve as a call to action for businesses around the world to join collective action initiatives, which increase public trust in business, deliver fair markets and level the playing field by fighting corruption."[29] The PACI initiative recognizes the importance of a multi-stakeholder, collaborative approach to combat corruption.

The Center for International Private Enterprise (CIPE), one of the core institutes of the National Endowment for Democracy, focuses on assisting developing countries in building multi-stakeholder business coalitions to fight against corruption. CIPE makes significant efforts to develop partnerships with local business associations, chambers of commerce, and think tanks to promote accountability in the private and public sectors in developing countries. For example, CIPE's projects were devoted to building the capacity of the Bangladesh Women's Chamber of Commerce and Industry, reforming the Pakistani Trade Organizations Ordinance, and assisting the Thai Institute of Directors in adopting the Collective Action against Corruption Declaration. Recognizing the importance of strengthening entrepreneurial organizations, CIPE developed governance principles for business associations and chambers of commerce, which were used in many countries.[30]

However, multi-stakeholder coalitions are not limited to business associations, they also include a wide variety of civil society organizations. For example, the United Nations Center for International Crime Prevention (UNCICP) proposes an integrated approach to incorporating social mechanisms to hold public administration accountable.[31] The UNCICP approach relies on civil society and business organizations as safeguards to monitor government agencies on a regular basis. The UNCICP pilot projects included the formation of social-control boards consisting of civil society representatives elected by neighborhood councils in Merida (Venezuela), Santiago (Chile), San Jose (the United States), and Costa Rica. Members of these social-control boards received special training from the UNCICP and were entrusted with the monitoring of public agencies' performance and proposing reforms based on citizens' complaints about public service delivery. The introduction of these social-control boards had a positive impact on the frequency of corruption, transparency, citizens' access to public institutions, and effectiveness in service delivery of the related public agencies. For example, social-control boards within the police force in the city of San Jose, the municipal governments in Merida and Santiago, and the judicial sectors in Costa Rica and Chile were responsible for the simplification of administrative procedures, a significant reduction in administrative discretion of public officials, the enhancement of citizens' access to information, and an increase in quality standards in public service delivery.[32]

Importantly, women's grassroots organizations have been increasingly active in providing societal accountability in developing countries. These organizations bring corruption and violations against women's rights to the attention of the appropriate authorities. The 2012 United Nations Development Programme

Report recommends supporting the institutionalization of successful female grassroots practices, funding women's organizations that develop and implement local anti-corruption programs, and promoting their partnerships with research institutions engaged in fighting against corruption.[33] Women's grassroots groups have a wide range of instruments that have proved to be successful in providing societal accountability. For instance, they can pursue a legal recourse, report corruption to public authorities, participate in local governments, educate communities on anti-corruption compliance, engage the media, mobilize female activists, and organize their collective action.

A good example of the role that women's organizations can play in the fight against corruption is the Balkan Coalition of Women's Business Associations. It was originally created in 2004 as part of a regional project in Romania conducted by the Center for International Private Enterprise. Over time, it evolved into a network of women's business associations from several countries. Currently, the network includes women's business associations from Central and Eastern European countries, such as Albania, Bosnia and Herzegovina, Bulgaria, Croatia, Greece, Kosovo, Macedonia, Serbia, and Romania. The Balkan Coalition of Women's Business Associations serves as an advocate for gender equality, a transparent business climate, and accountable public administration. Women's business associations submit protests to the government against excessive regulations and organize special trainings, seminars, and education programs for women on leadership, entrepreneurship, and citizens' rights. Their key objective is to support female entrepreneurs and give them a voice in the political sphere. Recognizing the fact that corruption disproportionately affects women, they focus on encouraging their members to be actively involved in anti-corruption efforts.[34] The experience of the coalition demonstrates how training, seminars, and education programs on anti-corruption compliance organized by women's business associations help female entrepreneurs protect their rights.

The rapid development of Balkan women's business associations and their success in mobilizing female entrepreneurs from different countries in this region can be a role model for other regions. At the beginning of their post-communist transition, the former Eastern Bloc countries faced severe challenges for entrepreneurial development, including the absence of independent business associations, especially women's organizations, and the lack of a general culture of associations. As Cornelia Rotaru notes, "Prior to 1989, no independent social associations were allowed in Central and Eastern European countries" because the Communist Party considered any free association among citizens a threat to the regime.[35] Due to this fear, the communist regime allowed each country to have only one women's association under the Party's control.[36] In comparison, in 2010, Romania had more than 60 women's associations and Albania had 64 women's organizations that were actively engaged in "increasing membership, opening branches in other territories, and developing networks of similar organizations both nationally and regionally."[37]

The Balkan experience shows the importance of collective action by women's grassroots groups and business associations against corruption. In the Balkan case, cooperation between different women's organizations expands beyond the national borders, which allows them to participate in regional politics. In comparison, in Russia, women entrepreneurs are not actively involved in anticorruption efforts. To a large extent, differences between Balkan and Russian entrepreneurial organizations and women's business associations, in particular, can be explained by various trajectories of their political regimes. In the 2000s, the Balkan countries managed to transform their communist regimes and centralized economies into pluralist democracies and market economies, while Russia was gradually sliding back toward authoritarianism.

Russian business associations focus their activities mostly on pursuing private interests, often at the expense of the interests of the entrepreneurial community as a whole. John Sullivan, Kim Eric Bettcher, and Aleksandr Shkolnikov refer to such organizations as redistributive associations.[38] They have a negative connotation due to their rent-seeking activities. Unlike market-promoting associations, they are not interested in improving the business environment and decreasing corruption in the economy. Quite the opposite, redistributive associations often participate in informal activities by taking advantage of their crony relations with the government. The prevalence of redistributive associations in contemporary Russia is explained by a confluence of historical, political, and social factors that shaped and constrained entrepreneurial organizations in the national economy.

Emergence of Russian Self-Regulatory Organizations in the Private Sector

Entrepreneurial organizations in the Russian Empire emerged relatively late in comparison with Western European countries, which is explained by the late industrial development and mobilization of the bourgeoisie. The first entrepreneurial organizations in Russia emerged in the second half of the nineteenth century. They borrowed most of their organizational structures and key principles from the already existing business organizations in Western countries, mainly Germany. In a very short period, they multiplied across the country. This process was fueled by the need of industrialists and entrepreneurs to represent their interests in the government.

At the beginning of the twentieth century, Russian entrepreneurial associations became powerful representative institutions. Their main objectives were to direct economic policy in the interests of industrialists and business groups and to serve as mediators between the state, entrepreneurs, and the public. To achieve these objectives, they used a wide variety of mechanisms, including filing petitions to government agencies, influencing public opinion through publications, and lobbying government officials. To distribute their views on economic policy, multiple self-regulatory organizations extensively published annual reports, bulletins, and special journals devoted to industrial and entrepreneurial development. However, the growth of self-regulatory organizations in Russia was interrupted by the Revolution of 1917. The Soviet political system considered entrepreneurial organizations a phenomenon of a capitalist system.[39] As a result, self-regulatory organizations were closed and only began to re-emerge after the collapse of the Soviet Union.

The first Russian entrepreneurial organizations were organized in the form of stock exchanges, with commodity committees as their permanent elected bodies. They represented commercial and industrial interests in the political sphere. For example, the 1870 statute of the Moscow stock exchange clearly defined its representational functions. According to paragraph 21 of this statute,

> an elected stock exchange committee is (1) to apply to public authorities for permits related to emerging trade and industrial needs, as well as to eliminate inconveniences that resulted from any orders or statutes regulating trade and industries; and (2) to give all kinds of suggestions to the Government to provide benefits and prosperity to trade and industry.[40]

Although state intervention in the activities of the Russian stock exchanges was comparatively limited, they were under control of public authorities. Stock exchanges comprised the largest group of collective business organizations in Russia.

Another form of self-regulatory organizations was represented by congresses of industries and commerce. The first congresses were held in Moscow in 1865, Saint Petersburg in 1870, and Nizhny Novgorod in 1896.[41] These congresses united entrepreneurs from all over the country. Their main task was to provide a platform for joint discussions of major problems in different industries. Congresses of industries and commerce also provided an opportunity for entrepreneurs to demand benefits and privileges from the government and advocate for protectionist policies. Participation of higher public officials in these congresses demonstrates their willingness to cooperate with the entrepreneurial circles. By the beginning of World War I, there were about 70 congresses of industries and commerce in Russia.[42] Their emergence gave a powerful impetus to industrial development.

At the beginning of the twentieth century, the first Russian chambers of commerce were organized to protect domestic industries and develop economic ties with foreign countries. They were also engaged in information exchange with analogous organizations in Western countries and represented the interests of Russian industrialists in international markets. In 1909, the Russian-English Chamber of Commerce was founded in Saint Petersburg. It had 433 members, including 27 industrial organizations and 98 enterprises.[43] Following its example, other chambers of commerce adopted their charters, namely, the Russian-Belgian Chamber of Commerce (1909), the Slav Chamber of Commerce (1909), the Russian-Italian Chamber of Commerce (1911), the Russian-French Chamber of Commerce (1911), and the Russian-American Chamber of Commerce (1913). Yet, their significance for entrepreneurs and small businesses was very limited because they represented the interests of large companies that were engaged in international trade.

"Entrepreneurial Spring" 121

In the nineteenth century, one of the most important characteristics of business associations in Russia was the lack of special laws regulating their organization and activities.[44] For a long time, various industrial ministries monitored entrepreneurial organizations based on different regulations. Only in 1906 did Russia's legislators adopt a special law on entrepreneurial organizations that universalized these regulations. For example, according to this law, all entrepreneurial organizations were subject to a mandatory application and registration process based on a set of official rules.[45] One of the advantages of this law was the formalization of Russian entrepreneurial organizations through the adoption of charters and normative documents. Figure 6.1 demonstrates an increase in registered charters by different types of entrepreneurial organizations: stock exchanges, chambers of commerce, congresses of industries and trade, and unions of industrialists and entrepreneurs.

In the second half of the nineteenth century, stock exchanges played the leading role in the representation of entrepreneurs and industrialists in the political sphere. Beginning in the twentieth century, their role was undertaken by congresses of industrialists and entrepreneurs. By the Russian Revolution of 1917, their number exceeded 70.[46] Interestingly, congresses of industrialists and entrepreneurs in Saint Petersburg, then Russia's capital, emerged relatively late in comparison with other large cities, such as Moscow, Yekaterinburg, Kharkov, and Odessa. For a very long period, entrepreneurs and industrialists in Saint Petersburg did not have influential representative organizations.

In his research on Russia's entrepreneurial organizations in the late nineteenth and early twentieth centuries, Yurii Tikhomirov proposes two reasons for the

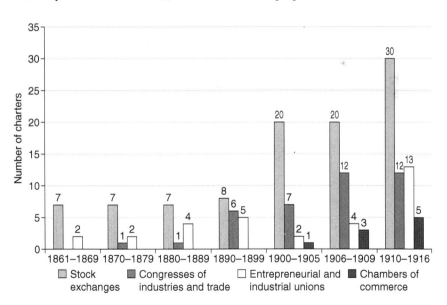

Figure 6.1 The number of charters adopted by business organizations in the Russian Empire in 1861–1916.

relatively late emergence of congresses of industrialists and entrepreneurs in Saint Petersburg.[47] First, the market position of metropolitan businesses was better than in other cities due to stable and solvent demand on their goods and services from the government and nobility in the capital. The second reason is related to the use of corrupt practices by businesses in the capital. Thus, Tikhomirov argues that "metropolitan industrialists and entrepreneurs [of Saint Petersburg] took advantage of their location in the capital to form personal connections with high-ranking officials, which allowed them to successfully resolve all problems confronting their businesses."[48]

Other historical studies of Russian entrepreneurship also point to the spread of informal practices in the capital. For example, William Blackwell notes that despite their extensive foreign connections and access to financial capital, "the Saint Petersburg entrepreneurs continued to live under the shadow of the Leviathan, and were more closely 'intertwined' with the tsarist bureaucracy than any other entrepreneurial group in the Russian Empire."[49] Interestingly, the contemporary survey conducted for this book also shows that entrepreneurs in Moscow, Russia's current capital city, tend to use corrupt practices, such as "grease" payments and personal connections with public officials, more often than in Saint Petersburg and Karelia.

At the end of the nineteenth century, entrepreneurs in large provincial cities were facing serious administrative problems which they often could not solve on their own. This is why they felt it necessary to create collective organizations in the form of congresses of industries and trade to represent their interests in the relations with state agencies. To resolve administrative problems, congresses of industries and trade often filed petitions to government agencies. Petitions were also a very effective way to give recommendations about economic and industrial policies to the government. Importantly, congresses of industries and trade worked in close cooperation with government agencies; sometimes they even included public officials as their members. The fact that the majority of petitions submitted by congresses of industries and trade were satisfied by the government points to their efficient cooperation.

Congresses of industries and trade had a wide range of instruments to enroll entrepreneurs as their members and influence public opinion about their activities. For example, they used their legislative right to organize libraries, exhibitions, museums, lectures, and educational courses, as well as the right to publish journals and books.[50] Importantly, in order to argumentatively present their perspectives on economic development before the government, entrepreneurial organizations invited distinguished experts, economists, jurists, and historians to participate in open discussions about business issues and problems.[51] These discussions were analogous to roundtables and forums used by contemporary self-regulatory organizations.

In order to form favorable public opinion about entrepreneurship, business organizations cooperated with publicists and journalists who specialized in economic policies. Their articles, reviews, and analytical and statistical reports were aimed at demonstrating a positive impact of entrepreneurship on social well-being. Business organizations owned numerous periodic sources, journals, bulletins, and newspapers, which constituted an important element in their system of public relations. In the 1900s, *Industry and Trade*, *The Southern Russian Mining Bulletin*, and *The Bulletin of Gold and Mining Industries* were among the most influential journals in the entrepreneurial circles, with the largest circulation of 2,000, 1,500, and 500 copies, respectively.[52] They were used to broadcast views of entrepreneurs about important economic issues and policies.

However, an analysis of publishing activities of congresses of industries and trade in Russia demonstrates that the majority of them represented the interests of large and medium-sized businesses and did not pay sufficient attention to issues that confronted small businesses and handicraft entrepreneurs. For example, the journal *Industry and Trade*, owned by the Board of the Congress of Industries and Trade, which was one of the largest entrepreneurial organizations in Russia, published only 12 articles about small businesses, handicraft production, and cooperatives between 1908 and 1917.[53] Most articles were devoted to issues of industries and trade in Russian regions, international trade, and the development of economic ties with foreign countries. Some entrepreneurial organizations, however, took significant efforts to enroll entrepreneurs and handicraft producers as their members. In 1910, there were 143 business organizations, including 36 organizations representing the interests of entrepreneurs in Russia.[54] Overall, entrepreneurial organizations were an important element in the system of the relations between the government and business capital. They had a significant impact on the nature and dynamics of Russia's industrial modernization and economic development at the national and regional levels. Their successful experiences as mediators between the state, entrepreneurs, and the public can serve as a role model for contemporary self-regulatory organizations in Russia.

Contemporary Russian Self-Regulatory Organizations and Their Anti-Corruption Activities

In contemporary Russia, self-regulatory organizations have gone through several development phases. Andrey Kiniakin distinguishes three waves of the re-emergence of Russian entrepreneurial organizations after the collapse of the Soviet Union.[55] The first wave began in the late 1980s and early 1990s. It was related to the structural transformation process in the political and economic spheres. The reorganization of the economy led to the emergence of national entrepreneurial associations that represented mainly the interests of large businesses. They included the Russian Union of Industrialists and Entrepreneurs, the Chamber of Commerce of the Russian Federation, and the Agrarian Union of Russia. The second wave in 1993–1997 was characterized by the acceleration of self-regulatory processes in the entrepreneurial sector that led to the formation of numerous professional and business associations, such as the Association of Privatized Enterprises and the Federation of Russian Producers. Finally, beginning in the early 2000s, the third wave was marked by the emergence of entrepreneurial organizations that represented the interests of small and medium-sized businesses, such as the Association of Entrepreneurs OPORA Russia.

Russian entrepreneurial organizations can be divided in three major types depending on their industrial status: (1) inter-industry cross-sector associations of entrepreneurs; (2) chambers of commerce; and (3) professional business associations. Table 6.2 describes their key anti-corruption functions.

According to the Ministry of Labor and Social Insurance, there were more than 250 self-regulatory organizations in Russia in 2015.[56] However, only a limited number of them had sufficient resources and social capital to promote the interests of their members in the political system. The largest and most influential cross-sector associations, with wide networks of regional offices, include the Russian Union of Industrialists and Entrepreneurs, the Association of Entrepreneurs OPORA Russia, the Russian Chamber of Commerce and Industry, and the Russian Public Organization *Delovaya Rossiya* (Business Russia).

Table 6.2 Types of contemporary self-regulatory organizations in Russia

Type	Key anti-corruption function	Examples of organizations
Inter-industry cross-sector associations of entrepreneurs	Development of proposals to the government and business community on how to create an entrepreneur-friendly environment in Russia and eliminate administrative barriers in different industries and sectors of the economy	The Russian Union of Industrialists and Entrepreneurs, the Association of Entrepreneurs OPORA Russia, the Union of Entrepreneurs in Saint Petersburg
Chambers of commerce	Development of standards for professional services in certain market segments, which determine a role model for business conduct, including issues of ethics and anti-corruption procedures	The Chamber of Commerce and Industry of the Russian Federation and regional chambers of commerce
Professional and business associations	Control and oversight over practices in certain industries (business associations) or occupations (professional associations)	The Russian Association of Lawyers, the Association of Pollock Fishers, the Association of Fertilizer Producers, the Russian Union of Leather Producers and Shoe Manufacturers, and other similar organizations

The Russian Union of Industrialists and Entrepreneurs was one of the first entrepreneurial organizations to initiate joint efforts and cooperation of the business community to combat corruption in the private sector. In early 2012, the annual Congress of the Russian Union of Industrialists and Entrepreneurs adopted fundamental principles of anti-corruption compliance for its members. In late 2012, these principles laid the basis for the Anti-Corruption Charter of Russian Businesses. Originally, it was signed by the largest entrepreneurial organizations. According to the Anti-Corruption Charter,

> Russian business[es] and employer associations that are Parties to this Charter, recognizing the need for targeted and consistent efforts to promote this Charter among their members, shall encourage the development and implementation of best corporate practices, such as performance evaluation and reputation enhancement systems, including through corporate non-financial social reporting.[57]

Not only entrepreneurial organizations, but also any domestic or foreign company can join the Anti-Corruption Charter.

According to the Anti-Corruption Charter, businesses are to develop and implement special anti-corruption programs and policies that regulate their internal activities and their external relations with other companies and public authorities. Major policies to be implemented by businesses include rejecting illegal preferences and benefits, supporting transparent and open procurement procedures, introducing rigorous financial control and auditing, providing anti-corruption training and education of staff, promoting law enforcement and cooperation with public authorities, disseminating anti-corruption information, and combating bribery of foreign public officials and officials of international public organizations. The signatories formed the Joint Committee for the Implementation of the Anti-Corruption Charter. In 2013, the Committee developed guidelines for assessing the compliance of businesses with the Anti-Corruption Charter. At its first meeting, the Committee approved the Consolidated Registry in the form of an automated database of organizations and businesses that joined the Anti-Corruption Charter. Figure 6.2 shows their regional distribution in 2015.

The Central federal district is the leading region, with the largest number of organizations that signed the Anti-Corruption Charter of Russian businesses. Most signatories from this district are located in Moscow. As of 2015, 87 organizations and businesses from Moscow signed the Anti-Corruption Charter. In Saint Petersburg, which is located in the North-western federal district, only ten organizations joined the Charter. In the Karelian capital city of Petrozavodsk, only one organization joined it in 2015. As of 2016, the Anti-Corruption Charter had been signed by 826 organizations and businesses.[58] Yet, an analysis of the Consolidated Registry shows that the vast majority of the signatories are open stock companies and large enterprises. Microenterprises and individual entrepreneurs comprised less than 8 percent of the total number of the Charter signatories in 2016.[59]

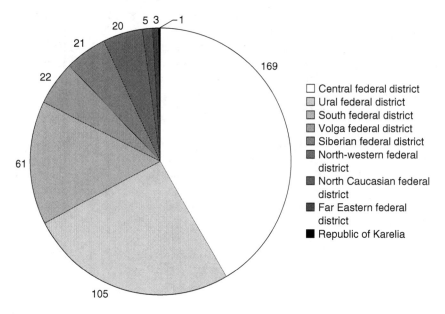

Figure 6.2 The number of signatories of the Anti-Corruption Charter of Russian Businesses, 2015.

This finding supports the results of the interviews conducted for this study, according to which most individual entrepreneurs and microenterprises are not involved in anti-corruption efforts. To a large extent, it can be explained by their limited size and resources. As the Council of Europe report, *Corruption Risks and Protection Mechanisms for Entrepreneurs in the Russian Federation*, indicates, "due to their size and scope of operations, SMEs [small and medium-sized enterprises] are often driven by the values of the owner" and have rather informal communication structures.[60] As a result, the implementation of codes of conduct based on the work split between different levels of management cannot be applied to SMEs because their organizational structures often consist of a single unit.

Another reason for the observed low involvement of entrepreneurs in anti-corruption initiatives is the ineffectiveness of business associations in organizing collective action. Most microenterprises and entrepreneurs do not track the development of anti-corruption initiatives themselves. This suggests that the only possible way for them to participate in the Anti-Corruption Charter is through their regional entrepreneurial organizations. After signing the Charter, regional entrepreneurial organizations should disseminate information about anti-corruption principles among microenterprises, individual entrepreneurs, and other entities. This, however, poses a severe challenge for entrepreneurial organizations because they often lack effective channels of information dissemination.

The interviews with entrepreneurs in Moscow, Saint Petersburg, and Karelia provide strong evidence that they do not have sufficient information about regional business associations, in general, and their anti-corruption activities, in particular. A similar situation was observed in other Russian regions. For example, an empirical study of Russian entrepreneurial organizations in the Volgograd region found that only a small fraction of entrepreneurs (3 percent of the total number of respondents) could find articles about local business associations in the regional media and most of them had little information about anti-corruption initiatives.[61] Taking this into account, regional business organizations should engage the media more effectively to target microenterprises and individual entrepreneurs.

A relatively low level of personal involvement of entrepreneurs in anti-corruption efforts is directly related to the current focus of Russian business associations on large and medium-sized businesses. This finding is consistent with other empirical studies of business associations in different Russian regions.[62] The interests of entrepreneurs and microenterprises are underrepresented in the economic and political spheres. Their inability to mobilize themselves in collective action leads to situations where their rights are systematically violated by public officials and regulatory agencies that impose additional administrative barriers and extort informal payments for routine government actions.

A 2016 report by the Wilfred Martens Center for European Studies and the Free Russia Foundation points to a rapidly deteriorating economic environment for Russian businesses and entrepreneurs who increasingly suffer from administrative corruption and predatory behavior of regulatory agencies.[63] One of the recent examples is the 2016 demolition of *kiosks* (small shops) by the authorities in Moscow and other major cities under the pretense of improving the urban scenery. Hundreds of entrepreneurs lost their bakeries, flower stands, and coffee shops. They were demolished by bulldozers in the middle of the night, which later came to be known as "the Night of the Long Shovels." Despite the public outcry over the demolition of the kiosks, individual protests failed to mobilize massive numbers of entrepreneurs. The same situation was observed with the 2015 introduction of additional burdensome fees on large trucks. The truckers "staged desperate and disparate acts of protest, but none of them made explicit political demands."[64] The failure of local protests of entrepreneurs not only demonstrates a low level of cohesion within the Russian business community, but also indicates the lack of effective leadership on the part of entrepreneurial organizations.

Weaknesses of Russian Self-Regulatory Organizations

According to regional surveys of entrepreneurs in Russia, most of them consider business associations mainly as consulting and lobbying organizations. These functions received scores of 4.36 and 4.00, respectively, on a 7-point scale, with 1 meaning the lowest importance and 7 the highest.[65] Also, Russian business associations received relatively low scores on the development of behavioral standards and ethical norms within industries and regions (a score of 2.99).[66] This finding confirms the results of the interviews with entrepreneurs from Moscow, Saint Petersburg, and Karelia who consider that Russian self-regulatory organizations are not efficient as moral and ethical role models.

An analysis of Russian self-regulatory organizations demonstrates that they have severe weaknesses that restrict their capacity to mobilize entrepreneurs and organize collective action against corruption. The most significant drawback is related to their organizational structure. A comparative study of Russian and German business associations demonstrates that they have similar organizational structures.[67] Despite these structural similarities, Russian and German business associations have different operational principles. In both countries, practices of reconciling economic and political interests are based on the neo-corporatist model that requires a partnership between the government and business stakeholders. However, the nature of this partnership differs significantly in the Russian and German political systems. While in Germany, this partnership is based on a pluralist democracy and is predominantly liberal, the Russian corporatism is characterized by authoritarian tendencies with elements of patron-client relations.[68] In Russia, this partnership mostly involves asymmetric relations where business associations provide their political support for the regime in exchange for government contracts and other favors for their members.

A recent study of Russian business associations demonstrates the tendency of an increasing one-sidedness in the dialogue between public agencies and businesses, which often turns into a monologue of the highly centralized government.[69] The interviews with entrepreneurs conducted in Moscow, Saint Petersburg, and Karelia illustrate this argument by showing how Russian business associations are used by their members to receive advantages and favorable treatment from the government. For example, an entrepreneur from Karelia expressed this idea in the following way:

> I do not trust entrepreneurial organizations at the federal level, especially if they are closely linked to government authorities. In most cases, they serve as "a career elevator" for their members. This means that if you demonstrate your loyalty and don't criticize the government, then you can get a promotion within the organization, make contacts with important people, and as a result, receive some privileges from the government, such as access to resources or procurement contracts. This is why when my rights are violated by government agencies, I never ask these organizations for help, but prefer to solve these problems on my own.

Another weakness is the lack of business associations that focus on individual entrepreneurs and microenterprises. The empirical study of business associations in Russian regions conducted by Andrei Yakovlev and Andrei Govorun showed that they mainly focus on companies with high revenues and businesses located in regional capital cities.[70] The interviews with entrepreneurs from Karelia confirm this conclusion. A Karelian owner of a transportation company puts it in the following way:

> National entrepreneurial associations are organizations affiliated with government agencies. All government agencies are working exclusively with large and medium-sized enterprises, and sometimes with small business with high turnovers. They do not protect the interests of entrepreneurs and microenterprises, with a turnover of less than 120 million rubles [about $1.7 million]. Officials are not interested in working with them as they cannot give large kickbacks. Because of corruption, microenterprises receive no additional support from government agencies.

The same situation was found in Saint Petersburg. An interview with a hostel owner from Saint Petersburg demonstrated that he shares similar problems with Karelian entrepreneurs:

> Programs for microenterprises should be developed at the municipal level. For example, in Saint Petersburg, there are 111 municipalities. However, when we came to the administrative heads of the municipalities, they told us that they had no funds. The federal budget allocates 2 billion rubles [about $286 million] annually to support small businesses, but microenterprises at the municipal level receive nothing. We are trying to unite microenterprises in the municipalities. The bureaucratic system ignores their interests and no one pays attention to them in the national entrepreneurial organizations. Entrepreneurs do not believe that these organizations can protect their rights. An alternative solution might be mobilizing microenterprises at the municipal level.

The majority of business associations created at the federal and regional levels are initiated by the government. A study of entrepreneurial organizations in the Volgograd region suggests that most entrepreneurial organizations are branches of national pro-government organizations.[71] As the study notes,

> The creation of such 'state' structures (represented at the regional level by such well-known organizations as the Volgograd Chamber of Commerce, OPORA Russia, the Volgograd Center for Protection and Development of Businesses, etc.) leads to the situation where small businesses perceive them as closed, inaccessible, and bureaucratic institutions with whom it is better not to have any dealings.[72]

In all Russian regions, the number of grassroots business associations initiated and organized by individual entrepreneurs themselves remains extremely low.

The interviews conducted in Moscow, Saint Petersburg, and Karelia identified that business associations in Russia suffer from numerous inefficiencies in their operational activities. The most important drawbacks include inefficient cooperation with the media, insufficient distribution of information about their activities among the public and individual entrepreneurs, restricted access to their resources and educational programs based on membership, and the lack of close cooperation between business associations and civil society organizations. These factors explain why many entrepreneurs are not actively involved in their activities and express unenthusiastic views about their creation. Another problem of Russian self-regulatory organizations is a low level of female entrepreneurs' engagement in their activities and the lack of attention to their specific problems and challenges.

A key feature of Russia's entrepreneurial organizations is the prevalence of redistributive over market-promoting associations. Redistributive associations focus on private interests pursued at the expense of the interests of the business community as a whole. This is especially obvious in the case of elite business associations that are directly or indirectly controlled by the government. Conversely, only a few grassroots entrepreneurial organizations with market-promoting objectives are dedicated to the protection of small businesses against oppression by the government. The dominance of redistributive associations in Russia can be explained by the recent regime shift toward authoritarianism, a low level of civil society development, and government incentives provided for elite business associations to engage in rent-seeking activities. In this way, the Russian government encourages "unproductive entrepreneurship." William Baumol, who coined this term in 1990, noted that "when there is a relatively high benefit to engaging in unproductive activities (e.g., rent-seeking and crime), entrepreneurs will take advantage of those opportunities."[73] In the case of Russia, elite business associations take advantage of the system of crony state capitalism to receive favors from the government in exchange for loyalty.

The prevalence of rent-seeking activities of Russian business associations leads to a deteriorating environment for the whole entrepreneurial community. On a more positive note, the allocation of entrepreneurship between productive and unproductive activities is not stagnant. According to Baumol, it can change over time together with the relative pay-offs assigned by society to such activities.[74] As the relative pay-offs are determined by both private and public actors, the focus of business associations on rent-seeking activities can shift toward market-promoting objectives through internal sources, such as leadership, or external sources, such as political, social, and international pressures. Reforming self-regulatory organizations is critically important for the creation of a business-friendly environment and climate in the Russian economy.

Notes

1 Shelley, L. I. *Dirty Entanglements: Corruption, Crime, and Terrorism* (Cambridge: Cambridge University Press, 2014), p. 71.
2 The investigation was dubbed the "*La Línea*" case because public officials from this customs corruption ring used a telephone number they called 'the line' (*la línea* in

Spanish) to bribe businesses in exchange for reduced import tariffs. This case led to the arrest of former president Pérez Molina and vice president Roxana Baldetti.
3 Washington Office on Latin America. *International Commission against Impunity in Guatemala (CICIG)* (Washington, DC: Washington Office on Latin America, 2015), p. 18.
4 Cited in Gagne, D. Claudia Paz y Paz, on the Revolution She Started in Guatemala. *InSight Crime: Investigation and Analysis of Organized Crime.* (2016). Available at: www.insightcrime.org/news-analysis/claudia-paz-y-paz-and-the-revolution-she-started-in-guatemala
5 Newman, K., & Fuentes, R. In Guatemala, a Justice Experiment Gone Right. *Al Jazeera America.* (2015). Available at: http://america.aljazeera.com/articles/2015/9/5/in-guatemala-a-justice-experiment-gone-right.html
6 Phillips, D. 'Operation Carwash' in Brazil Causes Normally Staid Business Meeting to Go off Script. *Washington Post*, November 17, 2014.
7 O'Donnell, G. A. Horizontal Accountability in New Democracies. *Journal of Democracy*, *9*(3) (1998), 112–126.
8 Ibid., p. 113.
9 Smulovitz, C., & Peruzzotti, E. Societal Accountability in Latin America. *Journal of Democracy*, *11*(4) (2000), 147–158.
10 Ibid., p. 150.
11 World Bank. *Fighting Corruption Through Collective Action: A Guide for Business* (Washington, DC: The World Bank, 2008), p. 4.
12 Ibid.
13 World Economic Forum. *The Global Competitiveness Report 2015–2016* (Geneva: World Economic Forum, 2015), p. 307.
14 Ibid.
15 See, for example, Albanese, J. S. *Transnational Crime and the 21st Century: Criminal Enterprise, Corruption, and Opportunity* (New York: Oxford University Press, 2011); Nichols, P. M. Multiple Communities and Controlling Corruption, *Journal of Business Ethics*, *88*(4) (2009), 805–813.
16 Tran, N. A. Corruption and Human Development, Working Paper series No. 2008/07. DEPOCEN (2008), p. 1. Available at: www.depocenwp.org/upload/pubs/Tran NgocAnh/ Corruption_and_Human_Development_-_Policy_Journal_DEPOCENWP.pdf
17 See, for example, Collins, J. D., Uhlenbruck, K., & Rodriguez, P. Why Firms Engage in Corruption: A Top Management Perspective, *Journal of Business Ethics*, *87*(1) (2009), 89–108; Powpaka, S. Factors Affecting Managers' Decision to Bribe: An Empirical Investigation, *Journal of Business Ethics*, *40*(3) (2002), 227–246.
18 See, for example, Mària, J. F., & Arenas, D. Societal Ethos and Economic Development Organizations in Nicaragua, *Journal of Business Ethics*, *88*(S2) (2009), 231–244; Morell, J., & Bettcher, K. E. *Approaches to Collective Action: How Businesses Together Can Lead the Fight Against Corruption* (Washington, DC: Center for International Private Enterprise, 2013); Sullivan, J. D., & Shkolnikov, A. *Combating Corruption: Private Sector Perspectives and Solutions* (Washington, DC: Center for International Private Enterprise, 2004).
19 Donaldson, T., & Dunfee, T. W. Toward a Unified Conception of Business Ethics: Integrative Social Contracts Theory. *The Academy of Management Review*, *19*(2) (1994), 595.
20 Ostrom, E. *Governing the Commons: The Evolution of Institutions for Collective Action* (Cambridge: Cambridge University Press, 1990).
21 For in-depth analysis of key principles of integrative social contract theory and its applications to anti-corruption action, see Donaldson & Dunfee, op. cit., pp. 252–284.
22 Boettke, P. J., Lemke, J. S., & Palagashvili, L. Polycentricity, Self-governance, and the Art & Science of Association. *The Review of Austrian Economics*, *28*(3) (2015), 315.
23 Ibid.

24 Center for International Private Enterprise. *Romanian Business Association Development Project Final Report, 2000–2003* (Washington, DC: Center for International Private Enterprise, 2003).
25 World Economic Forum. *Hedging Risk by Combating Human Trafficking: Insights from the Private Sector* (Geneva: World Economic Forum, 2014).
26 Ibid., p. 17.
27 Mantovani, M. The Business Case for Collective Action. In M. Pieth (Ed.), *Collective Action: Innovative Strategies to Prevent Corruption* (pp. 73–80) (Zürich: Dike Publishers, 2012).
28 Petkoski, D., Jarvis, M., & Frauscher, K. Fighting Corruption through Collective Action in Today's Competitive Marketplace. *Ethicsphere*, 5 (2009), 60–61.
29 World Economic Forum. *Partnering Against Corruption Initiative: Global Principles for Countering Corruption* (Geneva: World Economic Forum, 2016), p. 3.
30 Center for International Private Enterprise. *Combating Corruption: A Private Sector Approach* (Washington, DC: Center for International Private Enterprise, 2011).
31 Langseth, P. *Empowering the Victims of Corruption Through Social Control Mechanisms* (Prague: Center for International Crime Prevention, 2001).
32 Ibid.
33 Purushothaman, S., Tobin, T., Vissa, S., & Pillai, P. *Seeing Beyond the State: Grassroots Women's Perspectives on Corruption and Anti-Corruption* (New York: United Nations Development Programme, 2012), pp. 6–9.
34 Rotaru, C. *Women's Business Associations: Experiences from Around the World: Central and Eastern Europe* (Washington, DC: Center for International Private Enterprise, 2010), p. 12.
35 Ibid., p. 10.
36 Ibid.
37 Ibid., p. 11.
38 Sullivan, J., Bettcher, K. E., & Shkolnikov, A. *Business Associations, Business Climate, and Economic Growth: Evidence from Transition Economies* (Washington, DC: Center for International Private Enterprise, 2008).
39 In the *Great Soviet Encyclopedia* (New York: Macmillan Publishing Company, 1976), business associations were defined as "bourgeois organizations that unite capitalists ... so as to increase profitability, trample the rights of workers, do battle with foreign competitors, and manipulate foreign and domestic policies in the interests of monopolistic capital."
40 Rukosuev, E. Organizatsii predprinimatelei v Rossii v kontse XIX – nachale XX vv [in Russian]. *Ural'skii Istoricheskii Vestnik*, 40(3) (2013), 101.
41 Vorontsova, E. *Predprinimatel'skie organizatsii v Rossii: istoriografiya, istochniki, istoriya* [in Russian]. (Moscow: Eterna, 2013), pp. 490–494.
42 Ibid., pp. 196–197.
43 Fedorov, M. *Zhelatel'naya organizatsiya torgovo-promyshlennykh palat. Doklad obrazovannoy pri Sovete s"ezdov Osoboi komissii pod predsedatel'stvom chlena Soveta M.M. Fedorova* [in Russian] (Saint Petersburg, 1909).
44 Tikhomirov, Y. Predprinimatel'skie organizatsii Sankt-Peterburgskoi burzhuazii kontsa XIX – nachala XX vv (doctoral dissertation autoreferat) [in Russian] (Leningrad: Institute of the USSR History of the Academy of Sciences, 1990), p. 8.
45 Vorontsova, op. cit., p. 67.
46 Ibid., p. 371.
47 Tikhomirov, op. cit., p. 8.
48 Ibid.
49 Blackwell, W. The Russian Entrepreneur in the Tsarist Period: An Overview. In G. Guroff & F. V. Carstensen (Eds.), *Entrepreneurship in Imperial Russia and the Soviet Union* (pp. 13–26) (Princeton, NJ: Princeton University Press, 1983), pp. 17–18.

50 Vorontsova, op. cit., p. 197.
51 Ibid., p. 365.
52 Ibid., pp. 204–207.
53 Ibid., p. 367.
54 Rukosuev, op. cit., p. 105.
55 Kiniakin, A. Predprinimatel'skie assotsiatsii v sisteme politicheskogo predstavitel'stva interesov Rossii i Germanii: sravnitel'noe issledovanie (doctoral dissertation autoreferat) [in Russian] (Moscow: The Peoples' Friendship University, 2006).
56 Ministry of Labor and Social Insurance of the Russian Federation. Professional'nye assotsiatsii i ikh chleny [in Russian]. (2015). Available at: http://profstandart.rosmintrud.ru/centralnyj-katalog-professionalnyh-soobsestv
57 Conference of the States Parties to the United Nations Convention against Corruption. The Russian Anti-Corruption Charter for Business (No. CAC/COSP/2013/CRP.8). (2013). Available at: www.unodc.org/documents/treaties/UNCAC/COSP/session5/V1387976e.pdf
58 Anti-Corruption Charter of Russian Businesses. Konsolidirovannyi registr [in Russian]. (2015). Available at: http://against-corruption.ru/ru/reestr.html
59 Ibid.
60 Rupchev, G., Moiny, Y., & Kudryashov, A. *Korruptsionnye riski i mekhanizmy zashchity prav predprinimatelei* [in Russian] (Brussels: Council of Europe, 2014), p. 38.
61 Lobyzenkova, V. *Predprinimatel'skie struktury volgogradskoi oblasti: tendentsii razvitiya i upravleniya* [in Russian] (Volgograd: FGBOU VPO RANXiGS, 2012), p. 102.
62 See, for example, Yakovlev, A., & Govorun, A. Biznes assotsiatsii kak instrument vzaimodeistviya mezhdu pravitel'stvom i predprinimatelyami: rezultaty empiricheskogo analiza [in Russian], *Journal of the New Economic Association*, 9 (2011), 98–127.
63 Zaslavskiy, I. *The Tsar and his Business Serfs: Russian Oligarchs and SMEs did not Surprise Putin at the Elections* (Washington, DC: Wilfred Martens Center for European Studies & Free Russia Foundation, 2016). Available at: www.martenscentre.eu/publications/tsar-and-his-business-serfs-russian-oligarchs-and-smes-did-not-surprise-putin-elections/
64 Ibid., p. 8.
65 Pyle, W. Organized Business, Political Competition, and Property Rights: Evidence from the Russian Federation. *Journal of Law, Economics, & Organization*, 27(1) (2011), 41.
66 Ibid.
67 Kiniakin, op. cit., p. 3.
68 Ibid., p. 4.
69 Poltavskaya, M., & Lobyzenkova, V. *Biznes assotsiatsii v volgogradskoi oblasti* [in Russian] (Volgograd: Volgograd State Medical University, 2011), p. 45.
70 Yakovlev & Govorun, op. cit., p. 124.
71 Lobyzenkova, op. cit., p. 13.
72 Ibid., pp. 18–19.
73 Baumol, W. Entrepreneurship: Productive, Unproductive, and Destructive. *Journal of Political Economy*, 98(5) (1990), 893–921.
74 Ibid., p. 893.

References

Albanese, J. S. (2011). *Transnational Crime and the 21st Century: Criminal Enterprise, Corruption, and Opportunity*. New York: Oxford University Press.
Anti-Corruption Charter of Russian Businesses. (2015). Konsolidirovannyi registr [in Russian]. Available at: http://against-corruption.ru/ru/reestr.html

Baumol, W. (1990). Entrepreneurship: Productive, Unproductive, and Destructive. *Journal of Political Economy*, *98*(5), 893–921.

Blackwell, W. (1983). The Russian Entrepreneur in the Tsarist Period: An Overview. In G. Guroff & F. V. Carstensen (Eds.), *Entrepreneurship in Imperial Russia and the Soviet Union* (pp. 13–26). Princeton, NJ: Princeton University Press.

Boettke, P. J., Lemke, J. S., & Palagashvili, L. (2015). Polycentricity, Self-governance, and the Art & Science of Association. *The Review of Austrian Economics*, *28*(3), 311–335.

Center for International Private Enterprise. (2003). *Romanian Business Association Development Project Final Report, 2000–2003*. Washington, DC: Center for International Private Enterprise.

Center for International Private Enterprise. (2011a). *Combating Corruption: A Private Sector Approach*. Washington, DC: Center for International Private Enterprise.

Center for International Private Enterprise. (2011b). *Final Report to the US Agency for International Development for the Period of September 2002–September 2011*. Washington, DC: Center for International Private Enterprise.

Collins, J. D., Uhlenbruck, K., & Rodriguez, P. (2009). Why Firms Engage in Corruption: A Top Management Perspective. *Journal of Business Ethics*, *87*(1), 89–108.

Conference of the States Parties to the United Nations Convention against Corruption. (2013). *The Russian Anti-Corruption Charter for Business* (No. CAC/COSP/2013/ CRP.8). Available at: www.unodc.org/documents/treaties/UNCAC/COSP/session5/V1387976e.pdf

Donaldson, T., & Dunfee, T. W. (1994). Toward a Unified Conception of Business Ethics: Integrative Social Contracts Theory. *The Academy of Management Review*, *19*(2), 252–284.

Fedorov, M. (1909). *Zhelatel'naya organizatsiya torgovo-promyshlennykh palat. Doklad obrazovannoy pri Sovete s"ezdov Osoboi komissii pod predsedatel'stvom chlena Soveta M.M. Fedorova* [in Russian]. Saint Petersburg.

Gagne, D. (2016, July 29). Claudia Paz y Paz, on the Revolution She Started in Guatemala. *InSight Crime: Investigation and Analysis of Organized Crime*. Available at: www.insightcrime.org/news-analysis/claudia-paz-y-paz-and-the-revolution-she-started-in-guatemala

Great Soviet Encyclopedia. (1976) (3rd edn). New York: Macmillan Publishing Company.

Kiniakin, A. (2006). Predprinimatel'skie assotsiatsii v sisteme politicheskogo predstavitel'stva interesov Rossii i Germanii: sravnitel'noe issledovanie (doctoral dissertation autoreferat) [in Russian]. Moscow: The Peoples' Friendship University.

Langseth, P. (2001). *Empowering the Victims of Corruption Through Social Control Mechanisms*. Prague: Center for International Crime Prevention.

Lobyzenkova, V. (2012). *Predprinimatel'skie struktury volgogradskoi oblasti: tendentsii razvitiya i upravleniya* [in Russian]. Volgograd: FGBOU VPO RANXiGS.

Mantovani, M. (2012). The Business Case for Collective Action. In M. Pieth (Ed.), *Collective Action: Innovative Strategies to Prevent Corruption* (pp. 73–80). Zürich: Dike Publishers.

Màrìa, J. F., & Arenas, D. (2009). Societal Ethos and Economic Development Organizations in Nicaragua. *Journal of Business Ethics*, *88*(S2), 231–244.

Ministry of Labor and Social Insurance of the Russian Federation. (2015). Professional'nye assotsiatsii i ikh chleny [in Russian]. Available at: http://profstandart.rosmintrud.ru/centralnyj-katalog-professionalnyh-soobsestv

Morell, J., & Bettcher, K. E. (2013). *Approaches to Collective Action: How Businesses Together Can Lead the Fight Against Corruption*. Washington, DC: Center for International Private Enterprise.

Newman, K., & Fuentes, R. (2015, September 5). In Guatemala, a Justice Experiment Gone Right. *Al Jazeera America*. Available at: http://america.aljazeera.com/articles/2015/9/5/in-guatemala-a-justice-experiment-gone-right.html

Nichols, P. M. (2009). Multiple Communities and Controlling Corruption. *Journal of Business Ethics*, 88(4), 805–813.

O'Donnell, G. A. (1998). Horizontal Accountability in New Democracies. *Journal of Democracy*, 9(3), 112–126.

Ostrom, E. (1990). *Governing the Commons: The Evolution of Institutions for Collective Action*. Cambridge: Cambridge University Press.

Ovaska, T., & Sobel, R. S. (2005). Entrepreneurship in Post-Socialist Economies. *Journal of Private Enterprise*, 21(Fall), 8–28.

Petkoski, D., Jarvis, M., & Frauscher, K. (2009). Fighting Corruption Through Collective Action in Today's Competitive Marketplace. *Ethicsphere*, 5, 60–61.

Phillips, D. (2014, November 17). "Operation Carwash" in Brazil Causes Normally Staid Business Meeting to Go off Script. *Washington Post*.

Poltavskaya, M., & Lobyzenkova, V. (2011). *Biznes assotsiatsii v volgogradskoi oblasti* [in Russian]. Volgograd: Volgograd State Medical University.

Powpaka, S. (2002). Factors Affecting Managers' Decision to Bribe: An Empirical Investigation. *Journal of Business Ethics*, 40(3), 227–246.

Purushothaman, S., Tobin, T., Vissa, S., & Pillai, P. (2012). *Seeing Beyond the State: Grassroots Women's Perspectives on Corruption and Anti-Corruption*. New York: United Nations Development Programme.

Pyle, W. (2011). Organized Business, Political Competition, and Property Rights: Evidence from the Russian Federation. *Journal of Law, Economics, & Organization*, 27(1), 2–31.

Rotaru, C. (2010). *Women's Business Associations: Experiences from Around the World: Central and Eastern Europe*. Washington, DC: Center for International Private Enterprise.

Rukosuev, E. (2013). Organizatsii predprinimatelei v Rossii v kontse XIX – nachale XX vv [in Russian]. *Ural'skii Istoricheskii Vestnik*, 40(3), 99–109.

Rupchev, G., Moiny, Y., & Kudryashov. (2014). *Korruptsionnye riski i mekhanizmy zashchity prav predprinimatelei* [in Russian]. Brussels: Council of Europe.

Shelley, L. I. (2014). *Dirty Entanglements: Corruption, Crime, and Terrorism*. Cambridge: Cambridge University Press.

Smulovitz, C., & Peruzzotti, E. (2000). Societal Accountability in Latin America. *Journal of Democracy*, 11(4), 147–158.

Sullivan, J., Bettcher, K. E., & Shkolnikov, A. (2008). *Business Associations, Business Climate, and Economic Growth: Evidence from Transition Economies*. Washington, DC: Center for International Private Enterprise.

Sullivan, J. D., & Shkolnikov, A. (2004). *Combating Corruption: Private Sector Perspectives and Solutions*. Washington, DC: Center for International Private Enterprise.

Tikhomirov, Y. (1990). Predprinimatel'skie organizatsii Sankt-Peterburgskoi burzhuazii kontsa XIX – nachala XX vv (doctoral dissertation autoreferat) [in Russian]. Leningrad: Institute of the USSR History of the Academy of Sciences.

Tran, N. A. (2008). Corruption and Human Development, Working Paper series No. 2008/07. DEPOCEN. Available at: www.depocenwp.org/upload/pubs/TranNgocAnh/Corruption_and_Human_Development_-_Policy_Journal_DEPOCENWP.pdf

Vorontsova, E. (2013). *Predprinimatel'skie organizatsii v Rossii: istoriografiya, istochniki, istoriya* [in Russian]. Moscow: Eterna.
Washington Office on Latin America. (2015). *International Commission against Impunity in Guatemala (CICIG)*. Washington, DC: Washington Office on Latin America.
World Bank. (2008). *Fighting Corruption Through Collective Action: A Guide for Business*. Washington, DC: The World Bank.
World Economic Forum. (2014). *Hedging Risk by Combating Human Trafficking: Insights from the Private Sector*. Geneva: World Economic Forum.
World Economic Forum. (2015). *The Global Competitiveness Report 2015–2016*. Geneva: World Economic Forum.
World Economic Forum. (2016). *Partnering Against Corruption Initiative: Global Principles for Countering Corruption*. Geneva: World Economic Forum.
Yakovlev, A., & Govorun, A. (2011). Bizness assotsiatsii kak instrument vzaimodeistviya mezhdu pravitel'stvom i predprinimatelyami: rezultaty empiricheskogo analiza [in Russian]. *Journal of the New Economic Association, 9*, 98–127.
Zaslavskiy, I. (2016). *The Tsar and his Business Serfs: Russian Oligarchs and SMEs did not Surprise Putin at the Elections*. Washington, DC: Wilfred Martens Center for European Studies & Free Russia Foundation.

7 Conclusion
Protecting Endangered Entrepreneurs

The devastating impact of administrative corruption on economic development raises the question of how public and private actors can protect and promote the recovery of entrepreneurs endangered by a hostile institutional environment and burdensome regulatory regime. This chapter addresses this question by focusing on counter-corruption measures in both the public and private sectors. The chapter pays particular attention to public–private partnerships organized to mitigate the problem of corruption in the entrepreneurial sector. The analysis includes a diagnosis of what is wrong with the system, followed by some prognoses for how to fix these issues. In many cases, the proposed solutions represent only partial fixes due to the fact that the best options are not always politically feasible under the existing political regime.

An analysis of gaps in the current anti-corruption legislature in Russia is followed by several proposals. They include amendments of anti-corruption laws, deregulation reforms, and active cooperation with international enforcement agencies. An analysis of anti-corruption initiatives and programs developed in the private sector allows for several suggestions regarding a shift of business associations from redistributive goals toward market-oriented objectives, the promotion of favorable public opinion about self-regulatory organizations, their cooperation with civil society, the creation of a national online portal related to entrepreneurship, and the participation of women's grassroots organizations in collective action against corruption. It is also important to organize and maintain public–private dialogue in the policy-making sphere and public–private partnerships in the form of joint anti-corruption projects.

Counteracting Administrative Corruption in the Public Sector

Over the last decade, Russia has made significant progress in adopting new anti-corruption laws. In 2008, three interconnected federal laws were adopted in Russia. The first law, "On Counteraction to Corruption," established a general framework of anti-corruption regulation. The second law, "On Amendments to Certain Legislative Acts of the Russian Federation in Connection with the Adoption of the Federal Law on Counteraction to Corruption," developed provisions applicable to particular categories of government employees, public officials, judges, members of the State Duma, and persons holding state and municipal offices. Finally, the third law, "On Amendments to Certain Legislative Acts of the Russian Federation in Connection to the Ratification of the United Nations Convention against Corruption and the Criminal Law Convention on Corruption of the Council of Europe," amended the related national laws in accordance with the international conventions. These laws came into force in January 2009 and covered multiple aspects of Russia's anti-corruption regulation.

Although these laws introduced substantial improvements to Russia's anti-corruption legislature, there are still serious legal gaps which require immediate attention from policy-makers, including the criminalization of illegal enrichment, the protection of whistleblowers, and the development of legal mechanisms designed to facilitate asset recovery. In 2006, Russia ratified the United Nations Convention against Corruption, however, not completely. In particular, Russia did not ratify Article 20 of the United Nations Convention on illicit enrichment. Article 20 mandates criminal punishment for officials who fail to reasonably explain the origin of their income and wealth. The Federal Law, "On Counteraction to Corruption," requires state and municipal servants to report to their employer income, property and monetary obligations, which also covers their spouses and minor children. However, Russia has not yet adopted legislative measures necessary to establish illicit enrichment as a criminal offense.

Whistleblowers within public and private organizations play an important role in detecting corrupt practices. Whistleblowing involves high risks of reprisals on the part of accused organizations or persons, meaning that a lack of special programs and legislation in this arena undermines inducements to report misconduct of a fellow employee or superior within the organization. Special provisions on protection of whistleblowers are provided in the United Nations Convention against Corruption (Article 33). Furthermore, financial motivations for whistleblowing make this mechanism work more effectively. For instance, the False Claims Act, which was the first U.S. law adopted specifically to protect whistleblowers, gives financial incentives for people who report corrupt practices. Specifically, they receive a certain percentage of the money recovered or damages won by the government. In general, awards range from 15–30 percent of the total amount recovered under the False Claims Act. It has proved to be a very efficient tool in detecting misconduct of public and private employees. In 2016, the United States Department of Justice recovered over $4.7 billion of stolen money thanks to whistleblowers who filed cases under the Federal False Claims Act.[1]

According to Article 9 of the Federal Law, "On Counteraction to Corruption," a public official who discloses corruption to his employer, the prosecutor's office, or other government agencies is protected by the state. However, this law does not specify concrete measures of such protection. In 2015, a bill aimed at providing specific protection measures for whistleblowers who report corrupt public officials and private companies was introduced in the parliament. Yet, it did not receive enough support in the State Duma. It also remains unclear how effectively the whistleblowing law would be enforced in the case of its enactment. Currently, many agencies prefer to fire corrupt employees instead of reporting them to public authorities because of the potential threat to the organization's reputation. Yet, it is critically important to bring corrupt public officials to justice. As Elena Panfilova, the Chairperson of Transparency International Russia, indicates, "without bringing cases to the attention of the appropriate authorities, it will be impossible to create the system of 'zero tolerance' toward corruption."[2]

Apart from specific anti-corruption laws, policy-makers should be more actively involved in removing excessive bureaucratic procedures and administrative barriers that facilitate informal transactions in Russia's highly-regulated economy. In 2009–2010, the Center for International Private Enterprise together with the United States Agency for International Development (USAID) and Russian chambers of commerce in eight regions (Saratov, Astrakhan, Volgograd, Kirov, Smolensk, Novosibirsk, Perm, and Khabarovsk) conducted a project entitled *Improving Regulation to Reduce Corruption*. This project focused on the identification of legal loopholes, excessive bureaucratic discretion, and other issues in the laws guiding the relations between regulatory agencies and entrepreneurs. The project's proposals contain eight recommendations:

- the enactment of the Federal Law on Administrative Regulation;
- the creation of a single registry of state and municipal services;
- the development of procedures to monitor the effectiveness of administrative regulations;
- the analysis of regulations issued by government agencies based on the methodology developed by chambers of commerce;
- the execution of control by the Ministry of Justice over the implementation of federal laws at the regional and local levels;
- the adoption of legal concepts of government transparency;
- the establishment of legal review procedures;
- the active involvement of academia in the rule-making process.[3]

Yet, the existence of powerful "regulocracy" makes it difficult to implement these recommendations and enhance control over public agencies. Attempts to increase liability of public officials for administrative offenses and bribing are sabotaged by "regulocracy." In this respect, the 2015 presidential decree that decreased the minimum penalty for bribery is an example of a counterproductive policy. Specifically, in March 2015, President Putin signed an amendment to the Criminal Code, according to which the minimum penalty for accepting a bribe decreased from 15 to only five times its amount.

The development of comprehensive anti-corruption laws should be coupled with effective enforcement mechanisms. Special enforcement agencies play a critical role in preventing corruption in the public administration system. However, in Russia, law enforcement proved to be unable to prevent predations on businesses and extortion of informal payments by public officials. Moreover, the corruption of law enforcement exacerbates the already unfavorable situation for Russian citizens and entrepreneurs who suffer violations of their rights by regulatory agencies. Corruption of enforcement authorities is fueled by the low salaries of policemen and the lack of affordable housing. Financial and economic crises responsible for shrinking the formal incomes of enforcement officers further facilitate state predations on businesses. Together, these factors are responsible for the current institutional environment where law enforcement authorities often use their office not to defend the rule of law, but for their personal enrichment.

Another problem in Russia is weak coordination between multiple agencies aimed at preventing corruption, such as the Presidential Council for Combating Corruption, the National Anti-Corruption Council of the Russian Federation, the Anti-Corruption Parliamentary Commission, the Accounts Chamber, the Financial Monitoring Service, and the Interior Ministry's Committee for Economic Security and Combating Corruption. Their functions overlap, while their powers remain diluted and unclear. At the same time, their incentives for cooperation are weak and their practices fall far short of the policy's intent. Furthermore, key agencies with the authority to investigate and prosecute corruption cases in Russia, including the Federal Security Service and the Prosecutor General's Office, lack independence as their directors are nominated and can be dismissed by the President. These offices themselves are often criticized for corruption. For example, high-ranking officials of the Federal Custom Service, the Federal Security Service, and the Prosecutor General's Office were involved in one of the largest corruption cases (known as the Three Whales case), which centered around a furniture import company engaged in weapons and oil smuggling, as well as money laundering.[4] This case demonstrates that impunity of high-ranking officials from prosecution is a major weakness of Russia's judicial and law enforcement bodies.

International experiences provide evidence that a single independent agency with the authority to investigate and prosecute corruption could significantly improve the efficiency of anti-corruption campaigns. For instance, many studies point out that the key factor which made it possible to curb corruption in Hong Kong was the establishment of the Independent Commission Against Corruption (ICAC) in 1974.[5] Several important preconditions ensured its efficiency. First of all, being independent from the police and civil service, the ICAC reported only to the Colonel Governor. Second, officials working for the ICAC had the authority to investigate and prosecute corruption cases, including all relevant procedures, such as wiretaps, checks of bank accounts, searches without need for legal warrants, arrests, detentions, bails, and seizures of illegal funds. The ICAC also provided recommendations on legal and administrative reforms, as well as educational workshops for civil servants and the public. Third, officials at the ICAC were deterred from corruption by relatively high salaries in comparison with other agencies. In addition, they were protected from departmental transfers. Finally, special regular surveys monitored both corruption levels in Hong Kong and public trust in the ICAC.

From this perspective, the consolidation of multiple anti-corruption agencies into one entity could allow them to play a stronger normative and advocacy role in the development of anti-corruption policies. However, the creation of a single powerful and independent anti-corruption agency in Russia does not seem to be politically feasible. The reason is that anti-corruption campaigns conducted by public authorities often serve their short-term political purposes. Moreover, Russia's political elites lack the will to curb corruption because they depend on it for personal illicit enrichment. As a result, the existing myriad anti-corruption agencies resemble a feudal system consisting of separate fiefdoms that compete for public funds and resources, without the necessary accountability. Their current overlapping jurisdiction only adds to the complexity and ambiguity of Russian anti-corruption regulations.

In terms of international cooperation, corruption is a cross-border problem that requires coordination between countries across the world. Consequently, Russian anti-corruption agencies need to coordinate their efforts with international law enforcement organizations. Recently, many governments have recognized corruption as a common problem with shared responsibilities. Over the last two decades, a number of anti-corruption conventions have been adopted by international organizations. In 1999, the Organisation for Economic Co-operation and Development (OECD) adopted the Convention on Combating Bribery of Foreign Officials in International Business Transactions. In 2012, Russia signed this Convention. However, according to the 2015 Transparency International report on *Enforcement of the OECD Anti-Bribery Convention*, Russia and 19 other countries have "little or no enforcement" and lack effective mechanisms to deter bribery.[6]

In 1999, the Council of Europe launched the Group of States Against Corruption (GRECO). Apart from European member states, it includes a number of observers, such as Canada, Japan, Mexico, and the United States. In 1999, Russia signed the Council of Europe Criminal Law Convention on Corruption. By signing it, Russia automatically became a member of GRECO. In 2006, Russia ratified the Council of Europe Criminal Law Convention on Corruption and amended national laws according to its provisions. However, Russia has not yet signed the Council of Europe Civil Law Convention on Corruption which defines common international rules in the field of civil law and anti-corruption regulation. The latter convention contains provisions which are extremely important for Russia, such as compensation for damage from corruption, remedies for injured persons, invalidity of corrupt contracts, asset recovery, and whistleblower protection. Asset recovery, which is also a fundamental principle of the United Nations Convention against Corruption, is critically important because corrupt proceeds of Russian officials are mostly laundered in financial markets abroad, while stolen funds are often found in real estate in developed countries. For example, in 2016, millions of dollars stolen in the infamous Hermitage Capital case were tracked to accounts of Russian tax police officers in Canadian banks.[7]

The recent trend in enforcement of the Foreign Corrupt Practices Act (FCPA) by the U.S. authorities is the expansion of its extraterritorial reach. If money from bribery schemes has passed through its financial system, then the U.S. authorities can launch cases against foreign officials under the FCPA. The Department of Justice goes to extraordinary lengths to locate and bring FCPA violators to justice in the United States. Yet, in reality, it is extremely challenging if alleged FCPA violators are Russian nationals. The ability of the Department of Justice to prosecute foreign individuals is limited if countries are not willing to cooperate and assist in extradition. To begin with, Federal Rule of Criminal Procedure 4 requires U.S. prosecutors and law enforcement agencies to serve summons to individual defendants personally. This, however, requires permission from a foreign state, which might be difficult to obtain in countries that have not signed mutual legal assistance treaties with the United States.

Counteracting Administrative Corruption in the Private Sector

The analysis of Russian redistributive and market-promoting associations presented in Chapter 6 allows for several suggestions. First, there is a need to support the growth and development of grassroots market-promoting organizations founded at the local level by entrepreneurs themselves, rather than created through government initiatives. This measure is critically important because grassroots organizations based on voluntary memberships have more incentives to act as "the voice of business."[8] As the interviews with entrepreneurs in Moscow, Saint Petersburg, and Karelia demonstrate, most of them have to pay facilitation payments for routine government actions that they are legally entitled to receive. Therefore, they have strong incentives to protect entrepreneurial rights, resist oppression on the part of regulatory agencies, and fight against corruption.

Second, it is critical that Russian redistributive associations move away from the promotion of private interests and toward the use of open and direct mechanisms in representing the interests of the entire entrepreneurial community. Due to their close relations with public officials, entrepreneurial organizations directly or indirectly controlled by the government can be efficient in organizing public–private dialogue. Moreover, they could potentially play an active role in increasing the quality of decision-making in the political sphere by participating in joint activities with government authorities, providing informational support during the legislative process, and organizing public–private partnerships. A good example is a project conducted by the Center for Private Enterprise (CIPE) in Russia. It was aimed at assisting the Saratov Chamber of Commerce and Industry in developing an innovative approach to the fight against corruption at the regional level.[9] Their approach focused on finding gaps and contradictions between federal, regional, and local laws and closing these gaps through an advocacy campaign and partnership with public authorities. The results of this project included the reduction of administrative barriers in different areas, such as licensing, certification, and obtaining construction permits.

The interviews with representatives of self-regulatory organizations show that Russian business associations do not have sufficient public support. In this regard, they need to develop strong ties with the general public and civil society organizations. Public perceptions about business associations as an instrument for lobbying private interests discourage many entrepreneurs from becoming members. Not only do Russian entrepreneurial organizations need to attract new members, but they also need to receive support from civil society. The related task for business associations, therefore, is to persuade entrepreneurs and the public that their key objective is to increase the well-being of both business communities and ordinary citizens. As Chapter 6 shows, pioneering entrepreneurial organizations in the Russian Empire made significant efforts to form favorable public opinion about their activities. Contemporary self-regulatory organizations can achieve this goal through various methods, such as social networks, blogs on anti-corruption compliance in the private sector, online forums and courses, specialized Facebook groups, anti-corruption videos on YouTube, and online petitions, such as Change.org. Favorable public opinion and support by civil society organizations can be a potential force leading to synergies that entrepreneurial organizations would not be able to achieve independently.

Anti-corruption activities of civil society organizations and business associations are based on the same principles. Both can serve as mediators between the state, businesses, and the public. Therefore, it is necessary to unite the efforts of civil society activists with individual entrepreneurs and their collective organizations. The failure of Russian business associations to organize collective action by entrepreneurs suggests a need to combine their efforts with other social groups. Together, they can use a wide variety of bottom-up strategies, including civil disobedience, information dissemination about corruption, protests, petitions, strikes, social audits, digital resistance through social networks, and anti-corruption education. The key advantage of bottom-up anti-corruption strategies in the private sector is that they complement and reinforce top-down anti-corruption initiatives in the public sector.

Judging from international experience, a partnership between collective civil society organizations and business associations can be an effective tool for mobilizing isolated private actors and organizing massive anti-corruption campaigns. For example, based on 12 international case studies, Shaazka Beyerle demonstrates how civil society organizations and business associations played a critical role in pushing government agencies to follow transparency and accountability, even in countries characterized by pervasive corruption, such as Brazil, India, Uganda, and Afghanistan.[10] It is noteworthy that according to Transparency International, Uganda and Afghanistan have worse ratings on the Corruption Perception Index than Russia. In 2016, Uganda and Afghanistan were ranked 151st and 169th out of 179 countries, respectively, while Russia was ranked 131st.[11] Although Brazil and India have higher ratings on the Corruption Perception Index than Russia, they also have extremely complicated political and socio-economic environments. Successful anti-corruption campaigns in Brazil and India provide evidence that together civil society organizations and business associations can overcome the challenges posed by corrupt governments and public administration.

In terms of publicity, the interviews with entrepreneurs in Moscow, Saint Petersburg, and Karelia demonstrate that they do not have sufficient information about self-regulatory organizations and their anti-corruption activities. Taking this into account, self-regulatory organizations need to develop a system of information dissemination about their activities. They can achieve this objective by developing close cooperation with the media, publishing their own periodic sources, adding hotlines and feedback channels to their websites, and using social networks. The media sensitization of corruption-related issues is an important element of anti-corruption efforts. It facilitates legal and regulatory responses to rent seeking by government agencies. Moreover, the media inflates public concerns about this problem.

This task could be particularly challenging since Russia remains one of the most dangerous countries in the world for independent media due to numerous murders, detentions and arrests of journalists and human rights activists, denial of entry to international journalists, and frequent targeting of independent outlets by regulators.[12] According to the Committee to Protect Journalists, 36 journalists have been murdered in Russia since 1992.[13] The number of nonfatal attacks against journalists is even higher. In 2016, the Glasnost Defense Foundation reported 54 attacks on journalists and bloggers.[14] Among topics which are subject to particular political pressure are human rights abuses, government corruption, organized crime, and police torture. This is a serious cause for concern as free and independent media is a significant part of anti-corruption campaigns.

In authoritarian countries, where most media sources are controlled and censored by the government, Internet resources and social networks are becoming more important. For example, social networks played a significant role in the collapse of authoritarian regimes during the Arab Spring.[15] In Russia, the percentage of active Internet users of the total population was estimated at 68.3 percent in 2015.[16] In 2016, it increased to 71.5 percent.[17] The use of social networks can contribute to awareness-raising anti-corruption programs. For instance, social networks can help entrepreneurs and other business entities disseminate information about corrupt regulatory agencies and public officials, holding them accountable for their actions.

Most interviewed entrepreneurs from Moscow, Saint Petersburg, and Karelia support a proposal to create a national online portal that will combine the resources and efforts of businesses, self-regulatory organizations, and civil society activists. Specifically, this portal can be used to rank Russian regions based on the number of complaints about violations of entrepreneurial rights and extortion of informal payments by regulatory agencies. At the present time, it is impossible to find this information. Furthermore, such complaints should be automatically dispatched to public authorities for investigation and to journalists for publication in the local and regional media. This portal could also serve as an instrument for entrepreneurs to track the status of their complaints submitted to public authorities.

Another important aspect is the involvement of women's grassroots organizations in the development and implementation of anti-corruption campaigns.

Historically, women-owned businesses have long been underrepresented in male-dominated industries, such as construction, transportation, and warehousing. The low percentage of women-owned businesses in these industries points to certain difficulties in providing their credibility and competing in the male-dominated environment. For example, the interviews with entrepreneurs provide evidence that women in many sectors of the economy are not taken seriously and encounter serious challenges to prove their capability and credibility, and often have to overcome gender discrimination, sexism, and stereotypes. According to Transparency International, women are disproportionately affected by corruption in the following spheres: restricted access to decision-making due to an uneven playing field for women and men in corrupt societies; limited protection and advancement of women's rights due to a corrupt enforcement system; and reduced access to resources.[18] Taking this into account, women's experiences in this arena can contribute to collective action against administrative corruption. For example, in an interview conducted for this study, a female entrepreneur from Saint Petersburg described her motivation to participate in anti-corruption campaigns in the following way:

> I do not distinguish between the interests of my family and the interests of society. I live in this country and my well-being depends on a healthy social and business climate. I believe that it is impossible to build a happy family without taking social problems into considerations. Corruption distorts economic development, leads to an inefficient use of resources, disavows the purpose of public service, distorts incentives of businesses, and strengthens regionalism and nepotism. Moreover, it is linked to capital flight, which leaves our economy without necessary investment. As a result, the whole society suffers, including my family. If you like, my motivation can be defined as a maternal instinct.

Gender-specific incentives to participate in anti-corruption campaigns are well documented in the literature. For example, a pioneering study conducted by David Dollar, Raymond Fisman, and Roberta Gatti demonstrates that women are "more trustworthy and public-spirited" and less "individually oriented" than men.[19] The study shows that countries with a greater percentage of women in government tend to have a lower level of corruption than countries in which women are significantly underrepresented in the political sphere.[20] In Russia, it is still difficult for women to gain access to high-ranking positions. Although women comprise a large community of voters, they are significantly less active than men in working for a party or candidate in an election campaign. Women are also underrepresented in enforcement agencies, including the police. At the same time, Mexico and Peru's initiatives to recruit female police officers proved effective at decreasing the level of corruption in law enforcement.[21] Another example of the women's role in providing accountability is the Union of Cooperatives *Las Brumas* in Nicaragua that organizes special training, seminars, and education programs for female entrepreneurs on leadership and citizens' rights.[22]

As the United Nations report indicates, these programs and training were very successful in helping women in local communities to prevent corruption and protect their rights.[23]

In Russia, women play a critical role in the sphere of civil initiatives. In fact, the majority of NGOs were initiated and are run by women.[24] In this respect, they set a good example for female entrepreneurs to create collective business organizations "from below" at the regional and local levels. Overall, it is impossible to mitigate the problem of administrative corruption in the Russian entrepreneurial sector without women's contributions to collective action initiatives. The multilateral system of anti-corruption regulation combines the elements of self-regulation and traditional public regulation. One of the positive aspects of this system is the ability of women to transform public policies in the direction of equality. A major advantage of this system is that women and women's organizations can actively participate in the process of anti-corruption policy formulation and implementation. The integration of all stakeholders ensures the effectiveness of anti-corruption regulation.

Public–Private Cooperation in the Fight Against Corruption in the Entrepreneurial Sector

Public–private cooperation is a necessary element of successful anti-corruption campaigns. It can be organized either as public–private dialogue in the policy-making sphere or as public–private partnerships in the form of joint anti-corruption projects. Although public–private dialogue and public–private partnerships share similar principles, they represent distinctive stages of the policy-making process. In a broad sense, public–private dialogue means the participation of private actors in the policy formulation stage, while public–private partnerships require the involvement of businesses in the implementation stage of the policy-making cycle. Public–private partnerships (also known as PPP) can be defined as "cooperative institutional arrangements between public and private sector actors" that typically have a long-term nature.[25] In public–private partnerships, actors from different sectors jointly develop products and services based on sharing risks, costs, and resources.

The key objective of public–private dialogue is to improve the policy formulation through inclusive participation of private-sector actors. They can include representatives of the business community and civil society who have on-the-ground experiences with issues targeted by decision-makers in the public sector. Public–private dialogue can elevate issues of particular concern for entrepreneurs to the top of the government agenda, provide necessary data for the adoption of new laws, and give feedback on existing regulations. Public–private dialogue can be organized based on a top-down approach when public authorities ask particular entrepreneurs and business associations to provide their input on policies under consideration. An alternative bottom-up approach suggests that business leaders themselves initiate discussions about public issues through advocacy campaigns.

A view of the larger international context highlights key principles for the success of public–private dialogue between business associations and public authorities. For example, based on a study of 38 countries, Benjamin Herzberg and Andrew Wright distinguish eight strategies for persuading policy-makers to change inefficient administrative regulations:

- reach out to small businesses;
- strengthen business associations;
- define a network of government agencies involved in regulations;
- generate a two-tiered output, including legal proposals and policy papers;
- use branding and marketing with a clear mission statement;
- appoint a dynamic coordinator;
- manage expectations;
- be flexible and ready to involve new partners.[26]

Russian business associations can use these strategies to organize public–private dialogue at the national and regional levels.

A good example is the participation of the Turkish Coordination Council for Improvement of the Investment Climate in changing the national law on the companies' registration. Based on recommendations received by legislators from the Turkish Coordination Council, the national regulations were amended to decrease the number of bureaucratic procedures required to start a business from 19 to eight, while the time required for business registration decreased from 2.5 months to nine days.[27] Another example is the amendments to Vietnam's labor regulations based on recommendations received from the Vietnamese Business Forum. They resulted in more favorable policies for the hiring of expatriate employees by Vietnamese companies.[28] These are just a few examples of the importance of business associations' recommendations for the legislative process in the sphere of regulatory governance. Businesses and entrepreneurs benefit significantly from such public–private dialogue in terms of removing excessive regulations.

From a historical perspective, business associations in the Russian Empire made significant efforts to inform public authorities about their views on economic development. They often invited distinguished economists, jurists, and historians to participate in open discussions with public officials.[29] Contemporary forms of public–private dialogue include roundtables, forums, and working groups. They bring together representatives of public authorities, business associations, and individual entrepreneurs. Forums and roundtables are often used as a platform to discuss administrative barriers to doing business. One of their most important advantages is an intensive process of dialogue, which can provide new insights into the nature of corruption and promote action for responsible public administration.

Due to their collective bargaining power, business associations can be very powerful actors elevating problems of entrepreneurs to the top of the public agenda. A good illustration is the participation of Russian business associations in the development of the 2016 amendments to the Criminal Code to prevent unjustified criminal prosecution of entrepreneurs. Over the last decade, business associations have submitted numerous proposals to liberalize criminal legislation in the economic sphere. Their representatives have long demanded an expansion of the list of economic crimes exempt from criminal responsibility. Under pressure from business associations, in 2016, President Putin created a working group consisting of representatives of business associations and federal executive bodies. Their main task was to monitor and analyze law enforcement practices in the entrepreneurial sector. The results of their analysis were presented at several meetings of the working group with President Putin in 2016.

This working group identified several loopholes in the criminal and procedural laws that created myriad opportunities for law enforcement bodies to participate in illegal raiding and to facilitate unlawful asset seizures. One of these loopholes included the lack of legal procedures related to material evidence seized during the investigation, including documents, seals, goods, and other assets essential for business functioning. The group found that the law did not specify the amount of time during which enforcement authorities can keep this material evidence. In this respect, Sergei Ivanov, then Chief of the Presidential Executive Office, noted:

> The law enforcement officials open a criminal case against an entrepreneur and seize documents, hard disks, goods in stock, and other material assets during the investigation. We do not know how long the law enforcement officials can keep these assets. In the meantime, the company essentially comes to a halt in such conditions and the business collapses or, let's make no secret of it, is taken over by others.[30]

Another issue was the minimum value thresholds for the amount of damage required to launch criminal prosecution. These thresholds were established in the 2000s and, therefore, they did not reflect either inflation or the existing economic circumstances. As Sergei Ivanov noted:

> The result is that it is now possible to open a criminal case against a businessman for stealing 1,000 rubles [about $160]. Businesspeople can end up with several years in prison for what is really not large damages by today's standards. Now, the embezzlement of 250,000 rubles [about $3,850] qualifies as a serious crime, and embezzlement of one million rubles [about $15,390] as especially serious.[31]

In April 2016, several amendments to Russia's Criminal Code were submitted to the State Duma to liberalize laws related to economic crimes. These amendments extended exemptions from criminal responsibility for economic crimes, increased the amount of damage required to launch criminal proceedings, and allowed notaries to meet with detained entrepreneurs. The latter measure helped many entrepreneurs to delegate their right to manage their companies while they were held in pre-trial detention centers or under house arrest. Russian business associations and civil society organizations played a key role in developing these amendments.

The last decade also saw a clear trend toward cooperation between public and private actors in the sphere of joint programs and projects aimed at combatting informal transactions in the national economy. In 2010, the Saratov Chamber of Commerce and Industry in partnership with the Center for International Private Enterprise conducted a survey among Russian entrepreneurs and government experts to find out what counter-corruption measures should be given priority. The priority measures included monitoring government agencies, organizing anti-corruption education in schools and universities, and monitoring compliance with anti-corruption laws.[32] The implementation of these measures requires public–private partnerships. One example is a joint project organized by Citizens' Watch, a human rights NGO, and Saint Petersburg University of the Russian Interior Ministry. The main aim of this project was to make police ethics a larger part of education programs and address the problem of violations of human rights by law enforcement officers. Together with law enforcement officials, Citizens' Watch organized special training programs aimed at promoting ethical values among police officers and developing their social responsibility.

In another case, the Guild for Audio-Video Trade Development partnered with public authorities to assist in implementing new regulations that targeted counterfeit products. In 2003, the State Duma adopted a new law on licensing that became the basis of copyright protection. Its enforcement, however, was inefficient due to the predatory behavior of police officers who often both patronized establishments selling pirated goods and harassed legitimate traders with arbitrary inspections.[33] In 2003, law-abiding businesses from the Guild for Audio-Video Trade Development created a program aimed at improving this situation in the market. They offered their assistance in enforcing new regulations to the Moscow authorities by denouncing pirated trade and corrupt policemen. This partnership was mutually beneficial. The public authorities had an opportunity to receive necessary information from the private sector to combat corruption at the street-level policing. In turn, the Guild's members received legal protection of their businesses and certain guarantees of fair competition on the part of public authorities.[34] Although the situation with pirated products in Russia leaves much to be desired, the partnership of the Guild for Audio-Video Trade Development and public authorities contributed to a remarkable increase in a share of legal products in this market in Moscow.

Despite their effectiveness, public–private partnerships are underrepresented in the sphere of anti-corruption enforcement. The Center for the Development of Public–Private Partnerships distinguishes several problems in this sphere. First, there is no legal definition of public–private partnerships in Russia's federal legislation.[35] This often leads to misunderstandings and confusion for both private and public actors. An additional obstacle is the lack of public mechanisms to provide special benefits to private parties who participate in such partnerships. Another barrier that creates the greatest obstacles to the development

150 *Conclusion*

of public–private partnerships in Russia is a low level of skills and lack of experience of public officials in charge of such projects.[36] As a result, at the present time, the Russian entrepreneurial community does not fully realize the potential of public–private partnerships for the development and implementation of anti-corruption policies. In this respect, it is critical to organize special programs and seminars for public officials about the benefits and mechanisms of successful public–private partnerships. Finally, it is important to publicize the already existing public–private partnerships that ensure openness and transparency of arrangements between business associations and governmental agencies.

Lessons and Future Directions from Russian Entrepreneurs' Experiences

The major thrust of this book is to highlight two important directions of anti-corruption research which are often ignored by policy-makers who are in charge of administrative reforms. The first direction focuses on the role of self-regulatory organizations and collective action initiatives in mitigating administrative corruption and defending entrepreneurial rights against violations by public authorities. It relies on the following finding of the study: the vast majority of informal payments are made by entrepreneurs not to achieve illegal advantages, but to obtain property rights that they are entitled to receive under the law. To a certain extent, this finding demystifies widely accepted views about the cultural predisposition of Russian citizens to pay bribes. This study also suggests that membership in business associations is an important determinant of the frequency of informal payments in the entrepreneurial sector. In this respect, self-regulatory organizations are called on to support individual entrepreneurs in implementing better anti-corruption programs. They can provide a platform for various business entities to collectively participate in anti-corruption efforts.

The second direction of the research combines gender-specific attitudes toward corruption with an economic perspective on the role of female entrepreneurs in anti-corruption efforts. According to this perspective, gender-specific challenges related to economic competition in a male-dominated environment and women's traditional roles as family caretakers make them less tolerant of corruption. The practical implication of this finding is a need to enhance the role of women in the economic and political arenas, not only for the purpose of social justice and fairness, but also for overall social well-being. This study expands previous research into gender-specific attitudes toward corruption, by focusing on women's perceptions about "grease" payments. Not only do female entrepreneurs demonstrate more negative attitudes toward such payments, but they also use informal transactions in relations with regulatory agencies less frequently. This suggests that women's experiences can significantly contribute to the fight against corruption.

The active participation of female entrepreneurs and women's organizations in the development and implementation of anti-corruption programs could create an atmosphere encouraging ethics and gender equality. There are several possible explanations of behavioral differences between genders related to corruption. The interviews with female entrepreneurs conducted in the course of this research confirmed the argument about the "public-spirited" nature of women.[37] For example, one of the interviewed female entrepreneurs pointed to a maternal instinct as her motivation to participate in anti-corruption campaigns since the well-being of her family depends on the well-being of society as a whole. This study also confirmed another argument according to which women are often prevented from corruption by the existence of male-dominated clientelistic networks both in the political and economic spheres.[38] The survey conducted for this research found that female entrepreneurs are less involved in the activities of collective organizations in their industries.

This study contributes to the growing body of literature related to informal payments by focusing on motivations and perceptions of Russian individual entrepreneurs about the use of informal transactions. As Philip Nichols indicates, an understanding of attitudes toward corruption among the local population is critical for policy-making because these attitudes play an important role in determining the viability of anti-corruption regulations.[39] Therefore, the assertion that Russian culture embraces corruption should be tested in empirical studies. In this context, the book provides evidence that most informal transactions in the entrepreneurial sector are initiated by regulatory agencies whose rent-seeking activities impose a significant burden on businesses. Extortion of informal payments represents a disturbing trend in the Russian institutional environment. In turn, rent-seeking activities by regulatory agencies lead to the problem of overregulation in the entrepreneurial sector, which manifests itself in additional bureaucratic procedures for doing business in Russia.

When entrepreneurs place little trust in public institutions and business associations, they are unlikely to file formal complaints about corruption. As a result, most entrepreneurs prefer to solve administrative problems through informal methods. One of the most serious weaknesses of Russia's self-regulatory organizations is a relatively high level of their bureaucratization, especially at the federal level. On the one hand, the creation of elite business associations allows state agencies to control businesses. On the other hand, the concentration of large business associations at the federal level blocks the development of independent grassroots entrepreneurial organizations at the regional and local levels. The interviews conducted at the regional level showed that entrepreneurs do not trust large elite business associations because they promote the private interests of their members and take advantage of their crony relations with public officials. This suggests the importance of developing and supporting grassroots organizations initiated by entrepreneurs at the municipal and regional levels. Currently, their numbers are very limited, especially in provincial regions.

As civil society in Russia is not well developed, business associations can help its formation. Due to their representational role and economic leverage, business associations have better opportunities to organize public–private dialogue and draw attention to inefficient regulations. Recently, significant progress has been made on improving regulations related to the liberalization of criminal prosecution of businessmen charged with economic crimes. In 2016, under pressure from Russian business associations, President Putin introduced new amendments to the Criminal Code that limited the discretion of police officers and improved protection mechanisms against malicious criminal prosecution of entrepreneurs. In this respect, one of the positive aspects of self-regulatory organizations is their ability to react to new challenges faster than public authorities. The fact that their members share common objectives makes a positive impact on the regulatory process. From this perspective, the multilateral system of anti-corruption regulation, which integrates public and private actors, ensures the effectiveness of their efforts.

Collective action offers a way for small businesses and individual entrepreneurs to leverage their influence and power to counteract corrupt public officials. However, in order to be effective, self-regulatory organizations in Russia should move away from the promotion of goals of separate entrepreneurial circles toward the use of open and direct mechanisms of the representation of interests of the entire entrepreneurial community. The key objective of collective entrepreneurial organizations in the political system is to create a basis for an intensive dialogue between businesses and authorities and to increase the quality of decision-making through informational support during the legislative process and the organization of public–private partnerships.

Notes

1 Department of Justice. Justice Department Recovers Over $4.7 Billion From False Claims Act Cases in Fiscal Year 2016. (2016). Available at: www.justice.gov/opa/pr/justice-department-recovers-over-47-billion-false-claims-act-cases-fiscal-year-2016
2 Cited in Petrov, N. Transparency International: Rosatom zhestko boretsya s korruptsiei [in Russian]. (2011). Available at: http://infox.ru/business/company/2011/10/20/Transparency_Interna_print.phtml
3 Center for International Private Enterprise. *Improving Regulation to Reduce Corruption: The Role of the Russian Business Community* (Moscow, 2010). Available at: www.cipe.org/sites/default/files/publication-docs/saratovMethodologyEng2.pdf
4 Yasmann, V. Russia: Corruption Scandal Could Shake Kremlin. *Radio Free Europe/Radio Liberty*, September 26, 2006.
5 See, for example, Rose-Ackerman, S. *Corruption and Government: Causes, Consequences, and Reform* (Cambridge: Cambridge University Press, 1999), pp. 159–62; Langseth, P. *Integrated versus Quantitative Methods: Lessons Learned* (Vienna: Center for International Crime Prevention, 2000), p. 7; Quah, J. Curbing Asian Corruption: An Impossible Dream? *Current History*, 105(690) (2006), 176–179.
6 Transparency International. *Exporting Corruption? Country Enforcement of the OECD Anti-Bribery Convention: Progress Report 2015*. (2016). Available at: www.transparency.de/fileadmin/pdfs/Themen/Internationales/2015_ExportingCorruption_OECDProgressReport_EN.pdf
7 Leblanc, D. Investigators Track Millions of Dollars from Russian Tax Fraud Coming to Canada. *The Globe and Mail*, October 27, 2016.
8 Sullivan, J., Bettcher, K. E., & Shkolnikov, A. *Business Associations, Business Climate, and Economic Growth: Evidence from Transition Economies* (Washington, DC: Center for International Private Enterprise, 2008), p. 4.

9 Center for International Private Enterprise, op. cit., p. 15.
10 Beyerle, S. *Curtailing Corruption: People Power for Accountability and Justice* (Boulder, CO: Lynne Rienner Publishers, Inc., 2014).
11 Transparency International. *Corruption Perceptions Index 2016 – Results*. (2016). Available at: www.transparency.org/news/feature/corruption_perceptions_index_2016
12 Freedom House. *Freedom of the Press 2015* (Washington, DC: Freedom House, 2015).
13 Committee to Protect Journalists. 36 Journalists Murdered in Russia since 1992. (2017). Available at: www.cpj.org/killed/europe/russia/murder.php
14 Glasnost Defense Foundation. Konflikty zafiksirovannye FZG v techenii 2016 goda [in Russian]. (2017). Available at: www.gdf.ru/graph/item/1/1441
15 See, for example, Ray, T. The "Story" of Digital Excess in Revolutions of the Arab Spring, *Journal of Media Practice*, *12*(2) (2011), 189–196; Comninos, A. Twitter Revolutions and Cyber Crackdowns, Association for Progressive Communications, (2011), available at: http://gb1.apc.org/en/system/files/AlexComninos_MobileInternet.pdf
16 Federal Statistics Service of the Russian Federation. Monitoring razvitiya informatsionnogo obshchestva v Rossiiskoi Federatsii [in Russian]. (Moscow, 2017). Available at: www.gks.ru/free_doc/new_site/business/it/monitor_rf.xls
17 Ibid.
18 Transparency International. Gender and Corruption: Understanding and Undoing the Linkages. (2007). Available at: http://anti-corruption.org/pmb321/pmb/opac_css/doc_num.php?explnum_id=529
19 Dollar, D., Fisman, R., & Gatti, R. Are Women Really the "Fairer" Sex? Corruption and Women in Government. *Journal of Economic Behavior & Organization*, *46*(4) (2001), 423.
20 Ibid.
21 See, for example, Quinones, S. Stop! *Ms. Magazine*, December 24, 1999; McDermott, J. International: Women Police Ride in on a Ticket of Honesty, *Daily Telegraph*, July 31, 1999.
22 Huairou Commission. Grassroots Profiles. (2014). Available at: http://huairou.org/grassroots-profiles
23 Purushothaman, S., Tobin, T., Vissa, S., & Pillai, P. *Seeing Beyond the State: Grassroots Women's Perspectives on Corruption and Anti-Corruption* (New York: United Nations Development Programme, 2012), pp. 32–33.
24 Poltavskaya, M., & Lobyzenkova, V. *Biznes assotsiatsii v volgogradskoi oblasti* [in Russian] (Volgograd: Volgograd State Medical University, 2011), p. 180.
25 See, for example, Hodge, G. A., & Greve, C. Public–Private Partnerships: An International Performance Review, *Public Administration Review*, *67*(3) (2007), 545; Van Ham, H., & Koppenjan, J. Building Public–Private Partnerships: Assessing and Managing Risks in Port Development, *Public Management Review*, *3*(4) (2001), 598.
26 Herzberg, B., & Wright, A. Competitiveness Partnerships: Building and Maintaining Public–Private Dialogue to Improve the Investment Climate – A Resource Drawn from the Review of 40 Countries' Experiences. World Bank Policy Research Working Paper, No. 3683. Washington, DC: The World Bank, 2005.
27 Ibid.
28 Ibid.
29 Vorontsova, E. *Predprinimatel'skie organizatsii v Rossii: istoriografiya, istochniki, istoriya* [in Russian] (Moscow: Eterna, 2013), p. 365.
30 President of Russia. Meeting of the Working Group to Monitor and Analyze Law Enforcement Practice in Entrepreneurial Activity. (2016). Available at: http://en.kremlin.ru/events/president/news/51556
31 Ibid.
32 Center for International Private Enterprise, op. cit., p. 13.

33 Duvanova, D. Bureaucratic Corruption and Collective Action: Business Associations in the Post-communist Transition. *Comparative Politics*, *39*(4) (2007), 453.
34 Ibid., 455.
35 Center for the Development of Public–Private Partnerships. *Gosudarstvenno-chastnye partnerstva v Rossii* [in Russian] (Moscow: Center for the Development of Public–Private Partnerships, 2013), p. 12.
36 Expert Institute. *Bar'ery razvitiya mekhanizma GCHP v Rossii* [in Russian] (Moscow, 2010), pp. 31–32. Available at: www.niro.nnov.ru/?id=8164
37 Dollar, et al., op. cit., p. 423.
38 Swamy, A., Knack, S., Lee, Y., & Azfar, O. Gender and corruption. *Journal of Development Economics*, *64*(1) (2001), 25–55.
39 Nichols, P. M. The Fit between Changes to the International Corruption Regime and Indigenous Perceptions of Corruption in Kazakhstan. *University of Pennsylvania Journal of International Law*, *22*(4) (2001), 898.

References

Beyerle, S. (2014). *Curtailing Corruption: People Power for Accountability and Justice*. Boulder, CO: Lynne Rienner Publishers, Inc.
Center for International Private Enterprise. (2010). *Improving Regulation to Reduce Corruption: The Role of the Russian Business Community*. Moscow. Available at: www.cipe.org/sites/default/files/publication-docs/saratovMethodologyEng2.pdf
Center for International Private Enterprise. (2011). *Final Report to the US Agency for International Development for the Period of September 2002–September 2011*. Washington, DC: Center for International Private Enterprise.
Center for the Development of Public–Private Partnerships. (2013). *Gosudarstvenno-chastnye partnerstva v Rossii* [in Russian]. Moscow: Center for the Development of Public–Private Partnerships.
Committee to Protect Journalists. (2017). 36 Journalists Murdered in Russia since 1992. Available at: www.cpj.org/killed/europe/russia/murder.php
Comninos, A. (2011). Twitter Revolutions and Cyber Crackdowns. Association for Progressive Communications. Available at: http://gb1.apc.org/en/system/files/AlexComninos_MobileInternet.pdf
Department of Justice. (2016). Justice Department Recovers Over $4.7 Billion From False Claims Act Cases in Fiscal Year 2016. Available at: www.justice.gov/opa/pr/justice-department-recovers-over-47-billion-false-claims-act-cases-fiscal-year-2016.
Dollar, D., Fisman, R., & Gatti, R. (2001). Are Women Really the "Fairer" Sex? Corruption and Women in Government. *Journal of Economic Behavior & Organization*, *46*(4), 423–429.
Duvanova, D. (2007). Bureaucratic Corruption and Collective Action: Business Associations in the Postcommunist Transition. *Comparative Politics*, *39*(4), 441–461.
Expert Institute. (2010). *Bar'ery razvitiya mekhanizma GCHP v Rossii* [in Russian]. Moscow. Available at: www.niro.nnov.ru/?id=8164
Federal Statistics Service of the Russian Federation. (2017). Monitoring razvitiya informatsionnogo obshchestva v Rossiiskoi Federatsii [in Russian]. Moscow. Available at: www.gks.ru/free_doc/new_site/business/it/monitor_rf.xls
Freedom House. (2015). *Freedom of the Press 2015*. Washington, DC: Freedom House.
Glasnost Defense Foundation. (2017). Konflikty zafiksirovannye FZG v techenii 2016 goda [in Russian]. Available at: www.gdf.ru/graph/item/1/1441

Herzberg, B., & Wright, A. (2005). *Competitiveness Partnerships: Building and Maintaining Public–Private Dialogue to Improve the Investment Climate – A Resource Drawn from the Review of 40 Countries' Experiences*. Washington, DC: The World Bank.

Hodge, G. A., & Greve, C. (2007). Public–Private Partnerships: An International Performance Review. *Public Administration Review*, 67(3), 545–558.

Huairou Commission. (2014). *Grassroots Profiles*. Available at: http://huairou.org/grassroots-profiles

Langseth, P. (2000). *Integrated versus Quantitative Methods: Lessons Learned*. Vienna: CICP.

Leblanc, D. (2016, October 27). Investigators Track Millions of Dollars from Russian Tax Fraud Coming to Canada. *The Globe and Mail*.

McDermott, J. (1999, July 31). International: Women Police Ride in on a Ticket of Honesty. *The Daily Telegraph*.

Nichols, P. M. (2001). The Fit between Changes to the International Corruption Regime and Indigenous Perceptions of Corruption in Kazakhstan. *University of Pennsylvania Journal of International Law*, 22(4), 863–973.

Petrov, N. (2011). Transparency International: Rosatom zhestko boretsya s korruptsiei [in Russian]. Available at: http://infox.ru/business/company/2011/10/20/Transparency_Interna_print.phtml.

Poltavskaya, M., & Lobyzenkova, V. (2011). *Biznes assotsiatsii v volgogradskoi oblasti* [in Russian]. Volgograd: Volgograd State Medical University.

President of the Russian Federation. (2016). Meeting of the Working Group to Monitor and Analyze Law Enforcement Practice in Entrepreneurial Activity. Available at: http://en.kremlin.ru/events/president/news/51556

Purushothaman, S., Tobin, T., Vissa, S., & Pillai, P. (2012). *Seeing Beyond the State: Grassroots Women's Perspectives on Corruption and Anti-Corruption*. New York: United Nations Development Programme.

Quah, J. (2006). Curbing Asian Corruption: An Impossible Dream? *Current History*, 105(690), 176–179.

Quinones, S. (1999, December 24). Stop! *Ms. Magazine*.

Ray, T. (2011). The "Story" of Digital Excess in Revolutions of the Arab Spring. *Journal of Media Practice*, 12(2), 189–196.

Rose-Ackerman, S. (1999). *Corruption and Government: Causes, Consequences, and Reform*. Cambridge: Cambridge University Press.

Sullivan, J., Bettcher, K. E., & Shkolnikov, A. (2008). *Business Associations, Business Climate, and Economic Growth: Evidence from Transition Economies*. Washington, DC: Center for International Private Enterprise.

Swamy, A., Knack, S., Lee, Y., & Azfar, O. (2001). Gender and Corruption. *Journal of Development Economics*, 64(1), 25–55.

Transparency International. (2007). *Gender and Corruption: Understanding and Undoing the Linkages*, Transparency International Working Paper. Available at: http://anti-corruption.org/pmb321/pmb/opac_css/doc_num.php?explnum_id=529

Transparency International. (2016a). *Corruption Perceptions Index 2016 – Results*. Available at: www.transparency.org/news/feature/corruption_perceptions_index_2016

Transparency International. (2016b). *Exporting Corruption? Country Enforcement of the OECD Anti-Bribery Convention, Progress Report 2015*. Available at: www.transparency.de/fileadmin/pdfs/Themen/Internationales/2015_ExportingCorruption_OECD ProgressReport_EN.pdf

Van Ham, H., & Koppenjan, J. (2001). Building Public–Private Partnerships: Assessing and Managing Risks in Port Development. *Public Management Review*, *3*(4), 593–616.

Vorontsova, E. (2013). *Predprinimatel'skie organizatsii v Rossii: istoriografiya, istochniki, istoriya* [in Russian]. Moscow: Eterna.

Yasmann, V. (2006, September 26). Russia: Corruption Scandal Could Shake Kremlin. *Radio Free Europe/Radio Liberty*.

Appendix 1
Interview Questions

- Do you think that administrative procedures are burdensome for individual entrepreneurs in your region? Give examples if possible.
- In your opinion, how do individual entrepreneurs perceive "grease" payments to regulatory agencies? Give examples if possible.
- Do you think that individual entrepreneurs in your region are interested in organizing collective action to counteract "grease" payments?
- What organizations do you think should take the lead in counteracting "grease" payments"?
- What can be the role of self-regulatory organizations in such efforts?
- In your opinion, what solutions are the most successful in situations of excessive administrative procedures?
- Do you know any successful cases of mitigating excessive administrative procedures without "grease" payments? What are the major barriers for tackling "grease" payments in your region?
- In your personal experience, are self-regulatory organizations helpful for entrepreneurs in your region? How can they increase their potential?
- Are you a member of any self-regulatory organization? If yes, does your self-regulatory organization help entrepreneurs in situations of excessive administrative procedures? What organizational strategies do they use to counteract "grease" payments?
- What challenges and problems do individual entrepreneurs and self-regulatory organizations face in their efforts to counteract "grease" payments?
- What have been their major advances in counteracting the problem of administrative burdens in recent years?
- In your opinion, what anti-corruption initiatives should self-regulatory organizations focus on?
- Have you ever participated in collective action organized by self-regulatory organizations? Give examples if possible.
- Do you have any recommendations for individual entrepreneurs who find themselves in situations of administrative overregulation?
- What would you recommend for self-regulatory organizations to ensure that their strategies address concerns of individual entrepreneurs?

Appendix 2
Survey Questions

Part 1. General Questions

Region: Moscow □ Saint Petersburg □ Karelia □
Gender: Male □ Female □
Number of employees □
Participation in collective entrepreneurial organizations: Yes □ No □

Part 2. Specific Questions

1. In your opinion, how often do public officials and regulatory agencies extort "grease" payments in your region?

Please indicate your answer with "x"	Never	Very rarely	Rarely	Often	Very often

2. In your opinion, how often do individual entrepreneurs initiate themselves informal payments to regulatory agencies in your region?

Please indicate your answer with "x"	Never	Very rarely	Rarely	Often	Very often

3 Would you agree or disagree with the following statements?

Please indicate your answer with "x"	Strongly disagree	Disagree	Neither agree nor disagree	Agree	Strongly agree
A. The use of "grease" payments is always justified in situations of excessive regulation					
B. The consequences of "grease" payments are negative for businesses					
C. Individual entrepreneurs who use "grease" payments are more successful in their business than those who do not pay them					
D. Individual entrepreneurs feel humiliated when bureaucrats require "grease" payments for routine government actions					
E. Individual entrepreneurs in my region are interested in organizing collective action to counteract "grease" payments					

4   Which of the following solutions and how often do you use in situations of excessive administrative procedures?

Please indicate your answer with "x"	Never	Very rarely	Rarely	Often	Very often
Pay "grease" payments					
Use personal connections in regulatory agencies					
File a petition to public authorities					
File a complaint to regional associations of entrepreneurs, chambers of commerce, or similar self-regulatory organizations					
File legal actions within a court					

Thank you for your participation in this survey!

Index

Page numbers in **bold** denote tables, those in *italics* denote figures.

accountability: horizontal 113, **114**; societal 113, **114**, 117–118; types of 113, **114**; vertical 113, **114**; in public administration 5, 24, 29, 102, 116–117, 143, 145
Accounts Chamber 140
administrative barriers: case studies of 52–57, **52**; definition 47; and "regulocracy" 48–52; to doing business 10, 44, 47–48
administrative corruption: definition 4, 10; impact on entrepreneurial employment 1–3, 10, 59–64, **62**, **63**; linkages to political corruption 5, 10, 48; negative effects of 44–49, 91, 102, 127
Adygey region 60
Afghanistan 143
Agency of Strategic Initiatives 6, 61
Agrarian Union of Russia 123
Albania 118
Alexander the Second 20
Analytical Center under the Government of the Russian Federation 30
anti-corruption initiatives: fallacies of 2, 5; in the policy area **58**, 76, 85–86, 150–152; in the public sector 137–142; in the public-private arena 146–150; in the private sector 142–146
Anti-Corruption Charter of Russian Businesses 125–126, *126*
Anti-Corruption Parliamentary Commission 140
Anti-Terror Package 25
Arab Spring 11, 112, 144
Argentina 73
Association of Entrepreneurs OPORA Russia 2, 23, 49, 52–54, 78, 124, **124**, 129

Association of Joint Ventures, International Partnerships, and Organizations 22
Association of Privatized Enterprises 123
Association of Russian Lawyers for Human Rights 6, 9, 56, 61
Association of Russian Banks 23
Astrakhan region 60, 139
authoritarianism 8, 26–27, 102, 119, 128, 130, 144

Balkan Coalition of Women's Business Associations 118
Bangladesh Women's Chamber of Commerce and Industry 117
Bank for Development 29
Bashunov, Igor 100
"Basmanny justice" 99
Baumol, William 130
Beirut café 102–103
Belgorod region 60
Bitkov, Igor 26–27
blat 18
Bosnia and Herzegovina 36, 118
Bouazizi, Mohamed 112
Boyev, Valerii 100
Brazil 64, 73, 112–113, 143
Brod, Alexander 100
Browder, Bill 98, 103
Bulgaria 32, **33**, 34, **35**, 73, 98, 118
Bulletin of Gold and Mining Industries 123
Business associations: anti-corruption efforts 52, 85–86, 105, 113, 137, 143, 146–152; elite 9, 151; impact on attitudes toward "grease" payments 79–82, **82**; international 116–117; pre-revolutionary 11, 121; women's

162   Index

Business associations *continued*
  118–119; weaknesses of 58, 83,
  126–130, 142–143; in Russia 5,
  123–124, **124**
Butyrka Blog 105
Byzantine Greeks 19, 59

Canada 103, 141
Carwash case 112
Catherine the Second 59
CEFIR (Center for Economic and
  Financial Research) 47
Center for Information and
  Communications Research 55
Center for Political Technologies 92
Center for Public Procedures "Business
  Against Corruption" 96, **97**
Central Asia 19, 27, 59
Central federal district 125, *126*
centralization 21, 22–24, 30
centralized planned economy 18
Chamber of Commerce and Industry of the
  Russian Federation 22, 54, 124, **124**
chambers of commerce: anti-corruption
  efforts 78, 85, 116–117, 139;
  contemporary 5–6, 22, 58, 105, **124**;
  pre-revolutionary 120–121, *121*
Chechnya 60
Chelyabinsk region **97**
Chemezov, Sergey 26, 30
Chile 117
Chu, Steven 29
Chuvash Republic **97**
CIPE (Center for International Private
  Enterprise) 25, 116–118, 139, 142, 149
Citizens' Watch 149
Civil Initiatives Committee 8
civil society: activists 6–7, 91–92, 97,
  143–144; organizations 24–25, 26, 105,
  117, 130, 143, 149; protests 11, 112;
  and collective action 114, **114**, 116, 146;
  in Russia 2, 6–7, 23–24, 113, 130, 137,
  151
collective action: against corruption 2, 5,
  9, 11–12, 85–86, 105, 114–115, **114**,
  128, 137, 145; approach 116; definition
  114; initiatives 76, 115–118, 126–127,
  143, 146, 150; problem 115; theory 5,
  115
Colombia 73
Committee to Protect Journalists 8, 144
Communist party 16, 18, 21, 118
congresses of industries and trade
  120–123, *121*

Costa Rica 117
Council of Europe 85, 101–103, 126, 141
Council of Europe Civil Law Convention
  on Corruption 141
Council of Europe Committee on Legal
  Affairs and Human Rights 99
Council of Europe Criminal Law
  Convention on Corruption 138, 141
Croatia 32–36, **33**, **35**, 118
crony state capitalism 16, 27, 130
Czech Republic 31, 36

Demidov dynasty 20
*Demokratizatsiya, the Journal of Post-
  Soviet Democratization* 17
Deposit Insurance Agency 29
Deutsche Welle 105
"directly unproductive, profit-seeking
  activities" 45
Dozhd TV station 8
Dutch disease *see* resource curse
DWEN (Dell Women Entrepreneurs
  Network) 36
Dynasty Foundation 24

Eastern Bloc 10, 31–32, 115, 118
economic crimes 104, 148, 152
efficiency-driven economies 32
"efficient grease" hypothesis 74–75
Egypt 46
EkspoPUL 101–102
El Salvador 46
Emancipation reform of 1861 20
embezzlement 17, 105, 148
entrepreneurial ecosystem 34, **35**, 36, 38
entrepreneurial employment 6, 10, 44,
  59–64, *60*, **62**, **63**
"entrepreneurial spring" 11, 112–119
Estonia 32–36, **33**, **35**

facilitating payments *see* "grease"
  payments
factor-driven economies 32, 38
Fair Trials International 97, 99
False Claims Act 138
Far Eastern federal district *126*
FCPA (Foreign Corrupt Practices Act)
  73–74, 141–142
Federal Customs Service **50**, **51**, 140
Federal Security Service 140
Federation of Russian Producers 123
Female Entrepreneurship Index 10, 31, 36,
  38
Financial Monitoring Service 140

Forbes 28
"foreign agent" law 24–25
Foundation for the Development of Civil Society 55
Free Russia Foundation 127
Freedom House 8, 23

GEDI (Global Entrepreneurship and Development Institute) 36, **37**, 38
gender-specific attitudes toward corruption 6, 76–77, 80–81, **81**, 150
Georgia 32, **33**, **35**, 116
Germany 26, 98, 119, 128
Glasnost Defense Foundation 24, 144
Global Competitiveness Report 114
Global Entrepreneurship Index 10, 31, 36, **37**, 38
Global Entrepreneurship Monitor 10, 31–36, **33**, **35**, 38
Gorbachev, Mikhail 16, 21
Gorno-Altay region 61
"grabbing hand" 48
GRECO (Group of States Against Corruption) 141
Greece 118
"grease" payments: attitudes toward 77–82, **79**, **81**, **82**; definition 72; in institutionalism 75–76; in rational choice theory 74–75; in the legal school 73–74; in Russia 10, 18, 72–73, 82–86, 112, 150
Grudinin, Pavel 2
Guatemala 112
Gudkov, Gennady 92
"Guatemalan Spring" 112
Guild for Audio-Video Trade Development 149
guilds 20

handicraft entrepreneurs 123
Helen Dwight Reid Educational Foundation 17
Hermitage Capital Management 92, 98, 103
"household" corruption 4
human rights 7–9, 23–25, 112–113, 144, 149
Human Rights Watch 99
Hungary 31–32, **33**, **35**, 36

ICAC (Independent Commission Against Corruption) 140
Ikea 66n44
illegal business raiding *see reiderstvo*

illicit enrichment 4, 27, 138, 141
India 45, 76, 143
individual entrepreneurs: definition 3; classification 3; involvement in informal transactions 82–86, 151; involvement in self-regulatory organizations 58, 125–130, 143, 152; and administrative problems 52–54
Industry and Trade 123
infrastructure 34–36, **35**, 38, 46, 61–64, **62**, **63**
Ingush region 60
innovation-driven economies 32
inspections: misuse of 4, 18, 24, 49, 53–54, 101–103, 149; moratorium on 50–51; planned 50–51; unannounced 49–51, **51**; regime 47–48, 49–52, **50**
Institute for Information Freedom Development 24
Institute for Liberty and Democracy 45–46
Integrum group 30
Inter-American Development Bank 46, 116
Interior Ministry's Committee for Economic Security and Combating Corruption 96, 140
Interpol 91, 97–99
Interregional Tax Service of Saint Petersburg 103
Investigative Committee of the Russian Federation 56, 100, 102–103
Irbit 60
Ivanov, Sergei 148
Izvozchikova, Elizaveta 102

Japan 31, 141

Kabardin-Balkar region 61
Kaliningrad 6, 26
Kalmyk region 60
Karachay-Cherkess region 60
Karelia's Portal of Small and Medium-Sized Entrepreneurship 58, **58**
Katsnelson, Ilya 98
Kazakhstan 32–35, **33**, **35**
Khabarovsk 139
Khakass region 61
Kharkov 121
Khodorkovsky, Mikhail 98
Khudilainen, Aleksandr 55–56
Kievan Rus' 19–20, 59
kiosk entrepreneurship 19, 30, 127
Kiriyenko, Sergey 29–30
Kirov 139

kleptocracy 10, 11, 48
Koblyakov, Nikolay 98
kormlenie 72
Kosovo 118
Kostyuchenko, Nadezhda 100
Kozlov, Alexei 105
Krasnodar region 60, **97**
Krasnoyarsk 6
krugovaya poruka 17, 84

"La Línea" case 130n2
Las Brumas 145
Latin America 45–46
Latvia 32, **33**, **35**, 36, 73
lawlessness 93–94, **95**
League of Cooperators and Entrepreneurs of Russia 22
Leningrad region 55, 61
Levada Center 6–7, 24
likhoimstvo 72
Lithuania 36
Lukin, Vladimir 25
Lula da Silva, Luiz Inácio 112

MacArthur Foundation 25
Macedonia 32, **33**, **35**, 36, 118
Magadan region 61
"market capture" 9–10, 27–31
"maski shows" 97
Magnitsky, Sergei 103
Mamontov dynasty 20
market economy 23, 31, 119
market-promoting associations 119, 130, 142
Med syndicate 20
Medvedev, Dmitry 93, 96
Memorial 24
Mendeleev, Dmitry 59
Mexico 46, 141, 145
Miller, Alexey 28
Ministry of Economic Development of the Russian Federation **50, 51**
Ministry of Emergency of the Russian Federation **50, 51**, 102
Ministry of Labor and Social Insurance of the Russian Federation 124
money laundering 4, 94, **95**, 98, 140
monopolization 9, 20, 25, 27–28
Montenegro 36
Moran's I test 61–62
Morozov dynasty 20
Moscow: administrative barriers 44, 52–55, *52*; corruption 7, 61, 64, 92, 96, **97**, 99, 104, 127; entrepreneurs and self-regulatory organizations 6, 125, 128–129, 144, 149; facilitation payments 10, 77–78, 82–84, 142; governance 55–58, **55**; history 19–20, 59, 72, 120–122
Moscow Committee for Small Business Development 58, **58**
Moscow Economic Forum 1
Moscow region 56, 61, 92, 96, **97**
Movement for the Defense of Voters' Rights *Golos* 24
msdoimstvo 72
Muižnieks, Nils 25

National Anti-Corruption Committee 99
National Anti-Corruption Council of the Russian Federation 140
National Endowment for Democracy 117
Nelidov, Andrei 56
neo-corporatist model 128
NEP (new economic policy) 20–21
nepotism 17, 145
"new Russians" 17
Nicaragua 116, 145
"Night of the Long Shovels" 127
Nizhny Novgorod region **97**, 120
NGO (non-governmental organization) 7–8, 24, 97–98, 114, 146, 149
North Caucasian federal district *126*
North-western federal district 125, *126*
Norwegian Helsinki Committee 24
Novosibirsk **97**, 139

Odessa 121
OECD (Organization for Economic Co-operation and Development) 31–32, 53, 73–74, 141
OECD Anti-Bribery Convention 73–74, 141
OLS (ordinary least squares) 62, **63**, 81–82
Olympstroy (State Corporation for Construction of Olympic Objects) 29
ordered logistic regression 78–80, **80**
Orenburg 60
otpiska 83

PACI (Partnering Against Corruption Initiative) 116–117
padding 18, 76
Pakistani Trade Organizations Ordinance 117
Panama 116
Panfilova, Elena 85, 139
paradox of corruption 115

Paraguay 116
Paz y Paz, Claudia 112
perestroika era 9, 18
Pérez Molina, Otto 112
Perm 6, 60, 139
Peru 45–46, 145
Peter the Great 20, 59
Petrobras 112
Petrozavodsk 53, 57, 125
Poland 31–32, **33**, **35**, 36
police: corruption 24–25, 44, 57, 91, 94–96, **95**, 140–141, 149; discretion 101, 104, 152; inspections **50**, 102; reliability 114; violence 4, 24, 144
political corruption 5, 27
post-perestroika 16, 21, 23, 27
Potapenko, Dmitry 1
"predatory policing" 94
Presidential Council for Combating Corruption 140
Presidential Council for Civil Society and Human Rights 25, 91, 100
Primorsky region **97**
private-sector corruption 4
privatization 16, 18, 22; *see also* "velvet re-privatization"
procurement 16, 28–29, 47, 53–54, 83, 125, 128
Prodamet syndicate 20
Produgol syndicate 20
Prodvagon syndicate 20
prosecutor's office 25, 29, 51, 138
public-private dialogue 12, 137, 142, 146–149, 151–152
public-private partnerships 11, 55, **55**, 116, 137, 142, 146, 149–150, 152
Putin, Vladimir: civil society 24–25, 98; cronies 28, 30; corruption 8–9, 11, 91; policies 139, 148, 152; regime 23, 25–27, 93
"Putin's team" 28

RBC media group 8
Red Notices 98–99
redistributive associations 119, 130, 142
regional policies 6, **55**, 64
regulatory agencies: accountability 113, 139–140, 142, 144; corruption 5, 72–73, 93–94, 114; discretionary abuses 1–2, 11, 18, 48–57, *52*, 84–85, 91; facilitation payments 5, 10, 44, 77–80, 82, 127, 150–151; rent seeking 3–4, 47–48, 64, 101–102
"regulocracy" 10, 44, 48–49, 52, 139

regulatory environment 48, 61–64, **62**, **63**
reiderstvo: characteristics 92–94, **95**; definition 4, 91; by judiciary 99–101; by law enforcement 94, 96–99; by regulatory and registration agencies 101–103
rent seeking: definition 45; by business associations 119, 130; by public officials 1, 44, 48, 59, 76, 144; by regulatory and registration agencies 3, 10, 47, 64, 79, 101–105, 151
Republic of Karelia: administrative barriers 52–55, *52*; corruption 6, 8, 10, 44, 64; entrepreneurs and self-regulatory organizations 122, 125–129, *126*, 144; facilitation payments 77–78, 82–84, 142; governance 55–58, **55**
resource curse 38
Revolution of 1917 7, 20, 119, 121
Romania 36, 118
Romanova, Olga 105
Rosatom (State Nuclear Corporation) 29
Roskosmos 29
Rospotrebnadzor (Consumer Protection Service) **50**, **51**, 102
Rostec (Russian Technologies State Corporation) 26, 29–30
Rostov on the Don 60
Rostov region 61, **97**
Rotenberg, Arkady 26, 28
Rotenberg, Igor 26
"Rotenberg tax" 26
RT-Invest Transport Systems 26
rule of law 3, 38, 91, 99, 104, 140
Rus' Sidyashchaya (Jailed Russia) 105
Rusnano (Nanotechnologies State Corporation) 29
Russia: administrative barriers 45–48; anti-corruption policies 137–142; civil society 6–7; corruption 2–3, 17–19, 72–73, 99–105, 151–152; deregulation reforms 48–52; entrepreneurial development 1, 16, 31–38, 59–64; freedom of the press 8, 144; "grease" payments 76–84; history of entrepreneurship 19–23; political regime 8, 23–27; public-private cooperation 146–150
Russia's Civil Code 3, 104
Russian Committee Against Torture 24
Russian Criminal Code 56, 94, **95**, 103–104, 139, 148, 152
Russian Empire 7, 20, 22, 60, 119, *121*, 122, 143, 147

Russian Public Organization *Delovaya Rossiya* (Business Russia) 54, 96, 124
Russian Union of Industrialists and Entrepreneurs 22, 54, 123–125, **124**
Russian-American Chamber of Commerce 120
Russian-Belgian Chamber of Commerce 120
Russian-English Chamber of Commerce 120
Russian-French Chamber of Commerce 120
Russian-Italian Chamber of Commerce 120
Russian-Slav Chamber of Commerce 120
Russie-Libertés 98
Ryabushinski dynasty 20

Safra, Edmond 103
Saint Petersburg: administrative barriers 44, 52–55, *52*; corruption 7, 10, 64, 102–103; entrepreneurs and self-regulatory organizations 6, *124*, 125, 126–129, 144–145; facilitation payments 77–78, 82–84, 142; governance 55–58, **55**; history 59, 120, 121–122
Saint Petersburg Committee for the Development of Entrepreneurship and the Consumer Market 58, **58**
Saint Petersburg University of the Russian Interior Ministry 149
Sakha region 61
Samara region 61, 100
Saratov 6, 101
Saratov region 57, 61, 101, 139
Saratov Chamber of Commerce and Industry 142, 149
self-regulatory organizations: anti-corruption efforts 59, 76, 77–78, 82–86, 113–116, **114**, 143, 150; definition 5; pre-revolutionary 7, 11, 119–123, *121*; types 123–124, **124**; in Russia 127–130, 142, 144, 151; *see also* business associations; chambers of commerce; stock exchanges; unions of industrialists and entrepreneurs
Serbia 118
shell companies 104
Siberian federal district *126*
Slavneft 97
Slovakia 32, **33**, **35**, 36
Slovenia 32, **33**, **35**, 36
small business programs 62–64, **62**, **63**

Smolensk 139
Sobornoe Ulozheniye 72
social-control boards 117
Solidarnost' (Solidarity) 105
Soto, Hernando de 45–46
South Africa 73
South federal district *126*
Southern Russian Mining Bulletin 123
spatial error regression 62, **63**
Stalin 26
state capture 9, 27–28
state corporations 25, 28–30, 38
"state *reiderstvo*" 91
Stavropol' region 61
stock exchanges 20, 120–121, *121*
Stroganov dynasty 20
Sukhanov, Yurii 97

Tanzania 46
Tatarstan region 61
TEA (early-stage entrepreneurship activity) **33**, 34
"telephone justice" 17, 99–101
Temer, Michel 113
Thai Institute of Directors 117
Thailand 76
Three Whales case 140
Titov, Boris 5, 49, 92, 96, 104
TNK-BP 92
ToAz (TogliattiAzot) 99
tolkachi 17
Transparency International 2, 9, 141, 143, 145
Transparency International Russia 24, 85, 139
Tretyakov dynasty 20
Tunisia 112
Turkish Coordination Council 147
Tuva region 61

Ufa 60
Uganda 143
UNCICP (United Nations Center for International Crime Prevention) 117
Union of Industrial and Trade Enterprises of the Russian Empire 22
Union of Public Associations of Entrepreneurs and Tenants 22
unions of industrialists and entrepreneurs 105, 121, *121*
United Nations Convention against Corruption 138, 141
United Russia 24, 26
United States 31, 74, 117, 141, 142

United States Department of Justice 138
"unproductive entrepreneurship" 130
Ural federal district *126*
Ural region 59–60
USAID (United States Agency for International Development) 47, 116, 139
USSR Scientific and Industrial Union 22
USSR Supreme Council 16, 21–22

Valyavina, Elena 100
"velvet re-privatization" 93
Venezuela 117
"vertical of power" 11, 23–27
Vietnam 9, 147
Vietnamese Business Forum 147
Vikings 19, 59
Vimpelcom 101
Vladivostok 6
Volga federal district *126*
Volgograd Center for Protection and Development of Businesses 129
Volgograd Chamber of Commerce 129
Volgograd region **97**, 127, 129, 139
VSMPO-Avisma 25–26
vzyatochnichestvo 72

whistleblowers 138, 141
Wilfred Martens Center for European Studies 127
women's grassroots groups 118
World Bank 7, 9, 27, 32, 46–47, 72, 114, 116
World Bank's Doing Business report 53
World Economic Forum 9, 32, 116
World International Exposition of 1893 59

Yakovleva, Yana 105
Yarovaya, Irina 25
"Yarovaya law" *see* Anti-Terror Package
Yekaterinburg 60, 121
YUKOS 93, 98–99

Zakharchenko, Dmitry 96
Zygar, Mikhail 8